Global Economic and Cultural Transformation

Global Economic and Cultural Transformation

The Making of History

Mohamed Rabie

GLOBAL ECONOMIC AND CULTURAL TRANSFORMATION
Copyright © Mohamed Rabie 2013.

All rights reserved.

First published in 2013 by
PALGRAVE MACMILLAN®
in the United States—a division of St. Martin's Press LLC,
175 Fifth Avenue, New York, NY 10010.

Where this book is distributed in the UK, Europe and the rest of the World, this is by Palgrave Macmillan, a division of Macmillan Publishers Limited, registered in England, company number 785998, of Houndmills, Basingstoke, Hampshire RG21 6XS.

Palgrave Macmillan is the global academic imprint of the above companies and has companies and representatives throughout the world.

Palgrave® and Macmillan® are registered trademarks in the United States, the United Kingdom, Europe and other countries.

ISBN: 978–1–137–36777–8

Library of Congress Cataloging-in-Publication Data

Rabi', Muhammad, 1940–
   Global economic and cultural transformation : the making of history / Mohamed Rabie.
     pages cm
   Includes bibliographical references.
   ISBN 978–1–137–36777–8
   1. Economic history. 2. Social history. 3. World history.
4. Social evolution. I. Title.
HC21.R33 2013
330.9—dc23   2013020509

A catalogue record of the book is available from the British Library.

Design by Integra Software Services

First edition: October 2013

In memory of my parents who taught us the value of education and the price of dedication

Contents

Introduction	ix
1 A View of History	1
2 Stages of Societal Development	21
3 Processes of Societal Transformation	43
4 Social Transformation	59
5 Agents of Historical Change	79
6 Theories of World History	93
7 The Train of Time	107
8 Ideology and History	127
9 Cultural Determinism	155
10 A World in Transition	175
Concluding Remarks	195
Notes	199
Bibliography	207
Index	213

Introduction

As the 1990s advanced, most societies in the world entered a new period characterized by confusion and loss of direction. The profound transformations spurred by the information and telecommunications revolutions, the collapse of communism, and the advent of the Internet and globalization have affected all aspects of life of all societies in ways unknown before. They have influenced all cultures and economies and political systems, causing reality and our perception of it to change drastically. And since the forces of transformation have continued to gather momentum, our world has been thrown into a transitional period that does not seem to have an end in sight. Most ideas, theories, strategies, and institutions that helped shape and manage community life, national economies, domestic politics, and international relations in the recent past have been rendered inadequate and thus largely irrelevant.

Today, every society faces challenges that seem hard to define and harder to deal with. At the same time, social and economic systems in every society are becoming increasingly more complex and interdependent, and globalization is moving beyond the sphere of economics to engulf other aspects of life, particularly the cultural and security aspects. While older theories and strategies and road maps are fast becoming outdated, no new ones have emerged to take their place. The order of the day has become one of disorder.

Unconventional trends of change are slowly emerging as powerful forces affecting the nature, pace, and direction of societal developments in general and sociocultural and economic conditions in particular. These trends include wider economic integration across state lines, renewed political fragmentation and sometimes disintegration within state lines, deepened sociocultural segmentation within societal lines, and widened income and wealth and educational gaps everywhere. Because of their disruptive nature, these trends are weakening the state and undermining the cohesiveness of society and the particularity of national cultures and identities.

In the meantime, political plurality, the middle class, freedom of speech, and tolerance, which are the basic conditions for creating and sustaining democratic systems, are being undermined. While societies are slowly being divided into competing sociocultural groups, the middle class is being weakened and fragmented to the point of losing self-confidence and class consciousness. As for freedom of speech and the neutrality of the press, it has suffered a serious setback due primarily to the commercialization of the media. As a consequence, the traditional democratic institutions are slowly becoming dysfunctional, causing the promises of justice and equality to become more of an illusion than a reality.

Changes of this nature and magnitude suggest that the world is passing through a period of transition separating the recent past from the near future. In such transitions, the experience and wisdom of the past, and the logic that governed past history, usually become outdated and largely useless. People consequently are left with few theoretical tools to help them understand their present, and with no credible road maps to guide them into the future; they have to develop new tools and draw new road maps to suit the evolving, but yet to be defined, times.

This book is an attempt to define and explain this transitional period, to reexamine the old map in light of what is expected in the future, and to provide a new conception of world history to help us understand how we got here and where we are expected to go. Because societal maps are complex, the book will try to reexamine the relevance of some of the major ideas and systems, including ideology and its relation to society, culture and its role in change and conflict, as well as politics and development, the nation-state, and a few others.

I hope this book will make a contribution to improving our understanding of our past and present, and help foster our ability to deal with the challenges or our times and shape a more promising and just future for all.

Mohamed Rabie
www.yazour.com
Washington, D.C.

1

A View of History

World history is the record of past events that are perceived by most people to be important and interesting. It is the story of the development of human societies and their achievements in all fields of human endeavor, as well as the story of war and peace and their consequences. Because no one can confidently prove or disprove assertions about the past, any conversation about history is necessarily controversial. Therefore, all assertions made by historians should be considered probabilities, not facts beyond doubt. And if history contains no proven facts, then no history should be viewed as sacred, and no historical record should be considered beyond challenge. Indeed, unless we accept that the only fact about history is that there are no credible facts in history, we will continue to be largely prisoners of the past, unable to free ourselves from the chains of history, and move forward to envision a shared future for all humanity.

Since acts, ideas, inventions, and events that shape human history are not isolated from one another, the historical record reflects a chain of actions and reactions and interactions that form a process of continuous change and transformation. This process is an unconscious and unregulated movement of groups, nations, states, cultures, and civilizations toward higher, more complex, often undefined goals and societal formations. It is a self-propelled process that has no particular point of departure, and no clear destination. As it moves, it causes conflict, induces change, and transforms people's perceptions, ways of life, and life conditions in ways that do not necessarily reflect the desires or interests of most people.

For the historical process to continue, it requires motives to inspire it, forces to lead it, energy to fuel it, and a mechanism to coordinate its many activities. Traditionally, ambitious leaders, active groups, aggressive states, human needs and aspirations, and an uninterrupted stream of new ideas, technologies, and ideologies have played leading roles in motivating and energizing the historical process. Over time, relationships among

2 GLOBAL ECONOMIC AND CULTURAL TRANSFORMATION

these forces have variously been characterized by conflict, competition, and cooperation. Interestingly enough, however, the mechanism that has managed conflict, coordinated change, and moved the historical process in a seemingly orderly manner has been created unconsciously. Four major societal processes have gradually emerged as independent, yet complementary, vehicles to form a larger societal framework through which forces of change shape societies and their cultures and transform life conditions at any time. They are the sociocultural process, the political process, the economic process, and the infomedia process. How these processes emerged and what functions they perform and how they interact with one another is the subject of Chapter 3.

History and the Historian

History, being the record of big events throughout the ages, makes historical records the primary tool to understand what happened in the past, why and how it happened, and what lessons are there for us to learn. However, most records seem intended to glorify the victorious, idolize leaders, exaggerate achievements, dehumanize the vanquished, and often justify evil acts committed to achieve victory. Since there can be no winners without losers, and no heroes without villains, the vanquished have felt that history does not treat them fairly, and therefore they continue to criticize most historical records, call for their revision, and write their own versions of history. While these accounts are often substantially different, they are not necessarily more accurate.

Representatives of the vanquished peoples and decedents of slaves and minorities in general have engaged in rewriting history to reclaim their rightful place in it. To achieve this objective, they tend to view historical events that have changed their lives from a moral perspective, one that allows them to magnify their own suffering, belittle the victories of their conquerors, blame the victors for whatever had happened to them, and oftentimes dehumanize them as well. In fact, the glorification of the self and the demonization of the other are two faces of the same historical incident seen by two peoples facing each other across the confrontation line. History, therefore, is claims and counterclaims, overestimates and underestimates, and exaggerations and falsifications that may come close to telling the truth but never reflect it. Historical records leave the real truth hidden somewhere between many contradictory claims, but nowhere to be seen in order to be identified and evaluated.

Morality, which is an aspect of ideology and culture, has often been the tool used by historians to glorify and demonize freely. While the victors seldom feel the need to justify their acts to achieve victory, the vanquished are constantly searching for a justification to explain their defeat and criteria by which to judge and belittle their conquerors. Throughout history, the vanquished and the oppressed nations and minorities have acted as if morality lies exclusively within their domain. Yet, judged by today's standards of democracy, freedom, social justice, and human rights, almost all the leaders of the past, both winners and losers, would appear guilty of criminal acts; personal glory to them was almost always an end that justified all means.

Because history has always been contested, all historical "facts" remain meaningless and unimportant until they are evaluated and placed, along with their consequences, in certain historical perspectives. Every judgment of the past is usually made in light of the present moment as lived and understood by the historian who makes it. "We can view the past, and achieve our understanding of the past, only through the eyes of the present."[1] But these eyes see a particular view that is more relevant to the present as lived by the historian than to the past he tries to imagine and describe. Therefore, as the present changes, it causes our view of the past and general understanding of its culture and life conditions to change as well.

To provide an example, President Anwar Sadat of Egypt traveled to Israel in 1977 seeking peace despite the fact that a state of war had characterized the relationship between Israel and all Arab states at the time. Since such a trip amounted to a *de facto* recognition of the state of Israel, Arabs in general and Palestinians in particular condemned the trip and accused Sadat of treason. Fourteen years later, almost all Arab states, including representatives of the Palestinian people, participated in the Madrid Conference for Middle East peace. As a result, most Jewish and Egyptian historians vindicated Sadat; many credited him with courage and foresight. Both evaluations of Sadat's trip, however, were expressed in light of their own political context and time. But if we look at Sadat's trip today from a wider, more reflective historical perspective, both images of Sadat as traitor and as visionary would appear subjective and incomplete, particularly in light of the failure of the Madrid Conference and the death of the peace process that followed.

Sadat's trip to Israel was motivated by self-interest and a desire to regain lost Egyptian territory, and not by a desire to commit treason against other Arab states or to help Israel. But by signing a separate peace treaty with Israel in 1979, Sadat caused the Arab position *vis-à-vis* Israel to be vastly weakened; he practically eliminated all nonpolitical options, leaving the weakened Arabs at the mercy of a strong Israel backed by the United States. Sadat, therefore, was neither a traitor nor a visionary, a villain, or a hero,

4 GLOBAL ECONOMIC AND CULTURAL TRANSFORMATION

but a mere politician who sought to maximize his gain regardless of his action's consequences for others.

Many people and numerous historians seem to think that history holds the keys to understanding human development and to identifying the major forces that shape societal life in general and influence its future course. Because of this belief, theories of history were written, and continue to be written, to explain the nature of the historical process, its course, its logic, and its perceived final destination, assuming that there is a destination where history's long journey would eventually end.

Historians of each era can be divided into three general categories: adherents to the dominant ideology of the time, critics of it, and observers claiming neutrality. Historians in the first category tend to be apologists for, if not promoters of, the prevailing ideology and defenders of its actions and intentions. Critics and opponents of the prevailing ideology, in contrast, tend to highlight the shortcomings and excesses of it, as well as the sins and follies of its leaders. Historians who claim neutrality usually see history as a powerful force that does not differentiate between its subjects. They tend to see most leaders as less than heroes but more than demons, and view losers as neither victims nor innocent bystanders. Neutrality, however, is impossible to maintain, particularly in cases where people, and their lives and belief systems, are at issue. Every historian has his or her own worldview, values, life experience, and cultural and educational background against which he or she consciously or unconsciously judges the subjects of his investigation and their legacies. Because of these facts, historians continue to write controversial histories that deepen animosity and suspicion among peoples.

Although the historian "strives constantly to transcend his own present to recapture the past, to suppress his own personality in order to give life to generations long dead,"[2] he is a product of his own times and environment and life conditions. Every historian is a product of the culture and the particular ideology to which he owes his personality, identity, and intellectual qualities. Since cultures, ideologies, human environments, and life conditions continue to change and be transformed, every generation of historians is expected to produce records that try to reflect the spirit of old times while being colored by the cultural biases of the historian's times. Historians, no matter how hard they may try to transcend their present to recapture a past they never lived, are destined to produce history that is neither complete nor factual. Two historians writing about the same era or the same nation are likely to produce different histories. Thus, the history of every era and every nation is an ever-evolving, never-completed story. Every history, therefore, must be viewed as tentative, incomplete, and open to interpretations and revision.

"Any work of history is vulnerable on three counts," says Gertrude Himmelfarb, "the fallibility and deficiency of the historical record on which it is based, the fallibility and selectivity inherent in the writing of history, and the fallibility and subjectivity of historians."[3] Consensus among historians is rather rare, coming about only in regard to histories whose ideology is long dead, and has little contemporary political or emotional impact. Since there is no historical truth, good historians are only able to convey the spirit, the culture, the technology, and the general life conditions of times past.

R.G. Collingwood mandates that "the understanding of the past in a properly historical way requires, on the part of the historian, a re-enactment of past experience or re-thinking of past thought."[4] But neither the reenactment of past experience nor the rethinking of past thought is humanly possible. No historian can say with certainty what happened in the past without being a witness, why it happened, how it affected life conditions at the time, and how it may be of benefit to us. Collingwood in fact makes no distinction between an action and its causes. He claims that "when the historian knows what happened, he already knows why it happened."[5] Historical facts to Collingwood are the end rather than the beginning of inquiry. He further claims that "the full description of an action is at the same time its explanation."[6] But the description of an action that happened in the past can never be complete, nor can it be accurate. Once again, perhaps only a historian who can relive a particular past in his or her own memories—despite the passing of time—is able to describe that past, understand it, and draw valuable conclusions from it.

The Historical Connection

Historians in general have some type of connection to the histories they take as their major subject of inquiry. Chinese historians, for example, write more about the history of China than about the histories of France and Germany combined. Israelis are more interested in Jewish history and in the history of Arabs in general than in British or Italian history. Connections can be cultural, political, ideological, and/or circumstantial. Historians interested in world history strive to transcend their own cultural traditions, political views and ideologies to view the world as one entity and its development as a coherent historical movement. Since this book is about the making of world history and the transformations of world cultures and civilizations, I feel the need to explain my own connection to this history.

I have been fortunate to experience first-hand the development of human societies over time, and to witness the evolvement of more than one civilization and participate in some of their important events. And because civilizations go through difficult transitional periods before social, cultural, political, and economic transformations are completed and a new civilization emerges, living the life I have lived has given me a unique opportunity to see change as it evolved and feel the pains and hopes of people in such circumstances. My writings, therefore, are not a matter of only curiosity or imagination, but a commitment to convey the spirit of the times I have lived and identify the forces of change that transformed and continue to transform the world's many societies, cultures, and economies, and the way they are organized.

I was born in an enchanting agricultural community where neither electricity nor running water nor modern sanitation was available. People and animals were used to plow the land, plant the seeds, harvest the crops, and transport them to local markets. The community where most of my childhood was spent is quite similar to a typical agricultural community in Europe during the late decades of the nineteenth century, with a few exceptions; the existence of trains, cars, and radios were the major ones. As I was growing up and becoming aware of my social and economic environments, war erupted and caused my family and my generation to become refugees. The refugee camp in which I spent about five years of my youth was outside an agricultural town at the edge of a vast, desolate desert. For about two years, my older sister and I were assigned by our father the task of spending about two days a week roaming the neighboring desert to collect dry and dying bushes and shrubs needed to make fire for cooking. During the winter and early weeks of spring, the task was expanded to include the collection of wild vegetables to feed the family. Two of these vegetables are now domesticated, and every time I smell them and taste them I remember the days and events of a childhood lived as a hunter and gatherer who hunted no animals but gathered a lot of vegetables.

Other circumstances surrounding my life led me to share with nomads their food, listen to their songs and life stories, spend time in their tents, and observe their daily life. I was even able to see how men treat their wives and children, how younger men interact with older ones, and occasionally accompany shepherds as they perform their daily tasks. It was a life that represented the first stage of development of human society on its way to civilization. Having been uprooted from an affluent and secure existence and relegated to living in abject poverty and an insecure environment made me aware of the new life, evaluating every change and every tradition with a critical mind that never stopped thinking and wandering beyond the present and into the unknown.

By the time I entered high school, my family had moved to Jericho, the neighboring town, which is thought to be the oldest city in the world. Nevertheless, all nine of us lived in a one-bedroom apartment that had none of the basic modern amenities. The family, moreover, had neither the money nor the space to buy a desk, a table, a chair, or any piece of furniture that is today taken for granted in most agricultural communities. My father rented and cultivated a small piece of land on which we lived and whose produce provided most of the food the family needed for survival and a little money to support a mostly subsistence life; all children who were old enough to help in cultivating the land were required to do so. Domesticated turkey, chicken, pigeon, and rabbits provided the meat the family needed to supplement its mostly vegetarian diet.

Upon graduation from high school, I received a scholarship from the United Nations to study in Cairo, one of the largest and most vibrant cities of the Third World at the time. The trip from Jerusalem to Cairo gave me the first opportunity to fly in a plane and spend a night in a luxurious hotel in Beirut. Living and studying in Cairo gave me a chance to observe affluence and abject poverty coexisting side by side and watch modern and primitive cultures living their separate, estranged lives in one place, often in one building. Third World nationalism and socialism were thriving along with anti-imperialism in an atmosphere that inspired the young and gave hope to the deprived. It was only there that I was able to live in a house with electricity, running water, sanitation, a phone, and even a refrigerator. Life in Cairo represented what I call the transitional period between two civilizations, the agricultural and the industrial ones.

Five years later, I traveled to Germany, where I witnessed and participated in the so-called "German Economic Miracle" and lived for almost two years in a mature industrial society. In Germany, I pursued a graduate degree and worked a few months in a publishing house. Most of my free time was spent visiting as many German cities, towns, and villages as possible and immersing myself in the culture of the land. In the mid-1960s I moved to the United States, where I completed my higher education, earned a PhD degree in economics, and taught at a few American universities. While in the United States, I witnessed two of the most important social and political movements in modern US history: the civil rights movement and the anti-war movement that opposed the war in Vietnam.

In 1970, I left the United States for Kuwait to teach at its newly established university. And while at Kuwait University, I managed to change the educational system and the curriculum, introduce coeducation in Kuwait for the first time ever, publish a quarterly journal and two books and tens of papers and articles, and participate in the cultural life of the Kuwaiti society; I also got to know how the non-Kuwaiti communities lived and viewed life conditions in that part of the world. For six years, I witnessed a tribal society losing the major characteristics of its traditional culture as money was transforming it into what I call a "petroleum society." It is a society whose roots were still deep in the fourteenth and fifteenth centuries and whose aspirations were touching the twenty-first century, a society that thought it could buy anything and employ anyone with its money.

In 1976, I returned to the United States to teach first at Georgetown University in Washington DC and then at other universities. And while living in Washington, I witnessed the transformational impact of the Reagan and Clinton years on the American society, economy, and culture, which gave me the opportunity to live through the transitional period that took a mature industrial society into the age of knowledge. And in addition to teaching at a few American universities, I got involved in business, research, and publishing.

Between 1998 and 2000, I spent my time shuttling between Washington DC and Germany, giving lectures at German universities and research institutes and advising Erfurt University, which was being reopened after more than two centuries of closure following the religious wars of the seventeenth century. In 2002, I went to Morocco, where I spent two years teaching at Al Akhawayn University, and then I spent two more years living in Jordan. So for the second time in 40 years, I had the opportunity to observe how life changes during a transitional period separating the agricultural from the industrial age, where globalization has caused traditional cultures to lose most of their old traits and characteristics and be deformed beyond recognition.

Since boyhood, my life has been an ever-evolving, most fascinating story that took me to many interesting places in Asia, Europe, the Middle East, North Africa, and North and South America, enabling me to look back at the primitive roots from where I started my life journey and explore the unknown future in my thoughts and ways of living. And throughout the time since graduation from college, I have continued to travel, give lectures, write articles, and publish books. Thus my perspective goes beyond the ups and downs of ordinary life in one society, one region, or one civilization, and my connections to all the places and historical phases I have experienced firsthand have continued to fascinate me and challenge my intellectual capacities. As a result, I can say with confidence that I have experienced, within my lifetime, starting with the tribal age and into the knowledge age, the life of 500 generations, going back to the pre-agricultural times. I believe that no other person has lived my life, and no man or woman will ever experience my life experience because some of the times I had lived and many of the developments I witnessed have come and gone and will never come back.

Historical Discontinuity

My first reaction to the publishing of Francis Fukuyama's 1992 famous book, *The End of History and the Last Man* was direct and rather provocative: What has actually ended is not history per se, but the role of history in explaining the present and shaping the future. This assertion no doubt calls for an explanation, which will require an examination of the major forces that guide history, chart its course, and influence the development of human societies.

People everywhere are today experiencing one crisis after another; most of them are unsure of the present and fearful of the future. The world of the early 1990s went through a historical discontinuity from which it has not emerged yet; the discontinuity disrupted the historical process and dissolved the connection between the immediate past and the near future. As the history of the past was coming to an end, the history of the future was in labor unable to be born, leaving the present in a state of confusion, having no idea where to go and no identity of its own. While the present was reduced by the circumstances to a mere port where the past is ending its long journey, it was transformed into a staging platform for the future to begin its own voyage into the land of the unknown. Twenty years later, the process has not yet ended.

Historical discontinuities are relatively short transitional periods in the life of human societies, where the traditional forces that shape history and guide its movement become less effective, and new forces emerge rather suddenly to take the lead and cause fundamental social transformations. As a consequence, the normal historical pattern is disrupted and a new pattern emerges slowly to chart the future. But since change causes conflict, and conflict needs tools to manage, the emerging situation caused by a historical discontinuity causes all societies affected to experience confusion and a loss of direction. History during this period becomes more active, affecting all peoples and institutions, working at all levels, and moving in all directions but without a clear sense of direction.

It must be noted that Michel Foucault talks about discontinuity, but his emphasis is on the development of knowledge, particularly the sciences, rather than on history or the development of human societies. In explaining his concept of discontinuity, Foucault says, "It seems to me that in certain empirical forms of knowledge, like biology, political economy, psychiatry, medicine, etc., the rhythm of transformation does not follow the smooth, continuous schemes of development which are normally accepted."[7] In other words, Foucault talks about breakthroughs that happen in all fields of scientific research, and enable most fields of knowledge to make great leaps forward from time to time, and thus he does not

10 GLOBAL ECONOMIC AND CULTURAL TRANSFORMATION

talk about discontinuities that disrupt the established patterns of historical change. Therefore, Foucault's "knowledge discontinuity" and the historical discontinuity this book articulates must not be confused; they deal with different issues, are caused by dissimilar forces, and have different dynamics and implications.

A careful look at the political map of the world as we advance into the second decade of the twenty-first century reveals that most states face difficult political or economic or social and cultural challenges. None of the troubled states, including the richest and most powerful ones, seems able to deal with its problems with confidence or restructure its fractured societal systems. In addition, the traditional tools of economic analysis and financial management, as well as the old means of gaining and maintaining political control, have become inadequate. Thirteen years ago, Robert Reich wrote, "the pilots of the economy have never been here before. All of the old rules seem to be obsolete, and there are no maps and no guides."[8]

Experience of dealing with economic, social, political, and strategic issues is normally a good thing to have; nevertheless, all experience is limited in scope and time. If we were living in a traditional African or Asian country where life conditions change very slowly over time, past experience would be all that a leader needs to manage the challenges his community usually faces. But in a world that changes every second, experience rooted in the past is more of a liability than an asset. "Experts" tend to view the future as an extension of the past and to remain hostage to the old ways of thinking and doing things. Since we have never lived in a world as complicated and integrated and transient as the one we live in today, tools used in the past to manage economic and financial and security issues have become ineffective. Thus, putting the "experts" in charge of managing an evolving situation in a changing world is an exercise in futility; it is an attempt to recycle unrecyclable ideas and use unusable tools. Global challenges require global answers, and new times require new ideas and often new men and women as well.

For example, the complexity of life has rendered the nation-state, regardless of its size and power, too small to handle most international issues, and too big to deal with most domestic ones. A rupture in the historical process seems to have occurred, causing the past to lose its wisdom and become of little help to the future. The present, meanwhile, seems to have gotten lost between a largely discarded past and an unborn future, shaped by strange forces that defy conventional wisdom. In fact, the present, which was traditionally considered an extension of the past, has become more responsive to a future projected by futurists, advertisers, the media, and technological and scientific innovations. Historical discontinuities cause the future to become independent of the past we knew, and different from the present we live but unable to manage.

Every historical discontinuity is a unique development that makes people's experience similar to that of a driver entering an unfamiliar mountainous terrain. As he takes a long curve on a winding road, he loses sight of the familiar landscape that lies behind him, while the mountains he negotiates block his view of the landscape that lies ahead. As his speed and control of the vehicle become subject to the rough terrain, his expectations and confidence become subject to the ups and downs of the winding road. The familiar landscape that lies behind no longer helps; the horizon he faces is so vast and obscured that it provides little clues to what lies ahead.

This book is, in part, an attempt to explain this historical discontinuity and clarify its meaning by placing it in its proper historical and civilizational contexts. Recognizing the contributions of other historians and building upon their insights, I shall try to map the road that got us to where we are today. And using my own ideas and unique life experience, I will try to outline a vision of where we are expected to go from here. In so doing, I hope to be able to define the major forces of change and transformation that got us to where we are, identify the mechanism through which change is introduced and implemented in society, and explain the process of the development of human societies over time.

Richard Rubenstein says that there is a need for a new theory to help us understand the world in which we live.[9] Though this is true, the real need is for a theory to explain the nature and dynamics of intersystem relationships and how they influence our lives so that we may be able to develop a sense of how we got here, where we are going, and how to manage processes of social transformation. In other words, there is a need for a theory to connect the present to the future, rather than to the past, in light of how the present evolved from the past.

Robert Artigiani wrote years ago, "History teaches us to analyze the processes facilitating social revolution instead of trying to identify a vision of a feasible and desirable future."[10] While it is important to know history and learn its valuable lessons, we must realize that we cannot and should not be prisoners of our history, because history's logic changes as times change. Social change may be provoked by history and the collective memories it usually nurtures, but progress cannot be made without keeping an eye on the future; and this requires identifying the agents of historical change, describing the process of change, and understanding the role forces of change play in societal transformations.

The Historical Process

Since the dawn of history, human beings have formed societies with the primary objective of reaching higher levels of security and satisfaction. At the beginning, the pace of change was very slow, making societies seem frozen in time. But as people gained more experience and knowledge and developed better tools and technologies, the pace of change accelerated and life conditions became more complex. Complexity, in turn, presented people with more challenges to face, more issues to deal with, more desires to satisfy, more opportunities to exploit, and more change to endure. As a consequence, more players came to participate in shaping societal life, causing life to be organized in ways that made people and their social systems and problems and desires and fears more and more interdependent.

As societies change and move from one stage of development to another, or from one civilization to another, they pass through transitional periods that cause them to lose their traditional connections to their past. Since each successive stage represents a more developed and complex society with its unique culture and economy, transitional periods represent discontinuities rather than smooth links connecting one stage of societal development to the ones that precede and follow it.

During transitional periods, certain agents of social and at times technological change become more active than usual and new agents of change rise and intervene, causing the pace of change to accelerate and often alter its direction. As a consequence, the pillars of stability in society, particularly traditional values and norms and established social and economic systems, are undermined. Stability is replaced by instability, certainty by uncertainty, and confusion and fear of the unknown become prevalent. Many people are thus impelled to resist change and even to struggle to abort the process of transformation and reverse its course.

Nevertheless, humankind has demonstrated a remarkable ability to learn from actual life experience, adapt, accumulate knowledge, and use it to improve life conditions in general. Societies have seldom failed to use the accomplishments of each passing stage as a foundation on which to build new social and economic systems and structures, produce more and better products, reorganize economic life and social relationships more efficiently, and attain higher standards of living. Such progress, however, has never been accomplished without inviting conflict and causing unrelated changes that made life more complex and dynamic. Conflict and change, therefore, have kept shaping and reshaping human life, resulting in an ever-evolving world of increasing complexity over time.

In most cases, societal change leads to higher levels of security and satisfaction causing more knowledge to be developed and made available to succeeding generations to benefit from. Edward Gibbon said, "We may acquiesce in the pleasing conclusion that every age of the world has increased, and still increases, the real wealth, the happiness, the knowledge, and perhaps the virtue of the human race."[11] Nevertheless, with every new age, life has become more complicated and knowledge more sophisticated and specialized, causing our ability to produce and use knowledge to become decisive in making further social, cultural, political, and economic progress. Yet knowledge and the skills associated with it have always been unevenly distributed both within and among societies. There is today a knowledge gap between those who know and others who know less, and those who know less are less able to compete in an increasingly dynamic, knowledge-based economy. Continued change, moreover, causes this knowledge gap to widen and deepen with every passing day, and transform itself into a power and wealth gap.

As knowledge increases in society, it becomes more institutionalized, causing the influence of institutions through which knowledge in produced and disseminated to the public to increase at the expense of individual and group players. And as institutions and societal systems increase in numbers and complexity, change becomes multidimensional and largely uncontrollable and unpredictable, affecting all aspects of life, at all times. The people most involved with the production and application of knowledge tend to change faster, to benefit more, and to achieve higher standards of living, causing socioeconomic gaps and sociocultural divides within and between societies to widen further.

Historical records indicate that human beings have passed through numerous stages of societal development on their way to the present. Although it is believed that the first human society with a family organization and a language appeared about 95,000 years ago, the first society with a food economy appeared about 30,000 years ago only. For roughly 20,000 years thereafter, human societies were small, made up of bands and tribes that lived a nomadic life as animal hunters and food gatherers. But by organizing into small groups of hunters, people were able to enhance their ability to hunt and use the meat of some animals for food, the skin and fur of others for clothing, and certain bones as tools. A recent archaeological discovery made in Ethiopia in 1996 seems to indicate that humans developed an appreciation for music more than 30,000 years ago and used animal bones to make a musical instrument that can play more than one musical note.[12]

About 10,000 years ago, humans were able to domesticate several plants and animals and use them and their products for a variety of purposes.

Animals were employed to ease the burden of migration, to carry people and food across inhospitable terrain, and increase man's mobility and ability to launch and fight wars. The domestication of plants, on the other hand, enabled man to produce food in relatively large quantities leading people to attain a substantial degree of food security and some independence from nature. Plant domestication was probably the single most important development in human history; it paved the way for human societies to settle, causing populations to grow faster, cities to be built, states to be established, and what is called civilization to appear and slowly flourish.

Human societies that appeared about 30,000 years ago have continued to develop and become larger and more complex; they started with a primitive tribal society, passed through traditional agricultural society, which was followed by a relatively dynamic industrial society. Today, mature industrial societies are moving fast into the still evolving, but very dynamic, knowledge society. Each successive society represents a civilization that is economically and technologically superior to and profoundly different from all preceding ones.

"Culture" and "Civilization"

The words "culture" and "civilization" are often used alternately to refer to the same thing; it is oftentimes assumed that they have the same meaning. Although the terms bear similar definitions, their connotations differ from each other, which make their usage interchangeably inaccurate. Explaining the meaning of each word and the importance of its connotation, however, requires an explanation of how they relate to one another in a historical context. Such a clarification is important to understanding the course of societal development over time, and to identifying the issues that cause different peoples identifying with different cultures to misunderstand each other and at times to clash with one another.

Webster's Encyclopedic Dictionary defines "civilization" as "an advanced state of human society, in which a high level of culture, science, industry, and government has been reached." An alternative definition of civilization by the same source refers to "modern comforts and conveniences, as made possible by science and technology."[13] As for "culture," it is defined as "the sum total of ways of living built up by a group of human beings and transmitted from one generation to another."[14] In general, "culture" stands for the *way of life* that a group follows, and provides the social cement or social glue that binds its members together, while civilization stands for the *state of life* that a group enjoys, and defines the economic means that enables people to satisfy their needs and improve the material conditions of their lives.

The first definition of "civilization" as the achievement of "a high level of culture, science, industry and government," considers culture, just like science and industry, a component of civilization rather than its equal or other face. The definition also suggests that culture does not include science, industry, or government; it only includes intangible things that can be transmitted from one generation to another, such as traditions, customs, values, and attitudes. Culture, wrote Constantine Zurayk, is "the sum of the creative achievements of the human spirit in society."[15] Or, in Thomas Sowell's formulation, culture "involves attitudes as well as skills, languages, and customs."[16] Michael Naumann says, "Culture is a symbol for spiritual innovation, for satirical laughter, for imagination, for intellectual challenge—but also for comfort, for relaxation and for all those forms of entertainment that do not automatically dull people's minds."[17] Since civilization includes culture, and culture is only one component of civilization, neither concept should be used to refer to what the other means or is intended to mean.

The definition of culture concerns itself with the quality of what a society has developed over time in the fields of visual arts, literature, values, traditions, and similar things. It refers also to "the sum total of ways of living built up by a group of human beings," interacting with each other in what we call society. This suggests that culture includes traditions, attitudes, values, lifestyles, habits, belief systems, languages, worldviews, ways of thinking and relationships developed by a people or a nation and transmitted from one generation to another. Civilization, on the other hand, refers to both the quality and quantity of human achievements in the fields of culture, science, and industry; it is therefore a product of all peoples interacting with each other as well as with nature and technology over longer periods of time in countless places. Civilization tends to underline the comforts of life that are attainable through industry, science, and technology, as well as culture. These are comforts that reflect the accumulation and utilization of knowledge developed by all peoples in all places throughout history. While civilization concerns itself largely with the material aspects of life, culture concerns itself mainly with the nonmaterial aspects.

Because the interaction of human beings with nature is meant to discover nature's secrets and laws and exploit its resources, economic factors and technological tools and science have become decisive forces in making and shaping civilizations. Meanwhile, culture is the product of one people's continuous efforts to deal with life challenges that emanate primarily from the social environment in which they live. Civilization, therefore, is produced by humanity and thus it belongs to all peoples; culture is produced by society and thus it belongs to one nation. Consequently, culture is more particular and portable; civilization is more global and hardly transferable—the first is national, the second is universal.

16 GLOBAL ECONOMIC AND CULTURAL TRANSFORMATION

Since culture is a component of civilization and one of its many aspects, a civilization can and often does produce more than one culture or, to be more accurate, several shades of the same culture. Being an attribute of civilization, culture owes its very existence and basic traits to the particular civilization that produces it, and not to any other one, and therefore the fate of each culture is tied to the fate of its mother civilization. This means that as civilizations change and societies move from one civilization to another, cultures change as well.

Because cultures are products and attributes of civilizations, their development follows that of their mother civilizations. This is not to say that cultures do not influence or impact the development of civilizations. On the contrary, after a civilization is developed and becomes well established and largely stable, the cultural component of civilization assumes an active role in shaping change and influencing its direction and pace in society. Culture, being the sum total of ways of living, helps shape the way younger generations think and the attitudes they adopt toward other peoples, other cultures, the environment, the economy, science, and industry as well as time and work, education and technology. However, the most important elements of culture, I believe, are the values it espouses and the attitudes it impels people to adopt, particularly toward the environment, science, work, time, material gain, life, and freedom and tolerance.

Ancient "civilizations", such as the Greek, the Egyptian, and the Roman civilizations, were merely empires that covered large areas of land and ruled several peoples. All such empires had lived in the age of agriculture and therefore, they had similar cultures, not only to each other but also to other cultures that appeared in other places at the time. Describing life conditions and the way of life in Pacoma, a village in Bolivia, Jack Weatherford wrote: "in many ways Pacoma seems typical of village life across South America as well as throughout India, China and Sub-Saharan Africa."[18] A visit to the Van Gogh Museum in Amsterdam will reveal that the artist's paintings depicting rural life in Holland, France, and Belgium in the 1880s, particularly domestic life, could have been done a century later for Mexico, Thailand, or Morocco.

The Egyptian Pharoanic era of more than 5,000 years ago is considered one of the greatest civilizations of the past, if not the greatest of all. But Egypt of today is much more sophisticated and advanced than Egypt of the past, yet it is not considered a civilization. And what is true of the Egyptian civilization is also true of the Greek, Chinese, Indian, Mexican, Roman, Persian, and Islamic civilizations. These were empires having similar cultures and life conditions; however, their architectural and artistic achievements and social organizations were somewhat different. While people may talk of an American or a Japanese culture, no one talks about an American or a Japanese civilization. These are cultures produced by the industrial civilization and therefore the people of both countries have similar ways of living and states of living.

The industrial revolution of the eighteenth century has enabled peoples of Western Europe and North America to achieve higher levels of culture, science, industry, and government, causing the Western state of human living to be recognized as having reached the highest status of all civilizations. This civilization is the one commonly known as the "Western Civilization," but, to be more accurate, it should be called the industrial civilization. In fact, this civilization no longer describes life conditions in the West only, but in all industrialized societies of the West and East. Advanced civilizations produce refined cultures, and refined cultures reflect the achievements of advanced civilizations. The material and non-material achievements of each civilization, therefore, go hand in hand, and their internal and external dynamics and interactions are what make progress, stagnation, or regression possible or inevitable.

Culture in Historical Perspective

Some Third World intellectuals, particularly those belonging to older nations and great empires or civilizations of the past, tend to claim that the Western civilization is a civilization of material and technological achievements, but of little meaningful culture. They argue that human relations in the West in general, and in the United States in particular, are superficial, lacking passion and sincerity and, therefore, reflect lack of refined, humane culture. But in so claiming, such intellectuals conveniently ignore the superior Western achievements in the visual arts, music, literature, education, and architecture, as well as their contributions to the development of individual freedoms and human rights and environmental protection.

Although human relations in Third World societies in general are more personal and passionate, it is doubtful that they are always stronger or necessarily better than those prevalent in the West. In fact, human relations in a large Third World city like Lagos, Cairo, Manila, Calcutta, and Mexico City seem to be not only less conducive to change, but also less personal and passionate than human relations in a small Greek, Spanish, or British town. A United Nations study declared two decades ago that Manila and Bangkok have more in common with Tokyo and Washington than with their rural hinterlands. Globalization is exposing people to aspects of other cultures and causing all cultures to change and be transformed, often unconsciously.

18 GLOBAL ECONOMIC AND CULTURAL TRANSFORMATION

Third World theorists making the argument about the lack of culture in the West, tend to acknowledge, though unconsciously, that cultures are products of civilizations, and that an industrial civilization produces cultures that give priority to the material aspects of life. What causes human relations to become less personal and passionate and more formal and materialistic are powerful forces that include urbanization, industrialization, population growth, migration, and the diversification of interests and careers. Human relations and the social organizations of today are, as they were in the past, functions of environmental settings, human needs, belief systems, political and social and economic structures, interests, education, science and technology, and modes of production. As a consequence, cultures cannot stay the same while needs, interests, and economic activities change and multiply. In fact, history indicates that every civilization has produced its own cultures, and every successive culture has been less personal and passionate and more materialistic than the one that preceded it.

Most Third World peoples view Western cultures as strange ways of living that grew out of a colonialist mentality and are therefore inherently imperialistic, rather than humanistic. Since Western cultures are centuries ahead of Third World cultures in general, they are difficult for Third World peoples to understand and appreciate. On the other hand, Third World cultures stem largely from primitive needs and traditional belief systems and relations developed in small villages dominated by family life; many of them predate the Enlightenment and even the Renaissance age. Because of that, Third World cultures are difficult for Westerners in general to understand and appreciate. While some Third World intellectuals and humanists accuse Western societies of becoming largely materialistic, some Western intellectuals accuse the descendants of the great nations of the past of becoming the new barbarians of the present.[19] Although both views are wrong and rather racist, deeply rooted prejudices on both sides, and a failure to understand the dynamics of cultural change and the relationship of culture to civilization allow such claims and accusations to be made, believed, spread, and consequently persist.

Understanding a different culture that is old or new cannot be accomplished and should not be attempted without placing that particular culture in its proper civilizational and thus historical context. A culture of an agricultural society like Columbia is based more on values than on interests, and therefore more reflective of basic human needs and fears. As a consequence, it tends to be more conservative and personal and passionate, but less open to democratic values than an industrial culture. While every civilization, starting with the pre-agricultural one, had its own cultures and unique economy and society, no society could or did move from one civilization to another directly or promptly; all societies had to go through difficult transitional periods that represented historical discontinuities, causing cultures, economies, production relations, and ways of living to experience profound change. Each transitional period, while signaling the end of one civilization and the birth of another, is rife with all the apprehensions and changed expectations that usually accompany birth and death.

2

Stages of Societal Development

On their way to the knowledge age, human societies passed through a few stages; some historians and other social scientists have made the list lengthy, others have abbreviated it. However, each social scientist seems to acknowledge that the two greatest revolutions in human history were the agricultural and industrial revolutions, which gave birth to the agricultural and industrial civilizations. Historians also acknowledge that these two revolutions have had the greatest impact on people's cultures and economic conditions, or on their general ways of living and states of living. There is also an agreement on at least three major stages of societal development: the hunter-gatherer, the agricultural, and the industrial stage. Nevertheless, a growing number of social scientists think that the information and communications revolutions represent another revolution in human history that is destined to transform both the cultures and economic conditions of peoples of the world. This new stage is often referred to as the post-industrial age, the information age, or the globalization age. I call it the *knowledge age*, because knowledge and the recent technological innovations and scientific developments it includes are the major forces changing people's cultures, worldviews, relationships, and economic conditions everywhere.

Analyzing these stages and how they developed should make it possible to place all social, cultural, and economic transformations in their proper historical contexts and thus track the course of societal development over time. The intended analysis, however, is not meant to recount the history of each society or underline the accomplishments of each civilization, but to find that particular thread which runs through all stages of societal development forming the path of the *historical process*. Emphasis, therefore, will be placed on the major forces of change and transformation and the role they play in linking all stages of societal development to one another and differentiating them from each other.

22 GLOBAL ECONOMIC AND CULTURAL TRANSFORMATION

Historical records of older times seem to suggest that long before the development of agriculture human beings were able to get enough food and attain a sufficient level of security to survive and grow. Familial and tribal ties, as well as customs, norms, and traditions served as social glue that held early human societies together, and gave meaning to their communal life. This simply means that the roots of civilization came into existence probably 20,000 years before the dawn of the agricultural age and the establishment of permanent human settlements. However, it was a primitive civilization based on a food economy that depended primarily on the hunting of animals and the collecting of wild fruits and vegetables. Societies in that civilization were nomadic, and cultures consisted of little more than norms and traditions. The economic arrangements and social organizations were simple and informal and, because of that, early societies remained largely changeless for countless generations.

With the development of agriculture some 10,000 years ago, the economic base of life began to change profoundly, causing culture and the social and economic structures of society to change in ways that made them very different form the tribal ones. "Plant and animal domestication meant much more food and hence much denser human populations. The resulting food surpluses and the animal-based means of transporting those surpluses, were a prerequisite for the development of settled, politically centralized, socially stratified, economically complex, technologically innovative societies."[1] But after agriculture was established and its culture fully developed, the pace of change slowed, causing life conditions to become steady and seem perpetual. Most forces of change were either dormant or yet to be born. Nevertheless, the later centuries of the agricultural era witnessed important developments that included the development of writing, the birth of organized religion and the state, expansion of trade, and the incorporation of merchant life into the life of society, causing the pace of change to accelerate slightly but steadily. Trade helped societies connect with each other and facilitated cultural interaction and technological borrowing, and the state was able to regulate economic and noneconomic relations between neighboring communities, establish law and order, and protect agricultural settlements from invading tribesmen.

In the second half of the eighteenth century, the production of manufactured goods emerged in England as the most important, though not the largest, economic activity. This development heralded the coming of a new era, the industrial age, and the dawn of rapid change in all aspects of life. The coming together of major social, cultural, philosophical, scientific, and particularly economic and technological developments is what historians call the Industrial Revolution. It was a revolution that changed the mode of production and production relations, forcing other social and political and cultural systems and human relations to change drastically, profoundly, and irreversibly. The Industrial Revolution emerged as a continuous process of societal change that seems to have no end in sight. "Our fathers," wrote Charles Van Doren, "started the revolution and we are still living it. We could not stop it even if we wanted to."[2]

Around the middle of the 1990s, industrial society in general and the American society in particular began to experience a new wave of fundamental change or revolution. This new revolution was primarily driven by knowledge, particularly the information and communications revolutions, which caused the economy to shift quickly from the production of tradable goods to the production of tradable services and information and financial products. In the United States, "service employment accounted for 80 percent of employment in 2000. More people were at the time working in doctors' offices than in auto plants and more in laundries and dry cleaners than in steel mills."[3] Consequently, the Knowledge age began to impose its logic on the prevailing ways of living and states of living everywhere, causing all aspects of life in most societies to undergo fundamental and irreversible change.

The Age of Hunting and Gathering

The hunting and gathering age lasted longer and experienced less change than any other age; it started probably 100,000 years ago and continued without interruption until the development of agriculture 90,000 years later. People during this age lived in small families and tribes that survived on the hunting of animals and the gathering of fruits and vegetables. The domestication of animals about 11,000 years ago gave the tribal society and its social organization a new meaning; it enabled the nomads to strengthen their economic base, grow in size, and further develop their culture and way of life. Domesticated animals made tribal life easier and sustainable; the meat of some was used for food, the skin and fur of others were used for clothing, and the bones of some animals served other purposes, providing tools, weapons, musical instruments, and ornaments. In addition, people employed some animals such as the camel and the horse, as means of transportation, making it easier for them to move across difficult terrains, and interact peacefully and otherwise with others. The intellectual horizon of the tribal people, however, remained limited to their families and tribal loyalties.

Culture in this age was in essence a way of life based on age-old norms and traditions and a history of feuding with other tribes. The social and cultural aspects of life or what I call the *sociocultural process* governed the

24 GLOBAL ECONOMIC AND CULTURAL TRANSFORMATION

pace and influenced the course of societal change for thousands of years to come without challenge. In fact, the sociocultural process could hardly be called a process; it consisted of a simple set of traditions and customs that were passed from one generation to another without discernible change. Economic stagnation, the abundance of land and freedom, and lack of technological innovations made change difficult to conceive in this age. However, the basic goals of survival and security improved over time, but remained vastly constrained by nature, which set the limits and defined the space of social and economic activity.

Since economic conditions were basically the same everywhere, the environment became the primary force influencing the course of social change. And since environmental conditions were similar in most inhabited places, they produced similar patterns of living. Consequently, tribal cultures displayed almost identical characteristics in content, in character, in attitude, and in outlook; all had the same internal and external dynamics. The way of life of an African tribe, for example, had been found to be similar to that of a Middle Eastern tribe, which resembled greatly the way of life of Asian, Australian, European, and Mexican tribes. "Many events in human history seem to correlate very remarkably with environmental controls ... The historical theory that ascribes many events in the human record to environmental causes thus receives powerful support from geology."[4] All tribes lived in the same stage of societal development, had the same economy, and developed similar cultures. Members of each tribe were tied to each other by blood and kinship relationships, and believed and largely behaved as if they were members of one large family sharing the same history and destiny.

Yet strict tribal norms and traditions, while strengthening tribal unity they weakened individuality and initiative. On the other hand, internal tribal solidarity reflected an almost equal enmity toward the outside, causing tribal relationships to be shaped by suspicion, hostility, and a strong desire to avenge real and perceived past injuries to tribal honor. Tribes raided each other for a reason and often for no reason at all. Hostility toward the other had been, as the Rwanda, Burundi, and Somalia tragedies of the 1990s sadly demonstrated, an important aspect of tribal way of life. Contact between different tribes often meant war, whose consequences were recognized and largely accepted as normal. In other words, *tribal man fought to live and lived to fight*, causing life in general to start and end with fighting.

Nevertheless, places in which tribes lived were different in geography and topography, as well as in their endowment of plants and animals that lent themselves to domestication. Because of this diversity, argues Jared Diamond, some regions were able to develop first, enter the agricultural age, and make more progress than others. "Hence the availability of domestic plants and animals ultimately explains why empires, literacy, and steel weapons developed earlier in Eurasia and later, or not at all, on other continents."[5] In addition, nature and the dictates of a largely nomadic life denied people the opportunity to establish roots in one place, leading them to have no attachment to a country or develop a sense of belonging to a nation, even after the establishment of the state in the agricultural age. The family house, usually a tent, was the place to which tribal people exhibited most attachment, and the tribe was the nation to which they belonged and to whose customs and traditions and legacy they gave allegiance.

The Age of Agriculture

About 10,000 years ago, man began to domesticate plants and develop agriculture. Although no one knows how this discovery came about, historical records strongly suggest that agriculture was first practiced in present-day Iraq, Palestine, Syria, and Egypt. From there, it traveled slowly to other Asian, African, and European countries. It is also believed that agriculture may have developed independently in other regions of the world, particularly in China and New Guinea. It is significant that "the long transition from foraging to agricultural life ... happened in several places seemingly independently, yet within a few thousand years of one another."[6] Year-round warm weather, the abundance of water and fertile land, and the availability of domesticated animals made a semi-nomadic life possible. And this, in turn, enabled man to observe nature closely, follow its seasonal course, and ultimately discover the life cycle of plants.

Since tribal man was forced by nature and culture to spend most of his time foraging, I believe that the woman was responsible for the discovery of the life cycle of plants and thus the development of agriculture. In fact, women in many agricultural societies have continued to spend most of their time cultivating the land, tending plants, preparing produce for food, and preserving it for cold seasons and hard times. Even today, about 80 percent of all farm workers in the developing countries are women. And while women continue to work in the fields, men in some rural areas are busy developing bad habits, such as smoking and abusing their wives. Therefore, the woman should be given credit for causing the most important revolution in human history, and thus enabling humanity to develop civilization and enjoy its fruits.

The development of agriculture changed the economic conditions of life and the way of life of societies that adopted it; it changed the way societies and economies were organized and transformed human relations, as well as the relationship of people to their environment. Agriculture brought about a new civilization with its own society, economy, culture, social and economic structures, and political organization. "The change from hunting and gathering to agriculture involved more than a mere change in subsistence pattern; it represented a complete change in the social and cultural fabric of life." It "meant also a mental change."[7]

With agriculture, the ability of man to produce enough food to support a subsistence living was no longer in doubt. Because of that assurance, the importance of survival as an existential issue was vastly reduced, causing the life of the wanderer tribesman in constant search for food and a hospitable environment to become largely obsolete. As a consequence, the old way of life had to recede, and the building of a more advanced civilization in its place had to begin. And as agriculture was increasingly becoming a way of life for more people, permanent agricultural settlements began to appear and grow in size, and people began to build houses and communities and make roots in scattered hamlets and villages.

Farming the land and building permanent settlements transformed all aspects of human life. It changed the economic base, creating new activities over which man had some control, and caused land to acquire a new meaning that forced societies to reorganize themselves socially, politically, and economically. Domesticated animals, meanwhile, began to play an added role in the new economy as means to cultivate the land and transport agricultural products to markets. "Compared with the thousands of years humans spent foraging, the construction of villages represented another revolutionary change in culture, subsistence, technology, social organization and history. In many respects, humans still have not successfully completed this major transition."[8] The importance of land in the life of the agricultural society led eventually to private ownership of land, and this in turn led to dividing the agricultural society into two social classes separated mainly by land ownership.

In addition, the farming of the land on permanent bases caused people to develop a strong attachment to their environment, which led individuals and families to acquire a sense of belonging to a place and a community, and later on to a society and a state. As a result, people were forced to develop new traditions, initiate new internal and external relationships, and compete to improve the quality of their lives. And this, in turn, led them to develop and practice trade and acquire wealth, both portable and non-portable. And as trade expanded and agricultural communities grew in size and number, a need for a superstructure or a state arose to regulate access to water resources and fertile land and protect communities and traders from nomadic tribesmen. Consequently, politics and political structures and institutions, or what I call the *political process*, emerged slowly and began to play an increasingly important role in societal life in general. Therefore, the development of agricultural society and economy, and the building of the state superstructure, moved together; they reinforced one another, giving the new civilization its cultural and non-cultural institutions and characteristics.

The social relations that people developed in this age were, unlike those of the tribal age, based largely on cooperation and trust, not on suspicion and enmity. Learning from their experience and environment, people began to develop knowledge and make tools, causing land and labor productivity to rise and their needs and desires to grow and diversify in ways that affected their ways of living and social relations. Meanwhile, the accumulation of knowledge, the legalization and institutionalization of private property, and the ability to produce a food surplus worked together to introduce the idea of progress in human life, and accelerate the pace of societal development in four major areas:

1. State building, which led to strengthening the political process and its societal role as a force of stability and security;
2. Expansion of trade, which created a need to produce new tradable products such as clothing, and paved the way for the emergence of the economic process;
3. Development of tools of production and means of transportation, which led to improving labor productivity, facilitating trade and governance, and introducing a technological element to societal life; and
4. Cross-cultural interaction, which led societies to learn from each other, exchange ideas, and borrow available technologies, causing some people to make more material and cultural progress than others and become more aware of and interested in the world around them.

The need to share water resources among neighboring communities and resolve conflict among clans by peaceful means on the one hand, and the need to protect trade routes and communities from tribesmen on the other, strengthened the state's role as an institution to manage inter-community relations and provide a framework for cooperation and collective security. Subsequently, the state began to build cities as trade and political and cultural centers, form bureaucracies to collect taxes, build armies to protect communities from invaders, and expand state influence over larger areas and differentiated communities. Since most agricultural settlements at the time were small villages and isolated hamlets, they could not survive on their own; they needed state protection particularly from roaming

28 GLOBAL ECONOMIC AND CULTURAL TRANSFORMATION

tribesmen. And because the core purpose of an agricultural community was and still is to farm the land, not fight wars, the new society's capacity to protect itself against invaders was limited. In fact, mobility of fighting forces, which tribesmen had enjoyed, has been an advantage in all wars throughout history. Consequently, the state system evolved as a superstructure, having the authority and legitimacy and power to govern and influence the direction of societal change.

One of the new forces that played a pivotal role in the development of both state and culture was organized religion. Religion as we know it today was a major product of the agricultural age. It came in response to certain human needs, particularly the inability of man to explain nature, its workings, and many of its manifestations, as well as the meaning of life. Religion was also needed to provide ethical and moral codes of conduct and regulate social relations, especially during the formative stages of agricultural communities when the state was still unborn or ineffective. Since some of the questions raised by man thousands of years ago have continued to elude science even today, religious convictions have continued to play a major role in individual and group lives, influencing social relationships and people's outlooks and worldviews. Therefore, no one should doubt the importance of religion in human life or assume that it will disappear any time soon.

Since the material sources and means of survival during the agricultural age were almost the same everywhere, older cultures were similar in content and character. In a certain sense, the early agricultural societies shared similar but not identical cultures. The little change that cultures exhibited during those times came largely as a result of external rather than internal forces. These were forces that compelled individuals and groups to interact with each other through travel, trade, migration, and war and conquest.

While the same economic base caused nations to belong to the same civilization and exhibit its major characteristics and way of life, dissimilar environmental settings and varied internal and external challenges led societies to develop slightly different cultures. "The ways in which different societies responded to challenges distinguished Chinese civilization from that of the Aztecs, or Egyptian civilization from that of India. Problems produced unique responses and further differentiated one culture from another."[9] Nevertheless, the production and consumption of food has continued to be the focal point of the life of agricultural society in general. As a result, *agricultural man ate to live and lived to eat,* making food production and consumption and the enjoyment that comes with both activities the essence of cultures of the agricultural age.

With the expansion of trade and the building of empires, cultures began to play a more active role in individual and societal life, viewing external forces not only as threats to be avoided, but also as challenges to be faced and potential opportunities to be harnessed. Cultures that viewed external forces as challenges and possible opportunities were able to change faster and make more progress. In contrast, cultures that viewed external challenges as threats to be avoided became suspicious and inward-looking, and thus less able to change and make further progress. Culture consequently emerged as a force shaping peoples' attitudes, ways of thinking, and worldviews, defining individual and community identities and goals, setting priorities, and influencing the nature of responses to varied challenges. Such challenges were not limited to the physical environment and the other; they also included new ideas and philosophies, new technologies and scientific discoveries, and unconventional social, economic, and political arrangements. Nevertheless, cultures, regardless of their place and time, have shown little enthusiasm for change, especially change introduced from the outside or instigated by nontraditional forces and ideas.

Sociologists and political scientists often speak of a "national culture" and the role it plays in uniting people and giving them an identity of their own. While it is true that each people living in one state feel that they belong to one country and form one nation, no society has ever had one culture, except the tribal one. The moment the institution of private property was developed, no society could stay homogeneous. And since wealth is a source of power, and power is an effective tool to gain more wealth, the crystallization of private property caused the haves to feel and often behave differently from the have-nots. And this, in turn, served to differentiate the rich from the poor and the powerful from the powerless, causing the culture of the rich and powerful to acquire new traits different from those of the largely poor and powerless. As societies moved from the agricultural to the industrial age, the socioeconomic gaps that separated the rich from the poor widened further, and a new sociocultural divide was eventually created. Socioeconomic gaps reflect differences in income and wealth between rich and poor; sociocultural divides reflect educational levels and cultural sophistication that differentiate one group from another.

During the hunting and gathering stage, the tribe represented the society to which every member belonged. Each tribe had its own chief whose role was regulated by customs, and whose functions were largely limited to leading his people in times of war and mediating between them in times of peace. Life activities, including the economic ones were performed almost entirely outside the family home. But when the agricultural age and its civilization arrived, the tribal way of life lost its meaning and reasons for being. The extended family, or the clan, replaced the tribe and became the basic unit of a typical agricultural community, which consisted of a few clans. Each clan had its own head that was often chosen because of his knowledge

30 GLOBAL ECONOMIC AND CULTURAL TRANSFORMATION

and wisdom, and whose role was to maintain clannishness, manage conflict with other clans, and mediate between his clan and state authorities. In addition, most social and economic activities were performed inside the family home, not outside it.

With the full development of agricultural society, the history and historical logic of tribal society lost their relevance, causing tribal culture and social organization to become less efficient and civilized. So, as the tribal way of life was being outdated, the agricultural civilization with its own history and historical logic was being born. Although tribal history would retain much of its relevance within its own circles for thousands of years to come, it lost under the state much of its pastureland and freedom and momentum. It was forced to adopt a circular movement within an increasingly smaller and more confined physical, economic, and political space.

Consequently, the tribal society, being less free and less able to provide for itself as before, became dependent on the agricultural society; nevertheless, it retained a capacity to disrupt the life of agricultural society and temporarily impede its development. Even when tribes did invade, loot, and destroy states and empires and cause their demise, the invaders could not reverse the course of history. The conquerors were often absorbed by the more economically productive and culturally sophisticated conquered peoples of the world. History, being irreversible, has continued to move forward, making some of the most civilized peoples of the past the least civilized and developed ones of the present.

Since neighboring agricultural communities shared interests and had similar cultures, they had little difficulty interacting with each other peacefully and developing workable means of communications. And because relationships were essentially based on cooperation, trust, and mutual interests, language differences and a scattered existence did not present insurmountable obstacles. But since their cultures were different from those produced by a less sophisticated and civilized tribal society, they had difficulty communicating with tribal people and resolving conflict with them peacefully.

Communications between peoples belonging to cultures produced by one civilization has always been easier than communications between peoples belonging to cultures produced by different civilizations. Latin Americans, for example, have less difficulty communicating with each other than with North Americans, while the latter have less difficulty communicating with Europeans than with Asians. Third World nations in general, whose cultures are products of a largely agricultural civilization, find it easier to communicate with and understand each other than to communicate with and understand the industrial nations of Europe and

North America. Communications across cultural lines, therefore, must be defined as communications across civilizational lines, or across profoundly different cultures produced in different times.

Until the fifteenth century, no center of civilization anywhere in the world had experienced profound change to distinguish itself from other centers. Both Jack Weatherford and Paul Kennedy argued that throughout the Middle Ages the great centers of civilization in the world were at roughly similar stages of development and, because of that fact, "the world formed a single, albeit large, social system that operated at a much slower pace than that to which we have become accustomed."[10] But around the middle of the fifteenth century, the pace of social, cultural, political, economic, technological, and intellectual change began to accelerate and change direction in Europe. As a consequence, all societal systems were forced to enter a new period of transformation. Trade, which by then had become an important economic activity, led the ensuing change and paved the way for the economic transformations and scientific discoveries and technological innovations that were to follow, giving birth to what I call, the *economic process.*

Other developments occurred subsequently and played decisive roles in promoting change and accelerating its pace; they included improvements in navigation tools and maps, building better ships, producing more potent arms, growing competition between the major European cities and states, the development of printing, and the discovery of the New World. Due to these developments, manufacturing expanded; financial services were acknowledged as a legitimate business activity; and scientific, technological, and philosophical inquiry multiplied. Three centuries later, the Industrial Revolution took place in England, and traveled thereafter from there to other European and North American countries, transforming agricultural life in ways and to extents previously unknown. "Agricultural societies were transformed into urban industrial societies within the space of perhaps a hundred years, and all the accumulated norms, social habits and customs that had characterized rural village life were replaced by the rhythms of the factory and the city."[11]

The Industrial Age

In the second half of the eighteenth century a new way of organizing manufacturing began to emerge in England. Workers were brought to work together in one place for one master, who often was the sole owner of the means of production as well as the finished products. People, who worked for the new entrepreneur, were often landless and powerless laborers

32 GLOBAL ECONOMIC AND CULTURAL TRANSFORMATION

having nothing more than their labor to sell. Because of that powerlessness, workers were, especially during the first century of the industrial age, forced to work for long hours and live under intolerable conditions. When man is forced to sell his labor because of need, he is more likely to lose self-esteem and dignity and become vulnerable to exploitation and sometimes to slavery.

The Industrial Revolution, just like the agricultural revolution some 10,000 years earlier, ushered in a new wave of change that transformed all aspects of life in every industrial state. For example, workers were no longer free to determine their working hours and how to perform their work; tasks were assigned, working hours were specified, regulations were articulated and imposed by capitalists, and hierarchical relationships within the workplace were established and enforced. Income was tied to work, making survival a function of work availability and worker's capacity to work long hours and endure the pain of performing repetitious, largely boring, tasks. For the first time in history, the new worker could own neither the place of his work, the means of production, nor the end products he produced. His only source of income was his labor, and his labor was the only commodity he could trade. Industrial man in fact was transformed through manufacturing and money making into a machine, causing work to become the focal point of life. *Industrial man works to live and lives to work*, causing life to start and end with work, even for the majority of the rich capitalists.

The new conditions created by manufacturing forced workers to live near their places of work in clustered residential communities that lacked almost all health amenities. Slums, as a result, emerged and became homes for a growing rootless, powerless, poor, and at times angry social class, whose appearance was seen by many as inevitable. Intellectuals critical of this development, however, saw it as an evil act committed intentionally by heartless capitalists. Consequently, intellectuals called for change but failed to agree on the nature of the desired change, which led them to be divided along two major lines, one revolutionary, and the other utopian. But history, being the product of actions and reactions by many conflicting social actors and natural forces and societal processes, moved forward along neither the revolutionary nor the utopian line. History implemented change dictated by its own logic, the logic of the industrial age, where economic forces, interests, and financial institutions, or the economic process, had become the major forces causing societal transformation. And despite several attempts to build utopias and make revolutions, history has rendered both utopia and revolution unworkable in the long run.

Workers who were most attracted to the new job opportunities in manufacturing were the young whose families had earlier lived on land that was taken away from them by the landlords they had worked for. Being landless in a harsh environment, made them also rootless; they had to plant new roots, build new communities, and develop new traditions suited to their unique circumstances. Karl Marx, writing some 80 years after the birth of the Industrial Revolution, observed that "man's ideas, views and conceptions, in one word, man's consciousness, changes with every change in the conditions of his material existence, in his social relations, and in his social life, or in the state of his living."[12]

However, with the emergence of workers living in crowded slums, things began to change in society, and slowly a new social class emerged and began to seek change. Workers began to form labor unions to facilitate collective bargaining and apply collective economic and political pressure on the capitalists and the industrial state. Intellectuals, seeing the intolerable living and working conditions in and around factories, and the enormity of exploitation especially of children and women, supported the demands of the working class. Gradually, industrial workers developed a strong class consciousness that made them look and behave as a distinct social class. Union members who failed to achieve their goals peacefully resorted to strikes, demonstrations, and at times violence, which helped them become more assertive, forcing the state to recognize their grievances and move to address them.

While people were being uprooted and compelled to work and live under appalling conditions, members of the capitalist class were living in affluence and accumulating more wealth and power, causing both wealth and power to be transformed from the domain of land to the domain of capital. Wealth, meanwhile, enabled the wealthy to improve the quality of their lives and exploit more people as workers and domestic servants. More than a century later the number of servants living at the homes of their masters was used as a criterion to determine the social class to which the household belonged. But despite the fact that farmers and servants who worked on farms and in their masters' houses were by the end of the nineteenth century the two largest groups in industrial society, neither group was recognized or acted as a social class. Members of each group were weak and scattered and, despite sharing similar living and working conditions, were unable to develop a shared consciousness, which is a prerequisite for forming a distinct social class.

As the industrial revolution advanced, it expanded and diversified economic and financial activities, and thus it created new jobs, causing the number of people involved in manufacturing to multiply. And this in turn created a need for people to perform related tasks such as plant supervisors, accountants, labor relations personnel, transportation and trade managers, sales persons, banking and investment officers, technicians to service equipment, and innovators and engineers to develop new technologies and products. Consequently, a new class of largely urban dwellers was born; it was neither rich nor poor but in between. Because of its unique social position and economic functions, the new class shared neither interests nor traditions with either the rich or the poor; it has to develop its own way of life and claim its own place in society as a middle class.

Since wealth and power and social status move hand in hand, the new capitalist class was able to acquire more power, often at the expense of the landed aristocracy and always at the expense of the industrial workers. And with this shift in wealth and power and social status, the social and economic structures of society changed drastically, causing production relations and traditional cultural patterns to change as well. Though industrial society has developed its own culture and economy, the accumulation of change over time has led society to have three subcultures: one for the rich, another for the middle class, and a third for the poor working class.

Official recognition of labor unions and their right to bargain collectively on the one hand, and intellectual support of this right on the other, and governmental involvement were instrumental in facilitating association in society and strengthening democracy and political participation. Meanwhile, a middle class aware of its economic interests but limited political power, moved to support democracy because democracy guarantees political participation and economic freedom. And this in turn gave the middle class a societal role to play and a political forum from which it could air its grievances, protect its interests, and promote change in its favor. And while democracy was being strengthened and labor unions were growing stronger and getting better organized, life conditions in general were improving for all members of industrial society. Several factors had contributed to making this development a reality; noted among them:

1. Continued development of new products and technologies that improved productivity, reduced the cost of production, increased sales, and raised profit margins;
2. Increased demand for manufactured goods at home as well as abroad, which enabled capitalists to make more money and encouraged them to provide better wages and new employment opportunities for workers;
3. Increased state revenues from taxes, leading states to spend more on public health and education, improve infrastructure, and finance other services and welfare programs; and
4. Official recognition of the need to end labor exploitation, limit monopoly, and expand markets, which caused economic activities to expand and provide more opportunities and better-paying jobs for members of the middle class.

Meanwhile, migration from the countryside to urban centers in search of jobs caused the extended agricultural family or the clan and its traditions to ultimately disappear. The new communities that emerged in the industrial cities were composed of nucleus families sharing smaller living spaces and facing similar life challenges. Traditions and kinship ties that provided the social glue that held agricultural communities together for countless generations while minimizing change were no longer workable in the new environment. Old traditions and values and wisdom, therefore, could not be passed on from grandparents to grandchildren without questioning. Life conditions were changing so quickly that knowledge and wisdom of the past were fast becoming outdated and largely irrelevant. And because neither tribes nor clans could exist or function in the new industrial society, the state became more dominant in the life of people and allegiance to it was strengthened.

For example, the old family home on the farm lost much of its economic and social role in the industrial society. Being small and urban, the family home could not perform many of the tasks it used to perform in the village. The education of children, the making of clothes, the processing of agricultural products, and even entertainment moved almost entirely out of the home to new institutions run by specialists. Caring for the sick and the elderly also moved gradually to hospitals and special healthcare facilities, further weakening the old community structure and mutual obligations that held clans and agricultural communities together. Change in social and political relations and economic and social structures led to producing a new civilization, the industrial civilization, with its unique society, economy, and culture. Because these transformations were largely limited to Western societies, the new pattern of life was dubbed the "Western Civilization." Industrial civilization, like agricultural civilization before it, produced its own cultural varieties wherever it took roots.

Historians and philosophers of history, despite a wealth of books and fieldwork, are yet to agree on the forces that caused the Industrial Revolution. Some believe that economics and self-interest were the determining factors that led the transformation process. Others argue that the Protestant Reformation, which brought about many bloody religious wars in Europe leading to the separation of religion and state, was the decisive factor. Still others feel that the enclosure movement, which led landlords to confiscate or repossess land on which farmers had lived and worked for generations, created the first landless, rootless social class that provided the cheap labor whose sweat facilitated the building of the industrial capitalist system. Science, technology, inventions, new ideas, population growth, urbanization, political freedom, trade, and economic liberty are also cited as forces whose contributions to the Industrial Revolution were momentous. In fact, the Industrial Revolution was the product of all these forces and many more. The 300 years prior to the Industrial Revolution (1450–1750) were decisive in giving birth to new forces of change and undermining many of the older ones. These years represented a transitional period during which traditional agricultural systems and institutions and ways of thinking were invalidated, new ones were developed, and quantitative and qualitative societal changes were introduced and legitimized.

Karl Marx was one of the first philosophers of history to argue that the underlying economic forces in society are responsible for cultural products such as religion and ideology. Max Weber, in contrast, argued that culture produces certain forms of economic behavior and work ethics that facilitate economic progress. Both arguments, while basically sound, are partial and therefore cannot individually provide a satisfactory explanation of how societies respond to changes in the economic conditions of life or to transformations in traditions and value systems that regulate life. In a civilizational setting, culture plays the crucial role in changing economic behavior; in transitional periods, economic forces and technological innovations lead the way to change and cause sociocultural transformations.

The age of industry did not only expand manufacturing, it also helped agriculture expand, diversify, and become much more productive; it also expanded trade in agricultural products as well as in manufactured goods. Agriculture, consequently, became dependent on industry; it could not grow on its own to meet the growing demand for food, increase productivity, and improve the quality of products without the machines, fertilizers, improved seeds, and the new irrigation and farming systems that industry and its technological base had developed. In fact, without the advancement of science and technology, food production would have been less than adequate to support a growing industrial working class and feed urban dwellers. Rendering agriculture dependent on industry has also caused agricultural society in general to become dependent on the industrial society. The natural dependency of the agricultural society on the industrial one thus renders the *dependency theory* articulated by Latin American intellectuals largely baseless; it could neither explain lack of development in so many states nor help any of them transform its economy and overcome dependency and underdevelopment.

There is no doubt that the Western capitalist nations and their colonialist enterprise have worked hard to deepen the dependency of Third World economies on their own industrial ones and, because of that, colonialism did contribute to hindering the development of Third World economies and societies. Nevertheless, there was nothing that agricultural society could do to avoid dependency; dependency was and still is a natural historical development that no agricultural society could in the past or can now escape. In fact, there are societies such as Yemen that were not subjected to colonialism but still failed to enter the industrial age, while others that were subjected to colonialism such as Singapore and Malaysia, were able to join the community of the industrialized nations. Therefore, the dependency theory described by David S. Landes as "Latin America's most successful export,"[13] is not a model capable of explaining lack of development in the Third World; it is rather a sophisticated argument to blame the other and justify failure.

The discovery of the New World and the triumph of Christian nationalism in Spain at the end of the fifteenth century, which led to the expulsion of Arabs and Jews from Spain, marked the end of agricultural dominance, practically ending the great civilizations-empires of the past. For 500 consecutive years thereafter neither Arabs or Chinese, nor Indians or Turks or Persians were able to make notable contributions to world civilization. Agricultural society, becoming increasingly dependent on industrial society, could neither challenge industrial society nor could it impede its progress or undermine its cultural, economic, or political dominance. It could not even defend itself against the ideas, values, technologies, and armies of the new society. Because of industrial superiority, tiny England was able in less than 150 years of industrialization to rule over more than half of the world's population for the next 150 years.

The fundamental change in the state of living and way of human living ushered in by the Industrial Revolution was so profound and comprehensive, it made the history and the wisdom of all previous eras largely irrelevant. "The physical and mental world we inhabit has changed more—and faster and more often—in the past 200 years than it did in the previous 20,000 years."[14] Agricultural society, feeling threatened by the industrial state and its colonialist enterprise, became largely inward looking and more protective of its traditional way of living, leading many agricultural nations like China, India, and Egypt to retrench and become more conservative in their thought and outlook, and suspicious of others. This development served to further weaken the ability of such nations to initiate change on their own and transform their societies and economies and industrialize. And due to an expansionist industrial strategy and an aggressive capitalist class and imperialist industrial state, nations living in the agricultural age found themselves functioning within an ever-shrinking, and oftentimes besieged, political and economic space.

The evolvement of the industrial age strengthened the economic forces and institutions, giving capital and the capitalist system prominent roles in societal life. Slowly but steadily, the economic process began to assume

38 GLOBAL ECONOMIC AND CULTURAL TRANSFORMATION

a leading role in all industrial societies, greatly influencing their cultures, social relations, political systems and worldviews. The capacity of this process to contribute to every human activity has enabled it to grow in influence and visibility and to eventually replace the political process as the most dominant societal process. The decisive role played by industrial technology and money in winning World War II was instrumental in giving the economic process and its representatives the opportunity to gain the upper hand in industrial society, particularly in the United States, and claim special rights and privileges not available to the rest of the population.

Changing the state of human living as described above caused the history and the historical logic of the old era, the agricultural era, to come to an end; it no longer had valid experiences to share, or proven wisdom to give. The new society had to write its own history and depict its own logic while its social, political, and economic relationships were being rearranged on new bases. Nations that failed to understand this historical lesson were dwarfed by history and made to pay a heavy price in squandered resources, lost opportunities, and increased dependency on others. It must be noted, however, that both China and India and a few other Asian and Latin American states have managed after centuries of stagnation to face the challenges of our times and experience remarkable economic growth, technological progress, and cultural revival.

Soon after the economic process had become the most influential force of societal change, concerns began to be expressed regarding the damage manufacturing and mining was causing to the environment, and the negative impact that capitalism was having on the poor and social justice. Questions were raised as to the ability of the environment to sustain the prevailing production and consumption levels and meet the needs of future generations. Pollution control, sustainable development, the elimination of poverty, equality of opportunity, and reducing military spending emerged consequently as popular issues motivating intellectuals, scientists, liberal politicians, social activists, and students to challenge the capitalist system and expose its shortcomings. But the worst was still to come.

As the capitalist system was getting more productive, and money was getting more ruthless, a communications revolution and an information revolution were taking place and changing reality in mature industrial societies in new ways. These two revolutions are linked together and dependent on each other, and because of that interdependence they form one societal process, the *infomedia process*. The twin revolutions have transformed the media, leading it to become a powerful tool having the capacity to manipulate the other three processes and influence the course of change in society. As a consequence, they paved the way for the evolvement of a new age, the knowledge age, which has been transforming our economic and social and cultural lives for the last two decades, starting in the mid-1990s.

The Age of Knowledge

The age of agriculture lasted about 10,000 years before the Industrial Revolution occurred. Because of its long duration, it was able to transform the cultures and economic conditions of most tribal societies. When the age of industry arrived in the second half of the eighteenth century, probably more than 80 percent of the world's population was already living in the agricultural age. But when the age of knowledge announced its impending arrival around the middle of the 1990s, the age of industry was hardly 200 years old. Because of that, only about 30 percent of the world's population was living in the industrial age. Due to the complexity and knowledge requirements of the new age, it is not expected to transform the culture or economic conditions or society of an entire nation at any time. In fact, every nation or state will continue to need people to do certain jobs and be engaged in certain activities that are rooted in the industrial and agricultural civilizations.

As the age of knowledge advances, the infomedia process is expected to become more powerful and ruthless, because its services have become essential to the proper functioning of all institutions and organizations of every society, even the traditional ones. On the other hand, the dynamic nature of the knowledge age, and its educational requirements, will make the creation, commercialization, and utilization of knowledge and information and financial, health, and other services the focal point of economic activity. As a consequence, the major source of wealth will shift gradually from the domain of capital to the domain of knowledge and its applications, and a new man whose job is to create and process knowledge through learning will emerge. Because of that, *knowledge man learns to live and lives to learn.*

As we advance into the second decade of the twenty-first century, I feel that the transitional period leading to the age of knowledge is still incomplete; it still has about 15 more years before reaching its end. Therefore, it may be unwise to describe the expected characteristics of the new era in concrete terms, particularly since it is expected to be an era of continuous change. However, many far-reaching changes have already occurred and can be detected at all levels of individual and societal life. Values, traditions, needs, and convictions that provided the social glue that kept communities and families tied together throughout the agricultural and industrial ages have begun to fracture; some have even become dysfunctional. Basic

40 GLOBAL ECONOMIC AND CULTURAL TRANSFORMATION

assumptions that helped economists, political scientists, sociologists, and strategists to conceptualize, define, and analyze social, political, and economic units such as national economy, the nation state, society, culture, and class, have been either partially or totally invalidated.

National cultures, for example, are being divided into subcultures along ethnic, racial, religious, and socioeconomic lines. Shared traditions and values, same languages, and memories, and even religious convictions are no longer enough to maintain the cohesiveness and unity of any nation. Economic interests, lifestyles, hobbies, professional connections, and educational backgrounds are becoming more important in forming new communities and dividing older ones. And because such communities can and do often transcend political borders and ideological divides, they are producing a unique global culture with its own core of values and traditions and even language. National societies, moreover, are being divided into sub-societies along sociocultural lines in addition to the old socioeconomic ones.

Reactions to developments instigated by the advancement of the knowledge age are deep everywhere. People seem to have become overwhelmed by strange currents of change, and there is a feeling of a general loss of direction and control over unfolding events. The resulting reactions to this change range from denial to bewilderment, from political conservatism and religious fundamentalism to radical nationalism and extremism, from aggressiveness to retreat and retrenchment, from embracing the new values and lifestyles to cultural particularism, from universalism and globalism to tribalism, from tolerance to ethno-nationalism and racism. All of these reactions cause conflict and instigate change and, in the process, create new realities that transform perspectives and societies and make history more dynamic and irreversible. In fact, the new age of knowledge promises to make the coming future look like a *world in a permanent state of transition.*

In concluding this chapter, it is important to reiterate that each *stage* of societal development represents a unique civilization that comes after a difficult and sometimes long transitional period. Such periods, viewed from a wide angle, represent historical discontinuities that cause history of the passing era to come to an end, while paving the way for the new era to make its own history. And as one history ends, its logic becomes irrelevant, and the wisdom of the past becomes of little value to the new age and its peoples. Transitional periods are battlegrounds where war is waged between old values and new ones, between forces of stability and continuity and others of innovation and change. Such periods tend to be workshops for destructive creativity, where creativity is a tool of destruction and destruction is a condition for further creativity. As the first decade of the twenty-first century ended, almost all the nation of the world seemed to be, as Matthew Arnold once remarked, "wandering between two worlds, one dead, the other unable to be born."[15]

Each civilization has produced its own culture, within which similar but not identical sub-cultures have developed, causing societies living in the same era to have similar traditions, values, attitudes, relationships, and outlooks. In addition, each civilization or stage of societal development was largely dominated by one societal process. Although that particular process did not cause the elimination of the other processes, it dominated them, reducing their influence in society and making social transformation largely a function of its own dynamics. Since values and traditions are the essence of the sociocultural process, and values and traditions seldom change, societies dominated by the sociocultural process such as the traditional agricultural and tribal societies were unable to experience qualitative change for thousands of years. In contrast, due to the changing nature of interests, which represent the essence of the economic process, societies dominated by this process such as the industrial society have experienced and continue to experience change and transformation without interruption. The change in the relative role of each societal process, as history moves from one civilization to another, makes past history unable to repeat itself, shape the future or predict its course. Moreover, civilizational change makes it impossible for any societal process to fully regain a role it had lost.

As each new civilization got established, the societies of the preceding civilization could not successfully challenge the societies of the new one and, consequently, they became largely dependent on it and thus unable to transform themselves and make real progress on their own. They had to acknowledge the superiority of the new civilization, often implicitly, imitate it and accept dependency on it and its people and their scientific and technological accomplishments, or retreat into their civilizational shell and deteriorate slowly into irrelevance. The history of each stage, as a result, had to end with the transitional period, which marks the end of one history and the beginning of another, each having its own logic and dynamics and is relevant only to its own times. However, the new history and its particular logic will only become clear and easy to understand when the transitional period ends and the new civilization is established. As a result, all societies passing through a transitional period experience confusion, loss of direction, and a *trust deficit*. Since the issue of trust is important to understanding the role of culture in hindering communications between different peoples and creating obstacles that undermine the efforts of all developing societies in their transition to the industrial age, it will be explained in detail in Chapter 9.

The emerging knowledge age is creating a new society that seems destined to live in a state of perpetual change and transformation, or in a permanent state of transition. The infomedia process, which emerged at the end of the twentieth century as the leading societal process, is forcing all other processes to react to its unconventional ideas and values and technologies and become more active. While the sociocultural process is resisting almost all aspects of the cultural change promoted by the infomedia, the economic process is exploiting the economic changes associated with knowledge to promote free markets and maximize profits. The political process, meanwhile, seems to be lost, unable to decide where to go or what position to take, moving in all directions and making decisions that make little sense. This is the first time in history that the sociocultural, political, and economic processes find an environment suited for their activation at once. As a consequence, the way has been opened for never foreseen transformations and unprecedented opportunities for change in all fields of human endeavor. Since no change is neutral, the change societies are witnessing today brings with it a lot of pain and gain that tend to be unevenly distributed, causing some people to get most of the gain, while others feel most of the pain.

While the farming of the land was the development that represented the historical vehicle through which tribal society was transformed into an agricultural one, manufacturing was the economic and technological vehicle through which agricultural society was transformed into the industrial one. Today, globalization and advancements in the scientific and information and telecommunications fields represent the historical vehicle through which industrial society is being transformed into the knowledge one. And since each civilization produces its unique culture, society, and economy, as well as social and economic structures, capitalism and democracy, being products of the industrial age will have to change drastically to suit the new conditions being shaped by the knowledge age or deteriorate slowly into irrelevance.

3

Processes of Societal Transformation

In the not-distant past, natural resources, the environment, strategic locations, ambitious leaders, gifted individuals, creative ideas, cultures, and states played important, at times decisive roles as agents of change and forces of transformation. Lately, however, the roles of all such agents have been vastly and irreversibly diminished, and the roles of the societal processes of change have been enhanced at their expense. These processes are defined as the sociocultural, the political, the economic, and the infomedia processes. These are social mechanisms evolved over time to facilitate the introduction of change and the management of its consequences. And unlike social systems, the societal processes do not abide by certain rules or laws, and are not subject to effective control by any authority. Nevertheless, the degree of sophistication and activism of the dominant process always reflects the philosophical orientation of society and the developmental stage of its economy. Together, these processes form the larger societal framework within which all social systems and institutions function, and through which all change is introduced and managed in society.

Each societal process has specific tasks to perform, objectives to pursue, and logic to follow. But since no change can occur without affecting the roles and relative positions of other players in society, no process can function freely or independently; every process affects the other processes and is affected by them. Despite this relationship, in each civilization or stage of societal development one process distinguishes itself as the major vehicle facilitating societal change and influencing its direction. While the sociocultural process had dominated the life of tribal and early agricultural societies and determined the general direction of change, the political process dominates the lives of mature agricultural and early industrial societies and determines the direction of change. The economic process,

44 GLOBAL ECONOMIC AND CULTURAL TRANSFORMATION

meanwhile, dominates the life of mature industrial societies and influences the nature of societal change and its direction. Today, the infomedia process, in association with the economic process, determines the nature and influences the direction of change in almost all societies, particularly those passing through the transitional period to the knowledge age. Nevertheless, there are indications that the infomedia and economic processes are slowly merging and forming one societal process that would be hard to tame or challenge.

In an effort to become more effective in performing targeted tasks, each process exhibits, in varying degrees, a tendency to change, adapt, and be creative. This tendency is shaped by a desire to gain more power and outperform one or more of the other processes, which dictates that it must compete and sometimes cooperate with one or more of the other processes. Each process, therefore, is subject to change under the influence of four factors:

1. A built-in mechanism to adapt as circumstances change to remain relevant;
2. A desire to influence other processes and make them more responsive to its goals and needs, and less obstructive of its path;
3. A need to anticipate change by the other processes, particularly change perceived as threatening to its position and societal role; and
4. An impulse to react to actions taken by the other processes and changes they experience.

The sociocultural process is the oldest process of all; it was born as the first human society evolved to provide it with a system to organize and sustain itself over time. When religion and the idea of God were developed thousands of years ago, the belief system built around religion emerged as the core of the sociocultural process. And because religions in general claim to be based on universal values and eternal truth, the sociocultural process became a force of stability and continuity. But with every societal change, the sociocultural process and its religious core were forced to adapt to remain relevant and retain a societal role.

Centuries after the development of agriculture, political authority began to emerge and play a pivotal role in societal life, leading the political process eventually to become a major force in every society. In the beginning, the functions of the political process were limited in scope; but with the maturity of the agricultural age and the growth of populations and the expansion of trade, the political process assumed more powers and responsibilities, spurring the formation of states and empires and the building of large fighting armies. In a later, more advanced stage of the agrarian era, the economic process evolved slowly and began to play an active role in societal life, causing the roles of the other processes to change and decline. Today, the infomedia process is the major force facilitating societal change and influencing its direction.

The Sociocultural Process

The sociocultural process includes the social forces, institutions, ideas, values, and belief systems that define, shape, and manage the social and cultural affairs of nations. It performs its tasks by taking actions and sponsoring activities to preserve the cultural heritage of nations, emphasizing traditions and traditional values and belief systems; clarifying the dividing lines between ethnic, cultural, and religious groups within society; and responding to external and internal challenges and altered social circumstances. Since the major organizing principles of this process are values, traditions, and religious convictions, it represents the social forces of stability and continuity rather than change and transformation.

A stable core of values and convictions, and a simple, rather changeless agricultural way of life have given the sociocultural process the opportunity to dominate societal life and influence the nature of change for many centuries. The development of politics into a full-fledged societal process around the middle of the agricultural age and the emergence of the great empires of the past put an end to the dominance of the sociocultural process. And as the European agricultural society entered a transitional period leading to the industrial age, life conditions began to change rapidly and profoundly, causing the sociocultural process to enter a period of transformation characterized by chaos and crisis.

The expansion of trade, the discovery and exploitation of the New World, the questioning of the Church conduct, the increasing complexity of city life, the advancement of philosophy and science and technology, and the emergence of the nation state had combined to undermine most traditional values and question the rationality of certain beliefs. During the industrial age, the role of the sociocultural process was weakened; it could not lead unchallenged or influence societal life as before. Nevertheless, it continued to provide the social glue that held people together, giving them a community to belong to, while giving each nation an identity of its own.

In the second half of the twentieth century, the sociocultural process faced serious inside and outside challenges that forced it to lose balance and influence change in more negative than positive ways. While the dominant political and business elites began to promote social change and advocate building new relationships on the bases of interests and unconventional

46 GLOBAL ECONOMIC AND CULTURAL TRANSFORMATION

values and lifestyles, the conservative forces, fearing consumerism and materialism and liberalism, began to call for resisting change and retreat into their old cultural shells. As a consequence, traditional value systems and relationships were weakened, and the new ones were unable to gain wide popular acceptance. Although this change has influenced all societies, Third World societies in particular were traumatized by it, causing them to experience sociocultural polarization.

Two sociocultural camps consequently emerged in such societies; the first represents the liberal forces that are able to understand the nature of global change and appreciate the role technology and science is playing in transforming world society and economy; the other represents the conservative forces that perceive change as a threat to their traditional way of life and status in society. Having changed the way they view themselves vis-à-vis the other and the world, the liberal forces are advocating rapid change and promoting modernization. And because they see change as a force serving their interests, they claim that the economic and technological imperatives of the time demand a positive response to almost everything modern, including nontraditional lifestyles. The second camp, which represents the conservative forces, seems to lack the capacity to understand the nature of change and appreciate the role modern technology is plying in transforming the economic and noneconomic aspects of life. As a consequence, these forces are resisting change and calling for preserving traditional values and identities. Generally speaking, Third World forces of traditionalism and nationalism view the values promoted by the West and its media as a new wave of cultural imperialism that must be resisted. Meanwhile, no balance between the old and the new is sought anywhere, and no serious efforts are being made to reconcile the differences between the ideas of conservatism and liberalism.

Due to its inability to adapt to rapid technological, scientific, and economic changes, the sociocultural process in every society is today in a crisis. This gives rise to a new phenomenon in which a fragmented society is created in every city and state. One is characterized by affluence, consumerism, and liberalism; the other is characterized by poverty, traditionalism, and conservatism. And in between, there are a few more sub-societies that represent cultural, ethnic, religious, and socioeconomic minorities that feel lost and deprived of most things in life, except traditional values and convictions and memories that hold them together. Today, people belonging and claiming allegiance to the same culture, nation, state, and oftentimes religion, are living different lives socially, spiritually, economically, and intellectually. "The idea of culture as an identity . . . is going by the wayside in the realm of geopolitics."[1]

While growing socioeconomic gaps and sociocultural divides in every society are causing social fragmentation, economic and cultural globalization is creating three major cultures. One is global, to which the rich and the well-traveled and educated elites of the world as well as the youth belong; the second is national, to which the majority of each society belongs; and the third is a minority subculture based largely on ethnicity and religion, to which the poor and the ill-educated and culturally conservative minorities belong.

The Political Process

The political process includes the forces, activities, ideas, and institutions that shape and manage the political affairs of nations. It performs its tasks by responding to political needs at the local level, defining goals and strategies at the national level, and dealing with trade and security issues at the international level. Usually, political decisions are taken by the state, most political activities are carried out by national institutions, and goals are defined by the nation's overall philosophy and perceived need to advance the national interest, which usually reflects the views and interests of the dominant political and economic elites.

With the retreat of the tribal society and the disappearance of its social structure, the political process emerged as an extension of the sociocultural process to replace the tribe's chief and play his role. The growth of populations and the establishment of scattered agricultural communities in need of a superstructure to keep law and order and regulate the sharing of farmland and water resources were instrumental in forming states and defining the prerogatives of politics. Due to the enormity of these tasks, the political process was able to acquire substantial powers and dominate societal life in general for a long time. But as economic activity increased and diversified, and trade expanded and democracy spread in industrial countries, the state was impelled to recognize the rights of people to participate in shaping policy and determining the direction of politics. Consequently, the grip of the political process on societal life began to weaken, and the popular commitment to a national interest began to fracture.

Today, economic and cultural globalization, environmental concerns, world poverty, international terrorism, and a growing commitment to human rights are making political decisions and most politicians answerable to a world public opinion and subject to scrutiny by nongovernmental organizations and, at times, the world media as well. Meanwhile, the gradual disintegration of traditional society, wider recognition of the legitimacy of cultural diversity, and increasing life complexity have changed

48 GLOBAL ECONOMIC AND CULTURAL TRANSFORMATION

the way politics are organized, and how political institutions respond to internal needs and external challenges. Consequently, the political process of nations, particularly the democratic ones, has begun to lose coherence and focus. Politics today is seldom able to develop comprehensive and coherent sets of national objectives capable of winning popular support, causing the national interest to become a concept easy to speak of but hard to define. Consequently, national politics have become subject to the influence of external forces and global economic and noneconomic considerations that reduce states' capacities to take decisions and initiate actions freely.

Global developments since the early 1980s have reduced the ability of the political process to focus on issues of public concern. Such developments include international security and terrorism, the recurrence of economic recessions and financial crises, an open international trading system, economic migration, easy movement of jobs and investment capital from one country to another, and the integration of many industries worldwide. "Entrepreneurs built the national companies that destroyed local companies at the end of the nineteenth century, and they are building the global companies that are destroying national companies at the end of the twentieth century."[2] Forced to respond to many groups with varied and oftentimes contradictory objectives, the political process has become more reactive than proactive, and more vulnerable to the influence of the other societal processes, particularly the economic and infomedia ones.

The Economic Process

The economic process includes the forces, activities, ideas, institutions, and objectives that shape and manage the economic affairs of nations. It performs its tasks by responding to market forces that reflect the preferences of consumers on one hand, and the forces that motivate business people to engage in economic activities on the other. Opportunities created by technological developments and changed domestic and international conditions provide strong incentives for the economic process to expand globally and diversify its activities. Because profits are made by producing and selling goods and services, and since demand for such goods and services exists everywhere, the economic process functions at all levels, in all places, at all times, and pays attention to all potential markets and opportunities.

As a consequence of economic globalization, which internationalized investment and trading and financial markets, the state's role in managing national economies was weakened, and the role of the economic forces was strengthened at its expense. As a result, the multinational corporation felt free to expand, merge with other companies, downsize operations, outsource tasks, invest overseas, and pressure local and national governments to change laws and regulations in its favor. And as it seeks to increase market share, reduce production cost, improve competitiveness, and maximize profits, the multinational corporation neglects the communities where it operates and pays little attention to its workforce, creating winners and losers among states and regions. As a result, corporate social responsibility declined, national interest lost much of its meaning and appeal, and economic considerations outweighed all other considerations. Mergers of important industries and the increasing mobility of money and knowledge as well as knowledge workers are leading the economic process to become global and more powerful and ruthless.

Since profits are the major organizing principle of business entities in general, economic considerations rather than political or social ones guide this process and shape its relationships to the other processes. And due to the power it has gained since the mid-1950s, the economic process has begun to manipulate political and nonpolitical actors to strengthen its capacity to function freely. The political process, unwilling to surrender its traditional authority in society, is struggling to impose its will on the economic process, and provide adequate protection for consumers and the environment. While some states like China are able to control economic decisions; states like Germany and France are only able to influence such decisions; other states like the United States and Britain seem to have lost their capacities to do much to align corporate goals with the national goals.

In response to these developments, local politicians in America have become more active, demanding that the federal government gives more attention to job creation and worker training, while moving to acquiesce to corporations' demands, offering them subsidies and preferential tax treatment. Such actions are intended to provide financial incentives to entice new corporations to move to their communities and discourage others from leaving. But in both cases, local communities lose revenues that could otherwise be used to provide much-needed services related to education, labor training, healthcare, poverty, homelessness, and the like.

Economic and technological changes that occurred since the Industrial Revolution have increased the power and elevated the status of economics and businessmen in society. Most of the prestige and moral authority commanded by religious, political, and intellectual leaders in the past have been transferred to the domain of wealth. Corporate managers in the West in general, and in the United States in particular, have acquired more power than most politicians, are listened to more often than intellectuals, and are followed by more people than most religious men; the 2008 financial crisis,

50 GLOBAL ECONOMIC AND CULTURAL TRANSFORMATION

however, has changed this trend slightly. In his book *The Buying of the President,* author Charles Lewis wrote, "The wealthiest interests [in America] bankroll and, in effect, help to pre-select the specific major candidates months and months before a single vote is cast anywhere,"[3] causing the people who elect presidents, senators, and congressional representatives to become a mere afterthought of those elected.

According to conventional wisdom, "necessity is the mother of invention." But the institutionalization of research and development as part of the production process, and the media's involvement in the commercialization of products and services, have changed this perceived reality. While many new products and services are byproducts of scientific investigation and technological developments, media promotion of all types of products has been creating new human needs never existed or felt before. Decades ago, need was the mother of invention; today, invention has become the father of need. Every human need leads sooner or later to creating a new invention to satisfy it; every new invention leads, sooner rather than later, to creating a human need for it. So need instigates invention, invention feeds need, and the interaction of the two makes economy more dynamic, life more complex, and people's ability to reach a comfortable level of satisfaction largely unreachable.

For example, emphasis on crime in America has created a need for personal security and property protection. By heightening people's fear of crime, the media, in conjunction with the economic process, was able to develop in a few decades a multibillion dollar security industry. And due to sustained emphases on crime and terrorism, the need for security has continued to evolve and expand, leading people to upgrade older systems and get more protection. And as the need for security in the United States increased, people in most other countries have become aware of the need and the technology to satisfy it, leading security services to become a fast-growing international industry. Meanwhile, popular support for the imprisonment of criminals has made the building and management of prisons in the United States a huge business enterprise and the cornerstone of economic development in many impoverished communities that compete for housing more prisoners in their towns.

The Infomedia Process

The infomedia is made of the traditional media (newspapers, magazines, and books), radio and television, and the electronic and social media. As for the infomedia process, it includes the forces, activities, organizations, and groups that control the flow of information and news and manage entertainment programs in society. The infomedia performs its tasks by responding to events and crises, analyzing official policies while giving priority to certain issues over others, providing educational as well as entertainment programs, collecting and disseminating information, facilitating the flow of ideas worldwide, and following trends of change. And for a price, the infomedia provides leaders, politicians, and businesses with the means to promote their causes and reach their targeted audiences in a timely manner.

The twin revolutions of communications and information have vastly energized the media and expanded its reach. They enabled it to enhance its contents and activities, expand its national and international coverage, and transform itself into a powerful societal process. The ability of the infomedia to reach everyone, everywhere, at all times, and its willingness to provide information and entertainment programs continuously has given it the power to influence people's attitudes, to mold and remold public opinions, and to transform all cultures. And since all information and news has to pass through its channels, it is able to manipulate facts, politics, and people's hopes and fears as well as business decisions.

The infomedia process began to develop steadily and play a transformational role in society after printing was revolutionized in Europe in the fifteenth century. "Books became in the sixteenth century things for entertainment as well as instructions—a transformation as great as any in human history."[4] Before that time, most people in the world communicated by means of the spoken word, not the printed one. But since the spoken word is limited in its accuracy and ability to reach a large audience, ideas could not travel or spread easily; they encountered obstacles and were subjected to distortion and misinterpretation. But with printing, ideas were able to spread easily and exert an increasingly powerful impact on people's attitudes.

During the transitional period that took Europe from the agricultural to the industrial age, the media played a double role, facilitating the spread of new ideas on the one hand, and helping absolute rulers to control the flow of information and limit freedom of speech on the other. "In states that succeeded in controlling the press, most notably in Spain but also in Eastern Europe, the monarchs maintained their grip on religious, social and political thought."[5] In the twentieth century, the media also enabled states, especially Third World and communist states, to gain unprecedented power and use it to manipulate people and control most spheres of societal life. "Before the twentieth century, states could seek or claim such control. They could not exercise it. Now they can," [6] wrote Thomas Hugh.

Due to the immense power of the media, the political and sociocultural processes have tried to control it, subjecting its activities to certain regulations and ethical codes, but without any discernible success. In the West, particularly in America, the media functions freely, and the standards it has agreed to abide by are of its own making. Meanwhile, the economic process tried with great success to purchase media outlets and transform them into business concerns dedicated to promoting its ideas and making money. As a consequence, media elites, having their own unique identity and goals, emerged to promote a culture that reflects attitudes and values and lifestyles not necessarily shared by the public at large.

Members of these elites who own major media companies and manage news and other educational and entertainment programs find themselves almost always in conflict with forces managing the institutions of the sociocultural process. The culturally and religiously conservative forces in America and in other states like Saudi Arabia, realizing the power and influence of the media, were quick to establish their own media outlets, not just to counter what is perceived as disinformation disseminated by the liberal media, but also to launch their own misinformation and disinformation campaigns. And by so doing, the media has confused the public and vastly limited the freedom of speech to everyone, except to those who own a media outlet. In most Third World countries, the media cannot escape government control; it is strictly regulated and often owned and managed by state organs, causing freedom of speech to be denied to everyone, except to those who promote the ideas and lies of the ruling class and justify whatever mistakes they make and crimes they often commit.

As the media was gaining the power and freedom to collect, analyze, manipulate, and disseminate information regarding most aspects of life, this power was increasingly being concentrated in the hands of a few conglomerates and smaller groups of media elites. "Our 25 leading newspaper corporations own a third of all American newspapers, control two-thirds of circulation and have more than $30 billion in annual revenues, half of which come from non-newspaper activities,"[7] wrote Richard Harwood back in 1994. Merger activities since then and expansion in other fields like commercial education and publishing have made media ownership and power much more concentrated than ever before, while expanding its reach tremendously.

Freedom of expression, which most Western elites and traditional political parties preach religiously, has consequently become a victim of monopoly on the news, commercialization of entertainment programs, and lack of effective public oversight. Freedom of speech in my opinion has two basic requirements: having the freedom to say whatever you want to say, and having the ability to reach your targeted audience, which the media controls and seldom facilitates.

Moreover, media entrepreneurs have become increasingly more interested in making money than in educating or informing the public. They favor profitable programs that feature violence, crime, drugs, and sex, even programs that are socially harmful and morally corrupt. Richard Hardwood found that the dedication of corporate leaders "to journalism and its essential role in a democratic society is suspect. They are more responsive to the short-term demands of the stock market than to the values their industry supposedly represents."[8] In fact, while the forces of the economic process are busy polluting our physical environment, and money is busy corrupting politics and politicians, the forces of the infomedia are actively distorting our values and polluting our minds and social and cultural environments.

In the Third World, the development of transistor radio and television came at a critical time for the masses. They came while illiteracy rates were very high, giving the radio and television the opportunity to become the major sources of news, information, education, and entertainment. As a consequence, television and radio enabled the spoken word to make a great comeback, causing the desire for reading by students and the public to decline substantially, while causing book publishing, critical thinking, and intellectual thought to suffer a tremendous setback. Being the major source of information and education, a state-controlled media is able to manipulate the fears and desires of the masses, mold and remold their opinions, and color their views. The media has also created a consumer society in every Third World state whose members are interested in conspicuous consumption much more than in creative work and economic production.

Nevertheless, modern means of communications and the Internet and social media have created a more alert world public. Communications is in fact making people on all sides of the economic, political, cultural, and ideological divides more aware of what exists on the opposite side. It also provides people with the opportunity to link together, causing unprecedented social and cultural interactions that undermine the barriers that made communications across cultures difficult in the past; they also expose the excesses of dictators and sometimes the corrupt economic and political elites as well. The revolutions that swept Tunisia, Egypt, Libya, Syria, and Yemen in 2011 underscore the power of social media. In addition, fast and cheap means of communications have enabled the economic process to establish service centers in states where labor is cheap to serve customers worldwide; it has also encouraged the development of a world culture and facilitated the rebirth of minority subcultures.

54 GLOBAL ECONOMIC AND CULTURAL TRANSFORMATION

"The digital revolution allows once-ignored and even shunned groups to become organized."[9]

And as it facilitates the formation of subcultures, the infomedia facilitates the creation of global cultures that link young people and knowledge workers together across political lines. Kenichi Ohmae wrote, "In those societies open to the influence of the multimedia, the critical balance is already beginning to shift. Children and teenagers are, at deep levels of sensibility and knowledge, becoming much more like their counterparts in other societies similarly influenced than they are like the older generations within their own culture."[10] As a result, the young in societies exposed to the full influence of the infomedia have largely lost their ties to their traditional cultures and national identities; they have become followers of an emerging global culture that recognizes no political borders and abides by no ideological convictions. Ohmae adds, "The link among generations has been broken; a new link with those sharing similar experiences has been forged."[11]

Dynamics of Change

As explained earlier, the sociocultural process was the first societal process to emerge in history, followed by the political process. These two processes, concentrating primarily on continuity and stability, worked together and reinforced one another to dominate societal life for centuries. The economic process emerged slowly and grew gradually during the agricultural age, gaining momentum only after the Industrial Revolution. However, as it began to mature, the infomedia process emerged to challenge its dominance but not its goals. These two processes have worked together and continue to reinforce one another, concentrating primarily on change and transformation rather than continuity and stability. The sociocultural process produced great ideas and ideologies, of which religion is the most prominent one. The political process produced great leaders, empires, and political philosophies, of which nationalism, colonialism, and democracy are the most notable ones. The economic process produced great technologies, entrepreneurs, inventors, and industrial and trading companies as well as capitalism and communism. The infomedia process is producing great technological innovations, virtual communities, and global cultures, while systematically destroying many of the old ideological and cultural barriers.

The sociocultural process worked relentlessly to transform early human settlements into stable communities, using kinship, traditions, and belief systems to give each community an identity of its own. The political process, motivated by ambitious leaders and an ideological zeal, created nations, states, and empires that facilitated cultural interaction and helped expand trade. The economic process developed many products and activities that impelled people to build new associations on the basis of economic interests, causing all nations to eventually become largely economically interdependent. The infomedia process works today to link individuals together, create virtual communities on the bases of shared hobbies and interests, and transform the world into a global village that progressively renders political borders less meaningful, national cultures less particular, and ideology less sacred.

In addition, the infomedia provides the elites and masses with the means to communicate instantly and exchange information and ideas constantly. It uses sophisticated technologies and networks, as well as psychological methods to change attitudes and mold cultures, promoting certain values, undermining others, and encouraging the creation of new, unconventional ones. Since values are the heart of all cultures, some people accuse the Western media in particular of cultural destruction, while others call it cultural imperialism. Both views seem to acknowledge the importance of the infomedia but fail to find a way to use its potentialities to their advantage. And in conjunction with the economic process, the infomedia works to create a new world society free of rigid traditions and moral constraints, and an individual free of the usual national and cultural attachments.

In each age, the societal process that enjoyed most authority in society has claimed most of its talent. In the agricultural age, the sociocultural process attracted some of the most talented people, employing them in the service of religion to spread the faith and develop its doctrine. When the political process became the most dominant, it attracted the most talented individuals, employing them as bureaucrats, military commanders, and tax collectors. As a consequence, the sociocultural and political processes denied society the opportunity to use its talent to develop its economy, technology, and educational institutions, directing talent instead to ensuring continuity and maintaining stability and control.

The economic process also attracted most of the talented people, employing them in industrial production, innovation and technological development, and marketing and financial activities. Today, the infomedia process, along with the economic one, attracts almost all the talent in industrial and post-industrial societies, as well as a good portion of the talented individuals of the developing world. Talented people are being employed by profit-making enterprises primarily in the fields of research and development, and information technology and telecommunications. As the economic and infomedia processes employ world talent to develop

56 GLOBAL ECONOMIC AND CULTURAL TRANSFORMATION

the economic and financial services for the benefit of capitalists and bankers, they cause the socioeconomic gaps in every society to widen and the sociocultural divides to deepen further.

Every social, cultural, political, and economic activity involves the four processes of change and transformation. All change that societies have experienced throughout history has been the result of actions and reactions and interactions precipitated by agents of one or more of the four processes. When relationships between these processes are well defined and in balance, which rarely occurs, stability prevails in society, but only for a short time. When one process moves to expand its influence at the expense of another, conflict ensues, causing instability and provoking change. Instability, just like stability, is neither permanent nor necessarily bad. But for balance to be restored temporarily, a new relationship has to be built on new bases that alter the relative powers of all social forces involved.

Today, the sociocultural process is being pushed to abandon its traditional role of unifying nations and communities around shared values, traditions, and convictions. Emerging circumstances are forcing this process to move in two different and largely contradictory directions at once: the first is dictated by a need to accommodate the desires of an expanding economic process; the second is dictated by a need to accommodate the interests of minorities demanding cultural and political recognition. While the development of a global culture based on the values and lifestyles of Western consumerism accommodates an economic process eager to expand internationally, the creation of subcultures and *cultural ghettos* accommodates the demands of minorities for cultural and political rights.

Since the sociocultural and political processes are always searching for followers to lead and manipulate, and the economic process is always looking for new consumers and markets and investment opportunities to exploit, the infomedia has become the main vehicle facilitating the movement of all social actors, helping other processes achieve their goals. And by so doing, the infomedia has become the major forum to debate public issues, define national goals, and set public priorities. As a consequence, the infomedia process is able to assume the traditional role of the political party in democratic states, causing the democratic institutions to be undermined and become less able to function properly.

The sociocultural process tends to perform well at the communal level, fostering group unity and cultural identity. The political process tends to perform well at the national level, building nation states and developing national cultures and identities and economies. The economic process tends to perform well at the international level, linking economies and major markets and industries together and creating economic and political interdependences on the basis of mutual interests. The infomedia process tends to perform well at all levels; it helps integrate economies and industries at the global level, facilitate the fragmentation of societies and cultures at the national level, strengthen cultural ties and deepens religious beliefs at the communal level, and spread knowledge and make it accessible worldwide.

Interaction among the four processes causes relationships in society to change constantly. During periods of rapid change, relationships usually become chaotic, causing rules and regulations to become less effective, and traditional ways of thinking less helpful. At such times, intellectual activity and creativity is usually revived and encouraged to go beyond the known and traditional, which often leads to undermining the conventional wisdom and its logic and causes new worldviews to emerge slowly. In transitional periods, however, it is always easier to explain emerging situations than control them or predict their outcomes.

Chaos and order exist together in one world; they are two sides of one social process, and therefore neither one can survive long without the other. Order without some chaos, just like total cooperation without any competition, characterizes social systems that lack dynamism and are unable to adapt to new circumstances. Uncontrolled chaos, just like cutthroat competition, characterizes systems that are badly conceived, largely unproductive, and thus headed toward disintegration. Chaos and order are needed to build and sustain healthy societies characterized by dynamism and creativity. As Lester Thurow once said, "America has more than enough chaos to be creative, but too little order to use its ideas in the most efficient ways. Japan has more than enough order to be efficient but too little chaos to be creative." [12]

A new theory of social change capable of explaining chaos and order and how and why they erupt often unexpectedly is badly needed to bridge the widening gap between the reality of politics and the imperatives of economics in the evolving knowledge age. Such a theory should make it possible for us to use the certainty of order to regulate chaos, use the dynamics of chaos to transform order, and employ the propensities of both chaos and order to resolve conflict peacefully and make progress a reality shared by all.

4

Social Transformation

Social transformation means the restructuring of all aspects of life; from culture to social relations; from politics to economy; from the way we think to the way we live. Through time, societies have been transformed from small associations of individuals tied together by instincts, need, and fear, to small communities tied together by circumstances, kinship, traditions, and religious beliefs, to nations tied together by history, politics, ideology, culture, and laws. But for most of human history, the pace of change was very slow; no transformations in life conditions could be felt for several generations. However, "once tools were regularly made and used, they became a factor in human evolution, setting limits to behavior and opening new possibilities in both the organic and behavioral spheres."[1] Tools or technology in general have made change not only possible, but also inevitable. And once a society experiences profound transformations, the ensuing change becomes irreversible. "History, the truly relevant source of change, will not be reversed,"[2] wrote John Kenneth Galbraith.

Social transformation represents qualitative and quantitative change in all aspects of life, causing, as it evolves, social and political conflict. Depending on the extent and pace of the change, conflict can be mild, expressed largely in the form of intellectual dissent and spiritual revival, or severe expressed in political upheaval or civil war. Since each conflict has its own causes, no conflict can be resolved without the introduction of some change to address the basic causes of conflict.

In earlier times, man lacked the ability to control his physical environment, or even modify its behavior to be responsive to his needs and desires. Because of that inability, the environment was able to impose its will on human life, causing life conditions to stay static for generations. Tools that societies developed at the time were very primitive, and not in common use, and therefore could not have a noticeable impact on societal life. As a result, the life of the gatherer hunter as well as the tribal man remained

60 GLOBAL ECONOMIC AND CULTURAL TRANSFORMATION

the same for thousands of years; only war and mutual victimization were common occurrences during those times.

During the age of agriculture, the farming of land enabled man to acquire some capacity to influence his environment and make it more responsive to his needs and desires, causing social change to start moving. Internal forces representing changed environmental settings and new ideas and tools led to changing man's traditions, values, and relationships. Meanwhile, external forces representing military conquests and commerce led to cultural interaction among societies and instigated technological borrowing and the expansion of trade. Yet, meaningful transformations were not possible at the time because neither the internal nor the external forces of change were capable of conceiving a different future, let alone forcing it on societies whose cultures were based on traditions and rigid belief systems. Moreover, cultures of the agricultural age were similar to each other, making the impact of borrowing very little indeed.

In contrast, during the age of industry, the pace of social transformation accelerated due to the multiplication and diversification of the internal and external forces of change. The internal forces, which included manufacturing and changing the social and economic structures of society, were responsible for causing unprecedented transformations in the totality of life conditions in every industrial society. And due to expanding trade and launching the colonial enterprise, the external forces were responsible for causing similar, but smaller changes in most other parts of the world. Political freedom, high rates of economic growth, manufacturing, science, advanced technologies, education and health care, urbanization, and military power enabled the industrialized societies to change and change the world around them.

In the post-industrial age, due primarily to the information and telecommunications revolutions and economic and cultural globalization, societal change has become a dynamic process of transformation that has no end in sight. Since the services of the twin revolutions are in need everywhere, their impact stretches beyond all political borders and involves all cultures. And because the institutions through which these revolutions function are controlled by the rich and knowledge people, the ideas and actions of those people are having a great impact on the lives of all individuals, groups, nations, and states. In the wake of the collapse of communism and the end of the Cold War, the rich and knowledge people began to form global elite and use their power to gain control of the major economic, financial, media, and technological institutions worldwide. And to secure their interests and consolidate their power, the world's rich began to compete less and cooperate more with each other, free themselves from old ideological bindings and national causes, while keeping conflict manageable and change sustainable.

At the time of completing this book in June 2013, technologies to enhance our ability to deal with every aspect of life are being developed at the speed of light. Countless individuals and groups residing in hundreds of towns and villages, working through thousands of networks and organizations with varied, oftentimes contradictory, interests, are participating in this unique development process. As a consequence, a *world in transition* is slowly emerging, where many forces are instigating change and causing social transformations of immense proportions and implications. It is estimated that the last 30 years of the twentieth century had witnessed "tenfold increase in communication by electronic means and tenfold reduction in person-to person contact,"[3] causing writing and mailing letters and traveling long distances to meet with people to discuss issues of mutual concern to be vastly reduced. And since the pace of this change is accelerating, it is transforming our world into a place in a constant state of transition.

A world in transition describes a societal life in which no stable situations exist or could exist. Change in such societies moves in all directions, works at all levels, and affects all people and relationships at the very same time. And as it moves, it produces winners and losers, with both having different social, educational, and cultural backgrounds, as well as different needs and interests. Because of this complexity and dynamism, no particular trend of change can be defined with clarity and accepted as desirable or opposed as undesirable, causing future planning for change to become complicated. Technologies covering all areas of production, management, scientific research, education, and services are working throughout the four societal processes whose actions, reactions, and interactions are the major mechanisms that facilitate change and instigate conflict, and, in the process, cause profound social transformations.

Social Transformation in Earlier Times

During the age of hunting and gathering, a nomadic tribal society emerged and lasted thousands of years without meaningful change. Members of that society organized themselves around customs and were tied to each other by blood and kinship relationships. While customs had the force of the law, myth and magic played the role of science and technology. Since traditions and customs are forces of stability and continuity, and myths and magic are acts of deception and sources of fear, neither of which could instigate real change. Consequently, social transformation was not possible, and history was forced to move in place rather than in time.

62 GLOBAL ECONOMIC AND CULTURAL TRANSFORMATION

Animal husbandry and plant cultivation were the most important technologies developed by man about 10,000 years ago; they enabled societies to change and take a giant step toward civilization. A transition from the tribal to agricultural civilization represented a true revolution in the totality of the human condition, causing, as it unfolded, change, tension, anxiety, hope, and fear. "Every great change in human history has come at a high price, and the greater the change, usually the higher the price."[4] Tribal societies that choose to change were able to make material and cultural progress, while others that resisted change had to endure relative poverty and, at times, famine for the sake of a nomadic life that provided them with freedom and little else.

Religion appeared thousands of years after the development of agriculture, and developed over time into a sacred institution with a great deal of authority. At times, religion associated itself with the state; at others, it controlled the state. But often it competed with the state for influence and for people's allegiance and obedience. However, people in those times lived in smaller communities and isolated hamlets, and had a strong belief in faith and fate that led them to accept their lot in life, obey religious and nonreligious authority, and refrain from questioning their leaders' orders and intentions and, because of that, they changed very little.

Life under traditional agriculture is usually timeless and serene, enabling belief in faith and fate to prevail and perpetuate the forces of stability and continuity in society. Such life reflects tranquility and peace of mind, which breeds acceptance and stagnation, and limits man's curiosity and imagination. In fact, agricultural societies in general prefer feeling to knowing; people want to feel good and be secure. They usually lack the desire to know more than needed to run their daily lives, and to have little or no interest in knowing what might disturb life, particularly the inner life of faith and contentment. Generally speaking, agricultural people prefer believing to thinking, because the first is easier and more comfortable to entertain, while the latter in more difficult and less comfortable to contemplate. Due to the prevalence of such feelings and attitudes, it took some 10,000 years and numerous technological developments and scientific discoveries and countless ideas and wars before life under agriculture began to experience systematic and systemic change and witness genuine social transformation.

Around the end of the fourteenth century, commerce began to challenge both traditions and traditional authority in Italy and other Southern European countries. The expansion of trade caused economic and financial activities to expand and diversify, enabling cities and city-states to grow and prosper. As a result, a new social class of merchants emerged to manage trade, challenge the Church's economic doctrine, and promote financial services. Members of this class were city dwellers, some of whom were freed from the feudal system that had previously enslaved them. Because of their experience with slavery, most city dwellers felt and acted as free people. If democracy is "government of the people, by the people, for the people," as US president Abraham Lincoln said, the city-states in Southern Europe were "government of the merchants by the merchants for the merchants."[5] However, the conservative teachings of the Catholic Church and its economic doctrine made it difficult for cities and their urban populations to function freely and pursue their interests without Church interference. Consequently, conflict could not be avoided, and further social change could not be facilitated without the introduction and subsequent acceptance of change in the role of religion in society.

The expansion of trade, urbanization, and conflict with the Catholic Church were aspects and agents of social and economic change. As trade was expanding, a new economic philosophy, called mercantilism, appeared, dictating that the state make new laws and regulations to support manufacturing, protect national industries, and exploit the markets and resources of other, less fortunate nations. It was this philosophy that provided the engine of Western colonialism and paved the way for the development of the economic process. Although the establishment of financial institutions and the formation of large trading houses were instrumental in strengthening the economic process, "the manufacture of cloth was the chief industry of the age of agriculture, and in the end innovations in it indeed led to the transformation of the world."[6]

Between 1500 and 1650, Europe was a battleground dominated by religious and political wars from which the royal dynasties, the nation-state, and merchants and capitalists emerged as winners and warriors. The winners subsequently developed new technologies and military industries and used them to wage wars and expand the territories they controlled both within and outside Europe. "The West won the world not by the superiority of its ideas or values or religion but rather by its superiority in applying organized violence,"[7] says Thomas Hugh. That is how colonialism was able to control most of the world and establish colonies and settlements in many parts of it at the expense of the native peoples of the land.

The success of the Reformation movement in the seventeenth century was another manifestation of the social transformations that Europe had experienced during the transitional period from the agricultural to the industrial age. The success of the Reformation ended the conflict between the Catholic Church and Europe's political, economic, and intellectual elites in favor of the latter, while transforming religion into a social institution with moral, but without political or economic authority. Meanwhile, the emergence of the nation-state and its ability to acquire near-absolute

64 GLOBAL ECONOMIC AND CULTURAL TRANSFORMATION

powers caused obedience to the Church to be replaced by obedience to the state. However, the absolute reign of the nation-state and monarchs was short.

The American and French revolutions, which occurred in the latter part of the eighteenth century, changed the political cultures in Europe and North America fundamentally; they limited the powers of the state and gave people the right to elect their rulers. They forced the state to recognize the human rights of its citizens, while making the ruler accountable to the ruled, and thus they laid the foundations for modern democracy. The people, not the Church or the monarchy, soon became the sole source of political legitimacy. Two centuries later, democracy, just like all other social systems, reached it limits and began to experience the symptoms of old age, losing its vitality and ability to deliver on its promises.

Social Transformation in the Industrial Age

The industrial revolution, just like the agricultural revolution, transformed the totality of the human condition and changed the culture and social and economic structures of society, forcing people to change the way they organized their social, cultural, political, and economic lives. And as the age of industry advanced, power began to shift from the domain of the traditional land aristocracy to the domain of capital. A new class of business entrepreneurs slowly emerged to create wealth and gain power and use it to influence both economics and politics in its favor.

However, due to the conservative nature of cultures and their traditional religious core, the change that characterized the economic aspects of life moved faster and penetrated deeper in society than the change that characterized the sociocultural aspects. In fact, throughout history, change in the sociocultural arena has almost always come in response to changes in the economic and technological arenas and lagged behind it. At times, the response was rather quick and positive, but at most other times, the response had been negative or reluctant and slow. While the benefits of economic development and new technologies come about rather quickly, the benefits of sociocultural change are realized much later; only the negative aspects that disrupt social relationships and spread apprehension are evident initially.

One of the major manifestations of change that characterized the industrial age is the gradual transformation of farming into an industry. Around the end of the nineteenth century, for example, farmers constituted about 50 percent of the labor force in the West. A century later, they comprised about 5 percent in the West in general and less than 3 percent in the

SOCIAL TRANSFORMATION **65**

United States. However, the transformation of agriculture into an industry forced agriculture to become capital-intensive rather than labor-intensive, and more dependent on science and technology, chemical fertilizer, credit financing, and modern distribution and transportation systems. The dramatic shift of agriculture from a way of life to an industry was originally perceived as a threat to food security. But as farm workers were abandoning their farms to live in cities and work for manufacturing, agricultural machinery, chemical fertilizers, and new irrigation and farming systems were raising productivity and improving the quality of products.

As the farm populations were declining, the numbers of home servants were growing. Around the year 1900, the second largest group in the population and in the work force of every industrializing state was the on-site servants who worked and lived on the estates of their masters. "Census categories of the time defined a 'lower middle class' household as one that employed fewer than three servants."[8] In fact, almost all estates at the time had more servants than owners. 60 years later, this group of people had almost disappeared, because a new way of life had replaced the old one, leaving very little room for live-in servants. New household appliances, schools for small children, hospitals and nursing homes, and eating outside have reduced the need for the services of live-in servants tremendously.

As manufacturing expanded, the industrial working class grew rather quickly, and the public's awareness of its status and needs increased. The seemingly unlimited pool of workers leaving farming and domestic service to become industrial workers was instrumental in expanding manufacturing and increasing the size of this class: "The new class, industrial workers, was extremely visible. This is what made these workers a class. They lived perforce in dense population clusters and in cities."[9] Around the end of the nineteenth century, members of this class constituted about 5 percent of the labor force. Meanwhile, the growing size of the labor pool enabled the emerging capitalist class to exploit the struggling industrial workers, make large profits, and, in the process, accumulate huge amounts of wealth and power.

Due to the appalling living and working conditions of the industrial working class, it became the focal point of the philosophical writings of Karl Marx and other socialist thinkers. Such thinkers devoted much of their research to analyzing the historical origins of this class, its life conditions, and its rise in society; they also speculated about its sociopolitical role and future. As compared to the much larger groups of farmers and servants, the industrial class commanded unprecedented public attention. Marx predicted that it would eventually revolt against its masters and take ownership of the means of production. But despite the miserable working and living conditions of this class, "for farmers and domestic servants,

66 GLOBAL ECONOMIC AND CULTURAL TRANSFORMATION

industrial work was an opportunity. It was, in fact, the first opportunity that social history has given them to better themselves substantially without having to emigrate."[10] Eventually, the increased power of organized labor, public sympathy, intellectual support, and rising profits forced capitalists to pay their workers more and improve their working and living conditions.

Yet, just when it seemed that this social class was on its way to gaining control in industrial society, its fortunes began to decline rapidly. The industrial economy began to shift from manufacturing to services, some of which were knowledge-based, requiring specialized training and skills. Gradually, a new economy emerged, creating new jobs that required more schooling, special training, and changed attitudes the industrial worker did not have and could not afford. Such jobs have proved to be more of a challenge to the typical industrial worker than an opportunity. Other jobs that the new economy has been creating are service jobs that require little or no skills and pay low wages, making them of no interest to the industrial worker. Consequently, the size, power, and social status of the industrial working class began to decline gradually, even as it continued to organize strikes and win battles at the bargaining table.

The size of the American industrial class grew from a low of 5 percent of the labor force in 1900 to about 40 percent in 1950. It began thereafter to decline, reaching 25 percent in 1970 and about 15 percent by the end of the twentieth century, and by 2010 it was less than 10 percent of the labor force. Three major factors have contributed to the decline in the size of this class, and subsequently in its economic and political power:

1. Rising labor productivity and automation have increased production without needing more labor;
2. The emergence of a new group of industrializing nations having the capacity to produce high-quality products at low cost, causing America's demand for homemade products to decline; and
3. The movement of large corporations to relocate production operations to where labor cost is low, causing domestic demand for industrial labor in the West in general to decline.

The new economy, which began to take shape in the early 1990s, is knowledge-based and service-oriented. Because the role of knowledge in life is on the rise, and since the association of wealth and power with knowledge is strong and getting stronger, it seems that any possibility that the industrial working class will ever recapture its past glory has vanished. There is no chance that it will grow again and regain its confidence, independence, and class consciousness to have the required clout to cause economic or political change in its favor. Whoever gets enough knowledge and/or wealth today, even if his or her roots are in the industrial working class, is destined to have different values and outlooks and associations, and to entertain different dreams. In addition, the Western mass media and particularly the American media are constantly bombarding all social classes with information and images meant to falsify their consciousness, while the forces of religious fundamentalism are working hard to convince people to accept their lot in life and be content.

I believe that Marxism and the socialist system it built before 1990 may have been the last serious attempt launched by politics to control economics. The collapse of the Soviet Union and the shift of China to capitalism have put an end to that system as socialism failed to live up to expectations, empower the industrial working class, and undermine capitalism. And with that failure, economics won its last battle against politics. Nevertheless, economics has not won the war against the vanquished and impoverished peoples of the world. Therefore, the struggle for freedom, justice, and fairness will continue and make conflict a never-ending human tragedy.

By the end of the nineteenth century, socioeconomic and sociocultural transformations were able to create new facts on the ground and project themselves as prophets of hope and progress. Recurring economic recessions and social problems were considered setbacks and pauses, not signals of impending crises requiring a change of heart. In the twentieth century, which witnessed the greatest scientific and technological revolutions of all times, sociocultural and socioeconomic change became a dynamic process, transforming every aspect of human life. In contrast, social transformation in the Third World in general was grounded in the pre-industrial transitional period. Until the middle of the twentieth century, no non-Western nation, with the exception of Japan, had experienced the Industrial Revolution or seemed close to entering the industrial age. Nonetheless, almost every Third World nation had by then come into contact with the West and its industrial civilization and colonialist enterprise. Due to this mixed experience, most nations reacted to Western Civilization in two simultaneous, yet contradictory, ways. First, they began to adopt nationalism, build nation-states, and develop their economies, while resisting foreign domination. Second, they began to revive their traditional cultures and languages to protect themselves from the encroachment of Western culture, which they perceived as immoral, hegemonic, and discriminatory.

While nationalism was being adopted as a state ideology, religion was being revived and emphasized as the core of national culture. The combination of nationalism and religion, however, while serving to strengthen

68 GLOBAL ECONOMIC AND CULTURAL TRANSFORMATION

political unity and foster social cohesiveness, gave the sociocultural and political processes added legitimacy to become the most dominant processes in society. Thus, a state identity built around nationalism, and a national culture built around religion, did not evolve in the Third World naturally to meet internal needs; they came largely in response to external challenges and changed circumstances and perceptions. "Social identity becomes most important the moment it seems threatened; conspicuous forms of boundary maintenance become important when boundaries are under pressure."[11]

Social Transformation in the Knowledge Age

Around the middle of the 1990s, the advanced industrial societies of the West entered a transitional period leading to the knowledge age. It is an age in which scientific and technological knowledge are increasingly becoming the most valuable individual and national assets, and where the infomedia process is progressively becoming the most powerful force influencing the lives and perceptions of people everywhere. Since the emerging knowledge economy is more dependent on information and communications and ideas than on any factor of production, the rewarding new jobs that are being created are knowledge-based: "they require a good deal of formal education and the ability to acquire and to apply theoretical and analytical knowledge. They require a different approach to work and a different mind-set. Above all, they require a habit of continuous learning."[12] Knowledge workers need to learn how to learn, how to develop interest in learning, and how to update their knowledge continuously and apply it efficiently. As a consequence, education, including technical training, has become an important industry in and of itself, encouraging profit-making enterprises to enter the field and cause education standards to be lowered.

The new emerging economy is creating jobs for the knowledge worker and the unskilled worker, but little for other workers. And because of its transitional nature, the emerging economy is causing job insecurity to increase. The blue-collar worker, to acquire a decent position in the knowledge economy, will have to learn new skills, adopt new attitudes, and accept job insecurity as a fact of life. In other words, he has to change his culture because the culture of the industrial society is not compatible with the knowledge age. Since the knowledge requirements are expensive to obtain, and the cultural adjustments are difficult to make, large numbers of the lower and middle classes are losing their place in the new economy and status in the new society. The information and telecommunications revolutions are incapable of creating as many jobs as manufacturing did, and the better-paying jobs they are creating are for the knowledge workers and not for the displaced industrial workers.

As a consequence, it has become increasingly difficult for the industrial workers to change jobs, ask for more money, or bargain effectively through labor unions. Even unions that still have enough power to bargain and carry out strikes no longer enjoy public sympathy as before. The transformation of the free market philosophy into a virtual ideology has convinced the general public that members of such unions are driven by greed, not need. However, the Great Recession has changed this perception slightly; it proved that the managers of large banks and corporations and the infomedia establishments have decided to monopolize greed and force everyone else to live in need.

The knowledge age is also the age of the highly skilled and specialized worker who is able to find a good job anywhere in the world. Sophisticated computer networks have enabled knowledge workers to work out of their homes and out of small offices scattered in all corners of the globe, and to be connected to each other and to their workplaces; networks have also enabled knowledge workers to share information and coordinate projects instantly. Meanwhile, differentiated skills and varied specializations and scattered locations make it impossible for members of this group to develop class-consciousness and organize and create labor unions.

Specialization creates need to develop new, more complex societal systems to coordinate the work of knowledge workers and integrate the functions of the ever-growing numbers of organizations and institutions. It makes teamwork, work ethics, and flexible work hours essential to performing certain tasks and facilitating the creation of knowledge and wealth. It also makes both success and failure functions of knowledge and attitudes, while making knowledge and changed attitudes preconditions for individual and societal success. Peter Drucker argues that "With knowledge being universally accessible, there will be no excuses for nonperformance. There will be no poor countries. There will only be ignorant countries."[13] The availability and accessibility of knowledge facilitate the creation of new economic opportunities that make it easier for more people to succeed, while making it easier for those who hesitate to get the right education to fall behind rather quickly, and stay there permanently.

Knowledge workers in the new age are capitalists; they possess valuable social capital consisting primarily of specialized skills and unique attitudes that can be invested in several ways and in many places. Since knowledge frees people from need, knowledge workers have become less dependent on the state as well as on their families, sharing little collective memories with others, and committed to no particular ideology or nation. Their primary

70 GLOBAL ECONOMIC AND CULTURAL TRANSFORMATION

interest is to succeed, make the best use of whatever knowledge they may have, and get the most for it. As a result, knowledge workers have become modern nomads wandering from one place to another, from one organization to another, and from one country to another to advance technically and succeed materially. They are driven by self-interest and a competitive marketplace that forces them to become rootless and, for many, ruthless as well. But while most knowledge workers seem less committed to national and ideological causes, some seem more interested in human and environmental causes.

Since having a sense of belonging to a larger community is a basic human need, social and cultural clubs, new transnational organizations, and professional groups organized around special issues, as well as virtual communities are gradually emerging and replacing traditional institutions of community and political party and nation. Meanwhile, special interest groups are making governments and political elites in democratic states in general captive to short-term economic considerations, causing politics to replace policy and hindering the proper functioning of the democratic institutions.

Today, all societies are experiencing fundamental change and genuine transformations, some much more than others. Due to the nature and extent of this change, and because it affects different peoples differently, the traditional social links in all societies have been broken, causing societies to be fragmented along horizontal and vertical lines. As a consequence, societies are losing their traditional organizing principles and fast becoming colorful collections of groups of people clustered around ethnicity, culture, religion, interests, and nationality that compete more and cooperate less with each other. As a result, the concept of society, as it has traditionally been defined, has lost much of its meaning. Likewise, the common good as a national goal has become more abstract than real. Meanwhile, the assimilation of the many groups in society has become beyond reach, making the challenge facing every state in this regard one of how to politically and economically integrate rather than how to culturally assimilate its many sociocultural groups and minorities.

The American experience provides a vivid example of this unmet challenge. Rather than helping new immigrants assimilate and identify with the dominant majority and culture, the American "melting pot" has proved to be an idealistic notion without much substance. In a study of immigrant communities in the United States, Nathan Glazer and Daniel A. Moynihan reported decades ago: "rather than eradicating ethnic differences, modern American society has actually created new forms of self-awareness in people, which is expressed in a concern about roots and origins. Moreover, many Americans continue to use their ethnic networks actively when looking for a job or a spouse."[14]

Racial segregation and social discrimination in America, which came under attack in the 1960s, have since been joined by economic discrimination and intellectual segregation. While the former have been eased substantially, the latter seem to be tightening. In an age of continuous change and transformation, where wealth and knowledge are intertwined and knowledge is quickly becoming the major tool for advancement and integration, economic discrimination and intellectual segregation are denying most minorities the only opportunity that really counts. While getting quality education has become beyond the reach of the poor and even members of the middle class, intellectual segregation is denying minorities the opportunity to have an authentic leadership they can understand and trust. Minorities that have no trusted leadership are easy to manipulate, exploit, and keep submissive; yet, excluding minority intellectuals from public life robs America of a substantial portion of its human capital. The typical American intellectual is more likely to look at an intellectual belonging to a minority and whisper to himself: "you may belong to us, but you do not belong with us."

Classes in Society

The socioeconomic gaps that separate and largely define social classes in industrial society are increasingly becoming sociocultural divides in the emerging knowledge society, separating the many groups and leading them to live somewhat different lives. Since success is primarily a function of education and wealth and attitudes, socioeconomic classes have largely become manifestations of sociocultural divides. In other words, individuals and groups having the right education and the right attitudes are more likely to succeed and be rich; individuals and groups that lack the proper education and the right attitudes are more likely to fail and be poor. And as knowledge becomes the key economic resource and the major tool to climb the socioeconomic ladder, the knowledge elite is fast becoming the core of the leading class in society.

Recent developments seem to indicate that the knowledge society of the future is likely to be divided into five different groups, replacing the three socioeconomic classes of the industrial society. Since the United States is the first nation to enter the transitional period leading to the knowledge age, our description of how society is expected to be divided will focus on the American scene.

The Privileged Class

Members of this class are expected to represent less than 3 percent of the knowledge society; however, they are expected to control politics and the

72 GLOBAL ECONOMIC AND CULTURAL TRANSFORMATION

major business concerns as well as the media. Members of this class include the business, political, infomedia, and military elites, as well as lobbyists and many lawyers and physicians and economists. As a special elite rooted primarily in economics and knowledge, members of this class are expected to concentrate on accumulating wealth and power, and molding and remolding people's attitudes and views using the infomedia and philanthropy to achieve their goals. The major objectives of this class are to advance its social goals, foster its economic interests, maintain political control, and dominate the rest of the world.

The Upper Class

Members of this class are expected to represent about 10 percent of the population of a typical knowledge society and to include most scientists, engineers, medical doctors, college professors, and prominent media personalities and lawyers, as well as high-ranking officers of the armed forces, the intelligence community, and the militarized intellectuals. Being highly educated and motivated, members of this class will share with the privileged class its culture and, to some extent, its ambitions, but not its wealth or influence. As an associate class of the privileged one, the upper class will assist those on the top to tighten their grip on economic, political, and information power, and enable them to exploit the less fortunate members of society without having to interact with them. The militarized intellectuals, for example, are using think tanks and the media to spread fear in society and promote war in order to justify building every military system and enrich themselves and the military industry, causing the masses to be kept relatively poor and submissive.

The National Class

Members of this class are expected to represent about 40 percent of the population of the knowledge society and to include mid-level manager, school teachers, blue-color workers, skilled technicians, owners of small retail stores and service centers, and the bulk of the active and retired armed forces. This class represents the remnants of the middle class of industrial society, and, as a result, it will inherit its culture and way of life. Because of their makeup and cultural backgrounds, members of the national class are expected to be largely conservative and content, and less knowledgeable and ambitious. Being conservative and rather nationalistic, the national class will serve as a pillar of stability rather than a force of social change. Limited knowledge and job insecurity will make members of this class eager to work for the government and enlist in the armed forces, and, therefore, easy to lead and manipulate. For some, the armed forces will be the only opportunity to earn a decent income and guarantee a secure retirement. In contrast, neither the privileged nor the upper class will find enlisting in the armed forces an attractive option, or the military's doctrine a worthy cause.

The Alienated Class

Members of this class are expected to represent about 40 percent of the knowledge society. These are people who work on farms and in service jobs requiring little or no particular skills, the retired people who live on social security, and the poor who are largely uneducated and living primarily on government subsidies, as well as some immigrants and members of cultural and racial minorities that are discriminated against. Because of their diversified cultural backgrounds and poor economic conditions and lack of education, members of this class are expected to be more fatalistic and religious and less inclined to participate in politics and use it as a tool to change the system in their favor.

The Under Class

Members of this class are expected to represent about 5 percent of society and to include people who are disfranchised, imprisoned, convicted felons, chronically unemployed, and the homeless, drug addicts and others engaged in illegal drug trade and crime. Because of their varied cultural backgrounds and economic conditions and poor education, members of this class are expected to be divided between the angry and the submissive, and, therefore, the principal source of crime and domestic violence.

Members of the first two classes, the privileged and upper classes, are expected to form one sociocultural group, sharing the same culture but separated by wealth and power. The movement of members of the upper class toward the top will be possible but limited; it will be more a function of connections and luck than of knowledge and hard work, a function of who you know rather than what you know. Being individualistic and mobile, members of these two classes will have little or no community attachments. Traditional ethics and moral values are expected to play a small role in their lives as well as in the lives of the angry class, making trust between groups in the knowledge society hard to come by.

74 GLOBAL ECONOMIC AND CULTURAL TRANSFORMATION

The third and fourth classes, the national and alienated classes, will share similar cultures, but not the same culture, because each class includes different ethnic and religious minorities and socioeconomic groups. Because of such differences, the relationships between these two classes are expected to be difficult, at times conflicting. However, being group-oriented and settled, members of each class will retain collective memories that help them sustain solidarity while deepening their alienation from each other. Ethics and morality are expected to play a significant role in the lives of these two classes, making trust among members of each group an expression of belief in and attachment to traditional and religious values. Such a trust, however, is more likely to come at the expense of social trust, causing corruption to spread further and manipulation of the poor and weak by the rich and powerful to be endemic.

As for the underclass, it is expected to live in a different world having its own subculture, a culture shunned by other members of society. Members of this class will have little business ethics, will abide by no recognized rules or laws, and will have very little to tie them together. Being largely poor and hopeless, submissive and helpless, and rather angry and ruthless, the strong among its members are more likely to suppress, exploit, and even denigrate the poor and the weak, making life for such people cruel and largely inhumane.

Due to the huge income disparities and wide sociocultural divides, more people are expected to be imprisoned in the knowledge society. This development will not come as a result of more people committing crimes only, but also due to growing intolerance among the different classes. The United States, which is leading the way toward the creation of a knowledge society, may have given us an indication of what to expect in the near future; it is an example that must not be allowed to become the norm. Eric Schlosser, referring to the United States, says, "No other nation in human history has ever imprisoned so many of its citizens for the purpose of crime control." The state of California had by the end of 1998 "the biggest prison system in the Western industrialized world . . . the state holds more inmates in its jails and prisons than do France, Great Britain, Germany, Japan, Singapore, and the Netherlands combined."[15]

And though the United States has less than 5 percent of the world's population, it has almost a quarter of the world's prisoners. "The U.S. imprisons around 730 in every 100,000 people—the highest incarcerated population in the world—Department of Justice data shows." There are currently around 2.2 million people behind bars, "equal to a city the size of Houston," noted Bloomberg News. There are 4,575 prisons in operation in the United States, more than four times the number of second-place Russia at 1,029. According to California Prison Focus, "no other society in human history has imprisoned so many of its own citizens."[16] And while spending $35 billion on prisons in 1998, the United States spent $68 billion in 2010. Yet, high crime rates have persisted and the inmates' rate of increase has reached 13 times the population increase rate.

The privileged class will perform the role of the brain in the knowledge society, while the upper class performs the role of the heart and the nervous system. The national and alienated classes, meanwhile, will perform the role of the legs, feet, and hands that carry the body around and put the food in its mouth. The angry class will be viewed by the larger society as harmful parasites that need to be eradicated, not nurtured or treated.

Every society, regardless of its level of development and complexity, has social classes that reflect both sociocultural and socioeconomic differences. Each class has its own economic base and cultural shade. Social classes that are close to each other economically are likely to be close culturally. As sociocultural differences grow due to ideology and education, socioeconomic gaps widen, and as socioeconomic gaps widen, sociocultural divides deepen. This means that the sociocultural divides and the socioeconomic gaps are dependent on each other; the narrower the former, the smaller the latter, and the larger the latter, the deeper the former.

Since cultures are products of civilizations, people with different cultures often live in different civilizations or ages. Members of the privileged and upper classes are expected to live in the knowledge age and reflect its cultural values, ethics, and individualism. Members of the national and alienated classes will live in the industrial age and reflect its work ethics and religious values and community traditions. As for the angry class, its members will live in a world devoid of real culture where every act is permitted and every crime is justified.

As man developed agriculture and settled, law became more complicated, and its sources more differentiated. These sources were and to a great extent still, are rooted in traditions, religion, and politics. While ruler represented the law, his words had the power of the law, and while the religious man represented God, his words had the power of God's will. People, as a result, had little or no rights, only obligations. Whatever rights people may have had in such a society were not considered entitlements given to them at birth, but rather a grant from ruler or God. When politics controls and incorporates religious authority, ruler and God become practically one and the same. The former speaks in the name of the latter, and the latter can be reached only through obedience to the former.

In industrial society, law is made by people and subject to their free will. The primary objective of the law is to protect people from both religion and state. People, as a result, have rights and obligations that tend to be equal, tying personal freedoms to personal responsibilities. Yet, a desire

76 GLOBAL ECONOMIC AND CULTURAL TRANSFORMATION

to expand individual freedoms and get more wealth, and a belief in the goodness of the individual leads people to overlook the dangers inherent in the behavior of a market-oriented society, allowing white crime to spread and poverty to increase and become endemic.

In the knowledge society, because of increasing life complexity, law is becoming more complicated and less able to keep pace with change, leaving loopholes to be exploited by the rich and powerful. People, as a result, are gaining more freedom and becoming more individualistic, which leads them to feel that they have many rights and few obligations. Personal freedoms, most people seem to think, are limitless and must not be constrained. Money is allowed to buy justice and politics, making the law largely a tool to serve the interests of the powerful and protect the privileges of the rich. The pardons granted to criminals and fugitives by President Bill Clinton on his last day in office demonstrate the power of money and its ability to buy justice.

In a traditional agricultural society, leadership is largely authoritarian, and domination is legitimized by traditions and religion and exercised through coercion. In an industrial society, authority is largely democratic; it is legitimized by regular elections and exercised through the courts and governmental institutions. In the emerging knowledge society, authority is becoming weak and formless; it is legitimized by elite consensus, exercised through scattered centers of power and special interest groups, and facilitated by media manipulation of the masses.

Ideas, convictions, traditions, and values on the one hand, and technologies, institutions, systems, and interests on the other have had a competitive relationship throughout history. Wherever beliefs, traditions, and ideological convictions dominate, freedom is restricted, and technologies, institutions, and economies are used primarily as tools to foster ideology and enhance the power of its leadership. Iran, North Korea, Saudi Arabia, Sudan, and Zimbabwe are good examples of states where technology and economy have been used by ideological leaders to tighten their grip on power, limit freedom, and hinder change and thus social and cultural progress. On the other hand, wherever technologies, institutions, interests, and social systems dominate, freedom prevails but social justice suffers, and ideology remains able to react negatively to situations rather than shape destinies. Therefore, reducing the influence of ideological convictions, particularly religious convictions and traditional value systems, is a prerequisite for meaningful societal transformation.

Until a few decades ago, able, often charismatic leaders have symbolized the ideas and convictions that left a lasting impact on the lives of people. At the same time, no leader could claim greatness and lead unchallenged without being associated with an ideological idea and unconventional convictions. Perhaps not surprisingly, the recent decline in the role of ideology in general has been associated with a decline in the political role and impact of all types of leaders. The future therefore is unlikely to witness the appearance of a great leader or a grand ideology able to change the course of history in a meaningful way.

Historical records seem to suggest further that no nation had been able to enjoy freedom of expression and institute democratic rule and respect for human rights under the rule of charismatic leaders claiming greatness or divine authority. Charisma in society has always been in conflict with institutional bureaucracy because the latter works to enforce the law that seeks to limit the power of charisma. In societies still living in pre-industrial times, efficient institutional bureaucracy could not be developed, giving political leaders an opportunity to be absolutists. Absolute rulers, remarked Ottaviano Fregoso, are "always finding themselves obeyed and almost adored with such reverence and praise . . . They are subject to such boundless self-esteem that they take no advice from others,"[17] and have therefore no respect for the rights of anyone. In post-industrial society, in contrast, political power is weak and fragmented, allowing charismatic leaders to have some power but not enough to change the course of national or world history.

With the transformation from the pre-agricultural to the agricultural age, the role of man was enhanced at the expense of nature. With the transformation from the agricultural to the industrial age, the role of machines was enhanced at the expense of man. And with the transformation from the industrial to the knowledge age, the role of computers and robots is being enhanced at the expense of nature, man and machines. As a consequence, the nature of work has changed causing jobs and wages and job security to change as well.

In a world in transition, people are forced to shape their fate as individuals, groups, organizations, and communities through the workings of the processes of societal transformation. However, the social order that these processes have created and seem intent on perpetuating is one that borders on disorder, at times chaos. But disorder and even chaos usually signify the triumph of freedom over sacred order, choice over fate and ordinary people over ordained saints. Nevertheless, change initiated through these processes and managed by them is not necessarily desirable by everyone; it often fails to meet accepted standards of ethics and equity. Therefore, understanding the different roles of these processes and their actions, reactions, and interactions is very important to understanding social transformation and societal change in general and how to influence its course and the course of history in particular.

5

Agents of Historical Change

The societal processes of transformation explained in Chapter 3, the sociocultural, political, economic, and infomedia processes, represent together the mechanism through which change is introduced and managed in society. Therefore, they are not agents that provoke change and make history but tools to introduce and coordinate change. Nevertheless, no change can be initiated without the involvement of at least one societal process, and no social transformation can be completed without affecting the positions of the other processes. As a consequence, every change, regardless of its nature and magnitude, causes conflict and produces winners and losers, and thus it causes the balance of power relationships in society to change, sometimes drastically.

German philosopher Georg Hegel, as will be explained in more detail in the next chapter, saw freedom as being the "spirit of history" or the agent that motivates people to seek change and cause social progress to be made over time. Hegel was right, but freedom does not explain societal change by itself and thus human progress. Karl Marx, on the other hand, saw class conflict as the major agent of historical change that leads to societal progress. Marx argued that contradictions within the capitalistic system precipitate conflict between the capitalist class and the working industrial class, and that the resolution of this conflict creates new syntheses that reduce the intensity of conflict, leading to progress. Since the movement Marx described is supposed to continue until a classless society is reached, one can say that the search for social justice represents the spirit of history for Karl Marx. Marx was right in arguing that class conflict causes change, but class conflict cannot by itself explain societal transformations and human progress over time. Max Weber saw ethics and work ethics in particular as being a major agent of change that motivates people to work hard, save money, and invest, and thus cause progress to be made.

Weber was also right, but ethics cannot by themselves move history and cause society to be fundamentally transformed.

Paul Kennedy argues that technological developments and social transformations are the forces responsible for human progress. Kennedy, however, does not explain what causes technological developments and social transformations. Despite the importance of Kennedy's argument, he, just like the other philosophers of history, misses other important agents that have contributed and continue to contribute to causing change and making societal progress. Jared Diamond suggests that geography has had a decisive impact on people's lives and fortunes, and argues that humans, with the domestication of certain animals and the farming of wild crops, were able to take the first step toward civilization. Agricultural production, he argues further, leads to food surpluses, which support sedentary societies, rapid population growth, and division of labor, which means societal change and progress.

Agents of historical change are many, and every one of them gets an opportunity to influence societal life and cause change. However, how societies are organized, and in which stage of societal development they live and the nature of the environment that surrounds them give certain agents more opportunities to lead and instigate change than others. Thus, the agents that move history and cause progress differ from one place to another, and their roles vary from one societal setting to another. There is no doubt that geography, freedom, technology, ethics, and class conflict have played and continue to play important roles in societal life, but the role of each force was eclipsed at one time or another by the roles played by one or more of the other forces. I believe that the major agents that represent the spirit of history and cause change and progress over time are the following:

1. The development of the institution of private property;
2. The accumulation of capital which led to competition between individuals and business entities;
3. Technological developments and scientific discoveries, particularly those related to manufacturing, communications, transportation, and the making of tools;
4. New modes of economic production, which led to changing production relations and causing class conflict:
5. Sociocultural transformation, particularly in regard to traditions and attitudes toward work, time, the other, and nature; and
6. Man's continuous struggle and longing for freedom, particularly individual and political freedoms, and freedoms of speech and worship.

Private Property

The concept of private property appeared very early in human life, long before agriculture was developed and enabled man to take his first step toward civilization. The hunter-gatherer was the first man to discover private property, but his ability to own the things he wished to own was very much limited due to his nomadic way of life. Tribal man's property was also limited due to the circumstances surrounding his life; he could only own a tent, some clothes, and a few tools to hunt animals and defend himself and his family against the other. And because technology was almost nonexistent at the time, the hunter-gatherer as well as the tribal man experienced no noticeable change or social progress for tens of thousands of years.

The development of agriculture gave private property the opportunity to become a legitimate social institution, causing social stratification and injustice to spread and slowly deepen its roots in society. And because private property divided society into rich and poor, it acquired a sociopolitical role as well, enabling the rich to have more power and freedom. As a result, private property evolved slowly as a force motivating people to work hard, accumulate wealth, and use it to improve the quality of their lives and enhance their social statuses, often at the expense of others. Meanwhile, the inequality and injustice private property creates and perpetuates in society causes conflict to become a major characteristic of social relations, forcing the poor and powerless to seek justice and struggle for equality and freedom. Since the institution of private property was absent from tribal life, the tribal man lived his entire life largely free of oppression, exploitation, and injustice. The concepts of freedom and justice, therefore, had to wait for the development of agricultural and the evolvement of the private property institution before they could be born and appreciated and acquire a societal role.

The development of agriculture and the building of hamlets and villages enabled the concept of private property to expand and include land, tools, houses, domesticated animals, personal things, and more. And since land, tools, and animals constituted the bulk of the factors of production at the time, they enabled agricultural societies in general to produce more and attain higher levels of food and physical security. But since some people had more land, tools, and animals than others, the rich were able to enjoy relatively higher standards of living than those who did not have as much, and to employ and often exploit the poor farmers and farm workers. Meanwhile, improvements in making tools and farming methods enabled agricultural society to produce a surplus, causing the idea of progress to be born and civilization to emerge gradually. While producing a surplus allowed man to have more food and more time, it led him to trade his food surplus with others, and use the extra time to develop other aspects of life such as writing, science, philosophy, and religion. Individuals and groups, as a consequence, never stopped seeking more things to own, and societies never stopped experiencing change and making progress as a consequence.

Capital

As tools and means of transportation and sea navigation technologies were developed in the late agricultural times, trade expanded and capital began to play an increasingly greater role in individual and societal life. It caused the productivity of land and labor to increase, and while creating more wealth for its owners, it made work less stressful for peasants and slaves and workers in general. Slowly, capital emerged as a major factor of production, enabling societies to produce more and improve the quality of their lives. However, as capitalists were accumulating wealth and power and gaining more freedom, particularly during the industrial age, the poor and weak were losing their traditional power and freedom; the sources of wealth, power, and freedom were being gradually transferred from the domain of land to the domain of capital.

But with the advancement of methods of production and management systems, productivity of machines and labor improved and more goods were produced. As a consequence, capitalists realized that to make more money and accumulate more wealth, they had to expand markets for their products. And since industrial workers were the closest market they could expand and exploit, capitalists, driven by self-interest, moved to raise the wages of their less fortunate workers and share with them some of the economic gains they were making. Capital, as a result, became not only a force contributing to higher productivity, but also an agent of social change and societal progress. So, contrary to conventional thought, progress during the industrial age did not come as a result of cheap labor only, but primarily due to the availability of relatively cheap capital, technology, education, and economic freedom.

But no matter how much income the poor get, they always feel worse off compared to their rich neighbors. Contacts between the rich and poor in the workplaces, in shopping malls, and in estates owned by the rich make the poor aware of the extent of their poverty and weakness. Awareness of the size of the socioeconomic and sociopolitical gaps in society usually leads the poor and weak to seek justice and freedom, causing social conflict that leads to further societal change.

Nevertheless, by raising the productivity of land and labor, capital enabled society as a whole to produce more and have more free time to enjoy life, which encouraged people to allocate some of their free time to creative thinking and creative pursuits, causing more cultural and material progress. However, the continued accumulation of capital in the hands of the few caused the socioeconomic gaps in industrial society to widen further. No laws were enacted at the time to limit the reach of the rich and powerful and empower the poor and powerless. As a consequence, organized religion reemerged slowly as a force calling for fairness and social justice, comforting the poor, and asking the rich and powerful to be compassionate. Meanwhile, as workers moved to form labor unions and challenge capital demanding a larger share of the output of their labor, the capitalist state, fearing Marxist ideas, was forced to intervene to limit the reach of capital and provide social safety nets to protect the poor and needy, causing life conditions to change and the general standard of living to improve. In fact, the adoption of socialism by several states in Europe, and the idea of class conflict advanced by Marxism, had contributed more than any other factor to giving capitalism a human face and thus enable the Western industrialized societies to expand domestic markets and make further progress in all fields of human endeavor.

Science and Technology

Archeological discoveries suggest that man used tools before tribal society evolved to hunt and fight, which enabled him to feel more secure physically and get more food to survive. Tools, or technological devices in general, enable man to produce more of what he needs using the same amounts of resources available, or produce the same amounts as before with less time and resources. In both cases, however, progress is made because man gets more of the things he needs and likes to have, or gets more free time to use in activities that enrich his life and the lives of others. On the other hand, as people use their tools they learn how to make them better and more efficient, and develop new ones, causing technological knowledge to advance and accumulate. And this in turn enables man to produce more, change more, and make more material and cultural progress.

As economies grew and states were built and empires emerged during the agricultural age, trade expanded, roads were constructed, and more efficient means of transportation and fishing boats and ships were developed. Navigation systems were developed to enable merchants to travel long distances without much risk or fear. However, navigation systems could not be developed to the point of making it possible for sailors to travel deep and far in seas and oceans and come home safe without new scientific discoveries in areas related to geography and the solar

84 GLOBAL ECONOMIC AND CULTURAL TRANSFORMATION

system. So scientific discoveries were needed to facilitate more technological developments; meanwhile some of the tools and machines developed by technology facilitated new, more advanced scientific discoveries. However, the more economic and technological progress is made in society, the more the socioeconomic, sociocultural, and sociopolitical gaps widen, causing the rich to become richer and more powerful and freer, and oftentimes greedier and ruthless as well. The poor, meanwhile, feels poorer and deprived of many of the things he would like to have in life.

Freedom and Justice

People, since the dawn of civilization, have continued to struggle against whatever they thought is enslaving them or limiting their capacities to feel and act as free people, and thus call for equality and social injustice. Revolts were launched in older time by slaves against their masters, but such revolts did not lead to ending slavery because slaves were weak and societies were not disposed to supporting the demands of slaves for freedom. As a consequence, slavery continued for thousands of years before it was officially abolished in the twentieth century. Historical records suggest that no people could see an end to their struggle for freedom because man seems to view freedom as an open, limitless space; the more you see of it, the more you feel the urge to go further. Nevertheless, the tribal society was the only society in history to have all the freedom it needed to live a nomadic life; it therefore did not experience flagrant slavery or injustice, particularly since it was not divided into social classes. But with the dawn of the agricultural age some 10,000 years ago, the space of freedom began to shrink and appear limited, causing some people to get less and others more. As a consequence, conflict began to arise in society, and, with the creation of empires, conflict expanded to characterize relations between nations.

Today, people struggle peacefully and otherwise to free themselves from poverty and need, from political oppression and suppression, from ignorance and disease, from prejudice and discrimination, as well as from capital exploitation and foreign domination. No society is entirely free, and no social system is flawless; every society has more than one reason to feel that it must continue the struggle for freedom and justice, either to protect what they have, or to get what they feel they should have, or to regain what they had lost in the past. As societal systems evolve and production relations change, they produce winners and losers. While the first are encouraged to fight to preserve what they have, the latter, feeling cheated, are pushed to struggle to regain what they have lost. Therefore, the struggle for freedom and social justice and against oppression and injustice will never end.

Throughout history, every society has had certain social, economic, political, or cultural problems, such as political corruption, economic exploitation, racial discrimination, religious intimidation, denial of human rights, and media manipulation. Since each problem affects the fortunes of people differently, it distributes freedom and wealth and power and misery in society and among societies unfairly, allowing some to have more than others. Under dictatorships, for example, the leader of the nation monopolizes all attributes of political power and privileges of freedom, forcing ordinary citizens to have little freedom and almost no power. When large corporations are allowed to create oligopolies and monopolies, they confiscate great portions of the wealth of nations and create huge obstacles that prevent other business-minded people from entering the market, denying them an equal opportunity to participate in the economic life of society. When the mass media resorts to manipulating the news and substituting opinions for facts, they deny people the right to be informed and know the truth.

Therefore, when a group of people manages to control an aspect of societal life, be it economic or political or sociocultural, it confiscates some of the rights of others, and causes them to become less free and less satisfied. Everyone who does not enjoy his or her full rights is not free; everyone who is not free is unable to utilize his talents and be as productive as he could be. However, for people to feel free and demand freedom, they have to be aware of the meaning of freedom and the role it plays in individual and societal life. Since no state distributes freedom or wealth equally among its citizens, no society is entirely free or content, and thus the struggle for freedom and social justice will continue to play an important role in provoking conflict, causing change, and making history.

Accumulation of Knowledge

As man works, watches nature, develops his tools, thinks, and experiments with things around him, he gains more knowledge and transfers it to other people through his siblings, relatives, students, friends, neighbors, and the market, causing knowledge to spread and accumulate in society. Since knowledge cannot be reversed, and what is learnt cannot be unlearnt, knowledge increases man's ability to produce more and better products and service, develop new technologies and make further progress in all endeavors of human life. In fact, material progress or economic development has always moved in tandem with cultural and social transformation. However, material progress oftentimes moves first forcing social and cultural change to follow its lead; and sometimes, social and

86 GLOBAL ECONOMIC AND CULTURAL TRANSFORMATION

cultural transformations precede economic change. For example, when man developed land cultivation he produced a surplus and the surplus enabled him to have more time to think and build better, more productive tools and farming techniques, and develop new social systems. And as man became more productive and more thoughtful, he became more secure and innovative, allowing the new technologies to influence his life and relations to both man and nature.

Social and cultural transformations come either as a result of a great idea that influences how people think or in response to a cluster of small ideas that challenge the status quo and cause attitudes to change, or due to technological innovations that transform the economic base in society. Ideas, particularly grand ideas, can and do often change people's attitudes, leading them to change the way they think and behave and view others and the world around them. Religion in general, and the monotheistic religions of Judaism, Christianity, and Islam in particular, are grand ideas that gave the lives of their followers new meanings and enabled them to build cohesive communities of faith. But since religious teachings concern themselves primarily with the cultural aspects of life, religions were unable to change the material conditions of life, invoke scientific inquiry, or encourage technological innovations. Thus, religions were able to cause social change, but not societal transformation. In contrast, technological innovations usually transform the existing modes of production, causing production relations and social and economic structures to change, social and cultural transformations to take place, and progress to be made.

The Dynamics of Change

As explained above, each agent of historical change played and continues to play a role in the life of each society. Nevertheless, the nature of the relationships that tie these forces together, and the way they interact with one another are much more important to causing change and societal transformation and progress. In fact, no single factor is able to cause tangible change by itself because change affects the balance of power in society, causing one or more of the other agents to react in ways that foster change or hinder transformation. If the political and cultural environments, for example, were not hospitable to freedom as well as to initiative and creativity, it would be very difficult for society to make meaningful scientific or technological advances. On the other hand, no scientific or technological developments are meaningful if they do not affect the economic and sociocultural aspects of life. When new scientific discoveries are made and theories are developed, scientists use them to build new tools and machines that make man more productive and work more rewarding and life more interesting. Yet, for this to happen, society and its major institutions have to be ready for change.

Since each agent of change has its own role to play, it can take the lead and initiate change in society. For example, ideas that challenged the teachings of the Catholic Church in Europe during the Renaissance age, and others that motivated people to give priority to interests over values were the major forces that caused parts of Europe to enter the transitional period that paved the way for the industrial revolution. But since culture tends to be stable and resistant to change, it has to be challenged to become more open and conducive to change. Cultures are usually transformed through a process characterized by change and substitution that transforms some traditions and social relations, while substituting outdated attitudes and ways of thinking by new ones. But since values and traditions and belief systems do not accumulate over time, any change they may experience could be reversed rather easily. In contrast, scientific knowledge and technological innovations are developed in response to growing human needs and life challenges through a process characterized by accumulation and specialization; consequently, once made, scientific knowledge and innovations cannot be reversed.

Since industrial technology and management systems are tied to scientific knowledge, they tend to change as new scientific facts are discovered and accepted; they also tend to adapt as social and environmental settings change. Such technologies and systems are characterized by accumulation, substitution, and diffusion, which make them very effective in causing societal changes that cannot be reversed. The neutrality of most technologies and management systems, and their ability to adapt to different cultural and environmental settings allow them to serve most societies without difficulty. On the other hand, the ability of the ever-increasing new technological devices to make life easier and more enjoyable have enabled them to influence people's cultures in many ways, causing most people, often unconsciously, to change their traditions, values, attitudes, and ways of thinking and living.

In fact, it is rather impossible to make good use of advanced technological devices and management systems and institutions without adopting new traditions, attitudes, and ways of thinking compatible with the new machines and the tasks at hand, at least in the workplaces. Cultures, as a result, are forced to abandon some of the old ways of doing things and adopt new ones in their stead, causing social relations to change and sociocultural transformations to take place. New production relations as a consequence are developed and adopted, and new values related to science and technology and work find their way throughout society, making

88 GLOBAL ECONOMIC AND CULTURAL TRANSFORMATION

time and opportunity precious commodities to be used wisely, not wasted foolishly.

Due to these facts, no social or cultural change can succeed and endure unless it is made an integral part of a societal transformation process that includes the economic and technological aspects of life. In other words, for economic development to succeed, it has to be preceded by or accompanied by sociocultural transformation. Likewise, for sociocultural change to succeed and endure, it has to be preceded by or accompanied by economic development.

History seems to suggest that freedom is not a grant that rulers give away willingly to people they rule; it is rather a right that people have to claim and sometimes fight for to acquire. However, until few centuries ago, most people in the world were unable to grasp the meaning of freedom and appreciate the role it can play in their lives; they were unaware that they were missing something of value called freedom. As a result, most people could not claim what they did not know they had a right to. Since neither rulers nor the ruled thought they were doing something wrong at the time, the rulers were able to rule without challenge and enslave the ruled without feeling guilty. The ruled, meanwhile, were often happy to be ruled by dictators, accepting their lot in life and assigned role in society as an obligation of being members of a larger community.

Old cultural traditions, environmental settings, religious teachings, and family and tribal ties caused people to miss freedom without missing it. Since the tribal and agricultural ways of life emphasize mutual obligations and collective rather than individual responsibility, individual freedoms and individual rights had to wait for the industrial revolution before they could be properly conceived, developed, and fully appreciated. In fact, most Eastern cultures such as the Arabic, Persian and Chinese cultures still give communal rights priority over individual rights. As a consequence, rulers in general were able to ignore the needs and rights of the peoples they ruled without fear of retaliation, while the despotic ones were able to oppress and enslave them with impunity.

Whoever does not miss freedom is unaware of its meaning and importance; he is, therefore, unable to make others aware of its existence and appreciate its liberating feeling. In societies where women are controlled by men or oppressed by tradition, women are unable to make their children aware of the meaning of freedom, and thus raise them to think and behave as free people. As a consequence, children in such societies are brought up as members of a group dominated by a man who represents a higher traditional or political or religious authority, and accept subordination to authority and dependence on it. Because of such upbringing, individuals as well as groups are often denied their social and political and sometimes economic rights, giving the communal or national leadership the opportunity to confiscate such rights and distribute some of them as they wish. People are often treated as slaves responsible for whatever authority asks of them, while they have no right to hold authority accountable for whatever it does and does not do.

While the development of agriculture and the building of human settlements was the most important revolution in human history, it cost man a great deal of his freedom. First, it reduced his ability to move from one place to another freely; second, it paved the way for the development of the institution of private property, which led subsequently to feudalism and slavery; and third, it created the need for building the state superstructure which exercised control over many aspects of individual and national life. To regain a good part of the freedom he lost, man had to fight feudalism, the institution of slavery, empires, authoritarianism, state control, colonialism, capitalism, racism, and more. He also had to acquire the means to wage and win wars, which forced him to waste a good deal of his time and mental and material resources.

Nonetheless, man's longing for freedom and his struggle to gain freedom does not happen except when man feels that his freedom is compromised or confiscated by a higher, often illegitimate authority. Such a feeling, however, happens only when man becomes aware of the role freedom normally plays in sustaining his humanity, helping shape his future, and enhancing the meaning of his life. Therefore, freedom and the longing for it remain a cultural issue, which implies that traditional cultures need to be transformed first to enable people to feel free and commit themselves to stay free. However, for such a transformation to endure it must change the traditional relationships that tie the ruler to the ruled, and recognize that all people have rights and obligations that are equal. And as freedom holds people responsible for fulfilling their social obligations, it must hold rulers accountable for their deeds.

Cultures based on a religious core, and others based on ideological philosophies such as nationalism and communism are usually less aware of the importance of freedom and the role it can play in initiating change and facilitating individual liberty and societal progress. Freedom encourages people to discover their talents and enables them to employ such talents to advance their careers, and, in the process, enrich their lives and the lives of others. And regardless of its many aspects, freedom remains a human right, a moral value, and a basic requirement of societal development and human progress. Freedom, therefore, is not the spirit of history, but the spirit of humanity, without which no human being is complete.

On the other hand, private property has been most important in encouraging people to work hard and accumulate wealth, which led them

90 GLOBAL ECONOMIC AND CULTURAL TRANSFORMATION

to invest in economic activities and scientific research and technological development and improve the quality of the lives of everyone. However, the accumulation of wealth and scientific and technological knowledge has caused societies to be divided into social classes and groups separated from each other by incomes, cultures, education, wealth, and power, which created the right conditions for social conflict. For example, the tribal society, which preceded the development of private property, was a classless society that knew little competition and no social conflict. In contrast, the agricultural society, which witnessed the full development of the private property institution, was divided into two distinct classes, rich and poor, and as a consequence it experienced competition as well as slavery, change, and conflict. People who owned more land were able to exploit and often enslave others who owned little or no land at all, and use their wealth to produce more and enhance their power at the expense of the less fortunate ones. And this, in turn, planted the seeds of social conflict and led humans to struggle for justice and freedom.

During the age of industry, the pace of scientific discoveries and technological innovations accelerated and affected all aspects of life, particularly the economic ones. The industrial state and its large corporations were the first to realize that science and technology have a great capacity to help them advance their economic interests and political goals. As a consequence, scientific research and technological development activities were institutionalized, causing more knowledge to be produced and accumulated. While industry employed the new technologies to raise industrial productivity and diversify economic activities and enhance profitability, the state used industry to build armies and equip them with guns, cannons, and ships to invade other regions of the world, colonize their peoples, and exploit their resources. However, as economic activities multiplied and diversified and banking and trade services expanded to serve the growing industrial economies, a new society emerged having three classes: rich, poor, and a middle class.

Although the socioeconomic and sociopolitical role of the middle class was initially limited, it soon distinguished itself by having a high degree of awareness regarding its interests, its societal role, and its rights. Such awareness led this class to become an important player in industrial society, promoting democracy and employing it to enhance its status and protect its interests. However, the accumulation of wealth and knowledge in the hands of the few on the one hand, and the increasing cost of having the right education to maintain a middle class status in the knowledge age on the other, have served to weaken the middle class and deprive it of the power to influence events and state decisions in its favor. By the end of the twentieth century, and due to the advancement of the knowledge age, the middle class had lost most of its economic and political power and class consciousness. Today, no middle class anywhere has enough awareness and self-confidence to protect its interests and play a significant role in societal life.

Although no age has ever been free of competition, it seems that the more people advance technically and economically and educationally the more competitive they become. And as competition sharpens the divides between individuals, ethnic groups, and social classes, it causes conflict to become an aspect of everyday life. In older times, people often competed and fought trying to get the same things, making competition more negative than positive. During the tribal times, for example, tribes fought to steal the animals of other tribes and kill or kidnap their children and rape their women. Jared Diamond says in *Guns, Germs and Steel*, that until 7,500 years ago, people used to kill whoever they found in their way, suspicion rather than trust had characterized inter-tribal relations. However, stealing the property of others and hurting them did not change life in society; it made the defeated feel bad losing dignity and honor and property, while making the victors feel good having destroyed the life of another tribe. Conflict and competition, therefore, were between tribes that were largely equal, which made people and societies and history move in place, not in time; it is a zero-sum game that changed nothing as far as history is concerned. During agricultural times, things changed slightly as the nature of competition and conflict changed to become more than a zero-sum game. Nevertheless, the movement of society and thus history remained largely in place rather than in time.

During the industrial age, both conflict and competition were heightened as their nature changed substantially. While conflict that characterized class relations became a conflict between two unequal groups, competition became more positive than negative, concentrating primarily on producing and owning material things. As a result, incomes and profits became the major targets of conflict and competition, leading people to become less ideological and more practical, driven largely by interests rather than values and religious convictions. And this, in turn, caused industrial society to move in place and time at once without interruption, causing societal change as well as material and cultural progress to be made simultaneously.

As the knowledge age advances and services rather than manufacturing become the major economic activity, science and technology and money will take the lead role in changing life and transforming society. As a consequence, they are expected to heighten both competition and conflict and cause the socioeconomic gaps to widen and the sociocultural divides to deepen. The shift from manufacturing to services also causes the middle

92 GLOBAL ECONOMIC AND CULTURAL TRANSFORMATION

class to shrink and lose its position and most of the economic and political gains it had previously made. Since the middle class emerged as a result of industrial expansion and economic diversification, the retreat of manufacturing and most activities associated with it are causing the middle class and its role to retreat as well.

Hegel argued that the "eastern nations knew only that one is free; the Greek and Roman world only that some are free; while we [the Germanic world] know that all men absolutely are free."[1] Since freedom is the ultimate goal to which history aspires, Hegel believed that history will come to an end when freedom prevails. But since the struggle for freedom, as we argued throughout this chapter, will never end, history, therefore, will continue to unfold. Marx saw freedom as connected to economics and the private ownership of the means of production that causes exploitation and creates classes with conflicting interests. Marx argued that exploitation will end only when private ownership of the means of production is abolished. But since private property had played and continues to play a major role in motivating people to work hard, accumulate wealth, develop science and technology, and build the machines and tools that raise productivity and improve the living conditions of everyone, change will continue, and neither private property nor history will ever end.

6

Theories of World History

The history of the development of human societies from the age of the hunter- gatherer to the age of knowledge has been a long and turbulent one. It has involved conflict and profound change, countless bloody wars, and massive—at times chaotic—sociopolitical, socioeconomic, and sociocultural transformations due primarily to countless scientific discoveries and the development of innovative technological tools, machines and systems. These developments have affected all aspects of human life: the social and economic structures of society, culture, political organizations, modes of production, and environmental settings. Nature, geography, ideas, innovations, technology, religious and political leaders, states, and chance have contributed in different ways and to varying degrees to the making of human history. This chapter tries to briefly review the major conceptions of world history, explain their rationale, and expose their shortcomings, consequently paving the way for the introduction and articulation of a new conception of world history.

History books are records of important events and explanations of what caused such events to happen in the past and how they influenced life conditions in general. Interest in world history has led historians to rediscover ancient peoples and investigate the possibility that something larger than events, actions, leaders, states, and ideas might be driving history and charting its course. Conceptions of world history as a whole seek to present the history of humankind as a process that has a logic and life of its own. Theories of history, therefore, are attempts to detect the main currents of history, define the historical process, identify the forces that are driving it, and describe its path.

Despite the work of many philosophers of history, historians have not been able to agree on a unified theory of world history. Their individual points of departure and life experiences, varied cultural backgrounds, and specific interests have prevented them from reaching the same or even

94 GLOBAL ECONOMIC AND CULTURAL TRANSFORMATION

similar conclusions. The major theories that have been produced tend to see history in general as being linear, cyclical, or chaotic. Although the three conceptions are dissimilar, they have all survived, and none of them has been either completely discredited or universally accepted. The many contradictions of history seem to have convinced historians and students of history to find merits in each conception.

The Linear Theory

German philosopher Georg Wilhelm Friedrich Hegel is considered the father of the linear theory of history. He and Karl Marx were responsible for advancing the idea that contradictions exist as an inherent characteristic of social systems or formations, and that such contradictions cause conflict, which in turn causes the systems to collapse. As a consequence, new social formations or syntheses emerge to replace the old ones. And unlike the previous social formations, the new ones solve the major contradictions but give birth to new, less severe ones. As this process continues, contradictions become less basic, leading ultimately to the formation of a harmonious system where all basic contradictions are resolved. Both Hegel and Marx saw the continuous search for syntheses as a process reflecting the spirit of history. This process would, according to both Hegel and Marx, lead ultimately to solving all contradictions and creating conditions for a life without conflict. However, the contradictions that Hegel argued as being the driving forces of history are not the same contradictions seen by Marx.

Systems of thought and sociopolitical systems fall apart and disintegrate under the pressure of their own internal contradictions, Hegel claimed. They are then replaced by new, more complex systems that contain less fundamental contradictions. This seemingly an unending process of systemic change explains the notion of the historical dialectics put forth by the Hegelian and Marxist philosophies of history.[1] However, the basic contradictions in society, according to Hegel, are related to human freedom, and, therefore, the conflict they cause and the syntheses they produce are of a political nature.

Hegel argues that progress in history is a result of the blind interplay of human passions that lead to conflict, revolution, and war. For him, "nothing great in the world has been accomplished without passion."[2] He maintains that "the history of the world is none other than the progress of the consciousness of freedom,"[3] which itself is driven by passion. Hegel argued further that communities have very specific reasons for their own self-development and that these reasons drive human progress and chart the course of history. "Each [historical] period is involved in such peculiar circumstances, exhibits a condition of things so strictly idiosyncratic, that its conduct must be regulated by considerations connected with itself, and itself alone."[4]

There is no doubt that different communities have different reasons to seek change, but no community lives in isolation or is immune to outside influence; therefore, societal change cannot be based only on self-organizing principles that are beyond the influence of external forces. And though the process through which societal goals are normally defined, sought, and accomplished is often rational, outside forces oftentimes intervene and influence the course of change and thus its outcome. Nevertheless, Hegel argues that the history of the world is a rational, self-regulating, self-generating process; he asserts that "God governs the world; the actual working of his government—the carrying out of His plan—is the history of the world."[5] But for history to move and make progress, it has to have agents. Such agents, according to Hegel, are great historical men with visions to understand the issues of their times that reflect the will of the world's spirit. But this does not account for the actions of ideological leaders who are usually driven by blind passion to promote their own ideological zeal. Since such leaders' visions are usually narrow, they fail to understand the issues of their times and, as a consequence, they fail to reflect the will of the world's spirit, assuming that the history of the world has a spirit of its own.

Since history is a rational process as Hegel argues, it must have a destination or a goal toward which it moves with diligence. For Hegel, that ultimate goal is human freedom. "I am free when my existence depends upon myself,"[6] which means that freedom is individual rather than collective. History, according to Hegel, reaches its final destination and comes to an end when freedom prevails. Since the end of history represents the highest state of human consciousness, it can be attained only after many syntheses; freedom must thus travel slowly and be realized gradually. At one point in time, argues Hegel, the final synthesis emerges and conditions for political freedom and social harmony will be established. After the battle of Jena in 1806 gave birth to a liberal democratic state in Germany, Hegel declared the end of history. Hegel argues further that at history's terminus, the state blooms and prospers and its virtues become apparent. As a consequence, the great historical men would no longer be needed to play the role of history's agents; they would be replaced by the new democratic state, which would embody history's reason and spirit.

Hegel described the spread of civilization from the East to the West and ultimately to the heart of Europe via Greece and Rome over thousands of years. He wrote, "Eastern nations knew only that one is free; the Greek and Roman world only that some are free; while we [the Germanic people]

96 GLOBAL ECONOMIC AND CULTURAL TRANSFORMATION

know that all men absolutely are free."[7] This claim clearly indicates that Hegel saw history as a process moving from a primitive stage of development to a more civilized one, reaching its destination when all men and women are free under a democratic state.

Before Marxism appeared in the middle of the nineteenth century, the dominant view of history among its philosophers was based on the thought that idealism and morality were the causes of historical change, and that ideas, men, leaders, and states were the primary agents of change. Marx, in contrast, saw the basic contradictions in society as emanating not from certain social or political relations or moral considerations, but rather from society's economic structure. For Karl Marx, "the mode of production in material life determines the general character of the social, political, and spiritual process of life. It is not the consciousness of men that determines their existence, but on the contrary, their social existence determines their consciousness."[8]

According to Marx, the key to understanding a historical epoch, a social formation, or a chain of historical events lies exclusively in the domain of economics. Marx argues that the economic structure of society constitutes the basis "on which rise legal and political superstructures and to which correspond definite forms of social consciousness."[9] Social relations and political structures in the Marxist sense are an outcome of the mode of production; and, because of that, society is formed and reformed by forces over which people have little control and whose consequences they cannot escape. Marx wrote, "With the change of the economic foundation the entire immense superstructure is more or less rapidly transformed."[10]

The mode of production, according to Marxist thought, includes two components: the social forces of production and the relations of production. While the social forces of production represent man's relationship with nature, the relations of production represent man's relationship with other men in the workplace. And while these two components of the mode of production are tightly connected to each other, the ownership of the means of production governs the nature of their interaction; and thus the ownership of the means of production largely determines the course of societal change.

According to Marxism, people are the primary forces of production and the actors who invent and develop the material means of production or the tools of production; they are also the forces that set the means of production in motion. The human forces of production, however, do not include all people; they include only the working class, or the laborers who do the actual work. On the other hand, production relations are the social ties that develop among people during the production process as they perform their tasks as workers and capitalists. Production relations, therefore, are a function of property relations, or the ownership of the material means of production at any given time. Property ownership, in other words, determines the nature of the relationships that tie the social forces of production to the relations of production.

When property ownership is communal as it used to be in the primitive societies and is supposed to be in the communist one, argues Marx, society would be classless, and no basic contradictions would exist within its borders. But when property ownership is private, social classes appear, causing contradictions and antagonism to arise and conflict to ensue. Thus, change in the economic structure would be needed to resolve the basic contradictions between the social forces of production and the relations of production and lead to a new synthesis, or to a new social formation. But since the new syntheses contain within themselves their own less severe contradictions, societal change would continue creating one social formation after another until all basic contradictions are fully resolved and private ownership of the means of production is abolished and a classless society emerges. Nevertheless, Marx does not seem to think that this process will move slowly and transform society gradually until it reaches its final destination; rather, he argues that the working class will have to revolt against its capitalist masters and take hold of the ownership of the means of production and lead history to its predetermined end.

The revolution to settle class conflict and resolve the basic contradictions in society will be carried out by the social class that represents the core of the social forces of production, meaning the working class or the proletariat. Members of this class, according to Marxism, are the most exploited by capital or by the owners of the means of production and, therefore, its exploitation makes revolt against the existing relations of production inevitable. The proletariat, says Marx, is not "naturally arising poor." Rather, exploitation by capital renders members of this class "artificially impoverished."[11]

Notwithstanding this emphasis on the role of economics and material relations in the making of human history, Marx did not consider the economic structure of society to be the only active force driving the historical process. Nor did he consider social, political, and cultural superstructures to be passive actors in society. For Marx, non-materialistic forces, such as the environment, circumstance, and external forces also influence the economic structure in society and thus the course of history.

Progress in history, according to the Hegelian thought, is made as people gain more freedom, which is supposed to be "embodied in the modern liberal state."[12] The end of history would therefore come when freedom is universal and the liberal democratic state is established to represent its people and implement their desired principles of liberty and equality. Marxist

98 GLOBAL ECONOMIC AND CULTURAL TRANSFORMATION

thought, in contrast, rejects the vision of a liberal democratic state as the embodiment of liberty and equality; it also rejects the notion that the establishment of such a state would bring about the end of history. For Marxism, the liberal state had failed to resolve the fundamental contradiction in society, and the freedom it brought was only freedom for the bourgeoisie, or the capitalist class. Democracy, Marxism argues, is the tool used by the bourgeoisie to protect its interests, which are at odds with those of the proletariat. Marx envisioned the historical process coming to an end with the establishment of a classless society where class struggle ends and the state withers away. So, while Hegel saw the liberal democratic state as the guardian of freedom, Marx saw the abolition of the state as an outcome of the abolition of private property and exploitation, and therefore, a condition for the realization of both freedom and social justice.

The conceptions of history articulated by both Hegel and Marx are largely linear interpretations of world history; they see history going from point A to point Z through a well-defined path, solving sociopolitical and socioeconomic contradictions and producing more harmonious societies. Because each conception has its own end goal, both conceptions are deterministic, and therefore neither one gives people much choice. People, to make progress and move toward freedom and social justice, have to understand the course of history and respond to its spirit as articulated by either Marx or Hegel. All deterministic philosophies, in fact, narrow the options open to people substantially, and thus they limit people's abilities to think freely and change their ways of thinking and perceptions and decisions as life conditions change.

Religion, which received the attention of both Hegel and Marx, is also a linear theory of history that envisions a terminal station where history ends. But the forces and motives that drive history according to most religions are neither moral nor material; they are heavenly. Therefore, there is no process of history in religious thought; life, according to the three monotheistic religions of Judaism, Christianity, and Islam, is the first and last station before the end of history, which is also the end of all forms of life as we know it. The fate of every person and everything in life and even in the hereafter is predetermined by an outside, almighty force that no one can influence. God thus becomes the only force determining the beginning of history as well as its end; no human or nonhuman force can change that assumed fact.

Both Hegel and Marx considered the consciousness engendered by religion a form of "false consciousness." Hegel maintained that religions are "ideologies which arose of the particular historical needs of the people who believed in them."[13] And since human needs, life conditions, and perceptions of the world change over time, religious consciousness is particular, not universal, and transient, not permanent. Similarly, Marx wrote that it is "man [who] makes religion, religion does not make man." Religion, he added "is the self-consciousness and self-feeling of man, who either has not found himself or has already lost himself again."[14] He went on to say that "the abolition of religion as the illusionary happiness of the people is required for their real happiness."[15]

The Cyclical Theory

If Hegel is the father of the linear theory of history, Oswald Spengler has been given credit for developing the cyclical theory. Spengler's inquiry into the nature of the historical process led him to conclude that history moves in cycles. He rejected the linear interpretation of history and the division of history into the ancient, medieval, and modern ages, a division that implies the existence of a center and a progression from the primitive to the advanced.

Spengler viewed history as the story of cultures, of which the Western culture is but one. Cultures "are born, grow, mature, and die with the same superb aimlessness as the flowers of the field."[16] He argues that cultures, while similar, are not related to each other; each culture is an independent creature with a life of its own and, therefore, cultures "do not influence, or even genuinely stimulate each other. Thus, if there is any pattern in history, it must be sought, not in developments between the cultures, but in developments within them."[17]

According to Spengler's view of history, cultures are subject to certain laws, similar to those of biology that condition creatures for birth, growth, and decay. Nothing can be done to change this destiny in a fundamental way, he argued. Although cultures could die prematurely due to outside intervention, they could also linger on after old age for long without being able to produce anything of importance. The normal lifespan of a culture, Spengler speculated, is about 1000 years—through which a culture experiences birth, growth, maturity, decay, and death—unless outside forces intervene to interrupt this process. Spengler saw outside intervention as having a negative rather than positive impact on the course of the development of cultures. "Cultures never learn from one another, they never really understand each other, [and] what one cannot understand one cannot learn, and what one cannot learn one cannot be influenced by," Spengler wrote.[18] But if cultures are similar, as Spengler maintains, then cultures must have similar roots and similar reasons for being, as well as similar goals that lead them to have similar lives and be able to understand each other.

100 GLOBAL ECONOMIC AND CULTURAL TRANSFORMATION

As for the history of the world, Spengler felt that most of it is "historyless," and largely meaningless. "Considered as a whole, what we should normally call the historical past is a formless expanse of human life within which centers of meaning or significance—that is cultures—from time to time make an appearance and pass away."[19] This view suggests that nothing of value can be learned from history per se; only cultures and their patterns of development and life cycles are somewhat meaningful. The only thing to learn from history, Spengler seems to imply, is that cultures in general and Western culture in particular are destined to die and not rise again. New cultures will be born to keep history going, but their lives will be largely meaningless because cultures usually live a lonely life and normally die a natural death, leaving nothing of value behind.

Spengler made two basic mistakes in my view: First, he was unable to place each culture in its proper historical context and, therefore, could not see cultures as products of civilizations, which makes cultures produced by one civilization similar to each other and, at the same time, much different from cultures produced by another civilization. As products of civilizations, the fate of each culture and the pattern of its development are very much dependent on the fate of the civilization that produced it. And second, he failed to see the real impact of religion on people's consciousness; he said that "what one cannot understand one cannot learn, and what one cannot learn one cannot be influenced by." But looking at how the religiously committed people react today, one must conclude that the more mysterious a religion is the more influence it has on the consciousness and actions of its followers.

Arnold Toynbee, who was greatly influenced by Spengler's ideas and particularly his views regarding the decline of the West, was responsible for developing Spengler's conception of history into a fully cyclical one. Toynbee rejected the biological model advocated by Spengler to describe the life cycle of cultures, and replaced cultures with civilizations or nations in his historical inquiry. He also rejected the deterministic view of Spengler that sees cultures as creatures that rise, live, mature, die, and never rise again. Instead, Toynbee saw nations or civilizations as creatures that rise, live, mature, and either die or continue to live, depending on their responses to the challenges they usually face. Therefore, Toynbee claims that history has seen nations decline and rise again. He also saw cultural interaction as inevitable and positive, and one of the causes of cultural revitalization and national regeneration. While Spengler saw cultural interactions as contributing to the old-age ailments of cultures, Toynbee saw cultural old-age ailments as being curable by cross-cultural interactions.

And just like Spengler, Toynbee saw a positive role for religion in the life of civilizations or nations, especially at the beginning of their lives, or during the early stages of their development. However, Toynbee found that religion loses much of its role and influence in society as civilizations mature and intellectual and scientific challenges increase. He did recognize, however, that as civilizations enter their final life cycles, religion reappears and assumes an important but different role in the life of society. In the early stages of societal development, religion appears as a force that inspires young civilizations and nations; but in the last stage, it reappears as a system to comfort the dying.

While Toynbee identifies the West or the Western nations that appeared in the wake of the Reformation as a civilization, he fails to differentiate between the West as a civilization and older nations or states that appeared in the distant past. And because of this misrepresentation, his analysis loses much of its value; one cannot compare the Western world or the Western Civilization with smaller states that appeared and disappeared centuries ago. In fact, it is hard to consider any of the older states a nation, because no group of people during older times could develop a national consciousness to be considered a nation, or remold different societies and cultures and economies to be considered a unique civilization. Almost all successful older states had similar social formations, and were led, as Toynbee argues, by minorities that responded positively to the challenges of their times; as a consequence, they were able to build states like the Sumerians that lasted for a long time. Nations usually survive all historical upheavals as long as their languages and the core of their cultures survive, as the Chinese, the Arabs, and the Persians have demonstrated. (See Chapter 1 for an explanation of how cultures and civilizations relate to each other and differ from one another.)

Giambottista Vico, who lived and died before both Spengler and Toynbee, may have been the first modern philosopher to view history as cyclical. He wrote, "History moved in cycles, the change from one stage to the next being accomplished by a process both of growth and decay."[20] Spengler, as a moralist concerned with values, could not see "growth and decay" as simultaneous; he saw them occurring in a sequence. It is a view rooted in the belief that the ascendancy of money and machines or materialism in the West had come at the expense of culture, morality, and the individual,[21] and therefore, cannot continue forever. It is a view that would be expressed again by Max Weber and Joseph Schumpeter in the early and the middle twentieth century, respectively.

The Chaos Theory

The chaotic conception of history claims that history is a record of unconnected, non-causal events. History, the authors of the chaos theory seem to say, does not have any particular logic that guides its movement, and the

102 GLOBAL ECONOMIC AND CULTURAL TRANSFORMATION

developments that history experiences do not constitute in themselves a process with any discernible path or logic. Friedrich Nietzsche, Max Weber, and Leo Tolstoy are classified as adherents and architects of the chaotic view of history.

Nietzsche considered life a profound tragedy, a struggle from the beginning to the end. Therefore, he could not see any real logic or even purpose in history that would oblige us to accept the struggle of life as unquestionable or even worthwhile. His sensitivity to human weakness made him a moralist who sought to convince people that only they could make their own history. He regarded "traditional Christian morality as a slave morality, incompatible with the great life struggle."[22] And because of that view, Nietzsche criticized Martin Luther harshly, accusing him of restoring Christianity "at the very moment when it was vanquished."[23] Martin Luther is one of the leading figures who challenged the Catholic Church in the seventeenth century and caused it to splinter into several denominations.

Tolstoy, Weber, and Nietzsche, according to John Patrick Diggens, "all viewed history as essentially meaningless, an absurd succession of forces and effects that would remain without significance until the thinker strove to make sense of them."[24] Weber in particular adhered to a chaotic view of history, holding that "how humankind acts and confronts historical conditions is more important than any law supposedly governing history itself. History is what we make it,"[25] he asserted. And since what we make is subject to our individual and collective will and power, historical developments, as Weber argues, do not follow a consistent logic or a clear path; they are chaotic events of little meaning except to those who make them. "The concurrence of conditions that brought freedom into existence cannot be repeated, yet humankind rises to dignity only by making history rather than succumbing to it."[26] And this simply means that Weber rejects both the linear and cyclical views of history.

At another point, however, Weber seemed to say that history might yet be cyclical. For example, he predicted the inevitable return of aristocracy to democratic societies despite the successes of individualism and democracy, arguing that there is a possibility that history may reverse itself. He wrote that the "demagicalization of the world under capitalist and scientific secular forces cannot continue for long, emptying life of meaning and value without creating the conditions for countertendencies arising from opposite emotions and forces."[27] This suggests that Weber may have, perhaps unconsciously, accepted both the historical dialectic and the cyclical notions of history, even the Marxist theory that predicts class conflict. These observations were made by Weber after he had studied the American society and realized the far-reaching impact of materialism on the life of the American people.

But even if history is as chaotic as Weber and others claim, the modern chaos theory has proved that what seems to us chaotic is not in reality as chaotic as we might think. Nature has the capacity to organize and reorganize complexity and make sense out of chaos.[28] Chaotic developments, therefore, regardless of their nature and causes and extent, tend to eventually produce discernible patterns of change that lead to new, more stable systems and relationships within the natural and human spheres. The history of rivers, for example, attests to the ability of nature to organize water emanating from rain and snow and ground springs, and to form rivers and streams with clear paths leading to serene lakes and turbulent oceans to keep them alive.

Theories that have a clear, deterministic conception of world history tend to condition life and determine peoples' fate, giving people little choice and limited options. The options they usually give people are confined to the following:

1. To ride the tide of history by joining the forces of change and hope for positive change;
2. To try to slow down the movement of history by creating obstacles in its way and, in the meantime, lose time and energy needlessly; or
3. To accept fate as determined by history and do practically nothing besides subjecting themselves to its will.[29]

Religion, as a theory of history, is even more restrictive of choice and freedom of action. It demands that man should accept fate without questions and be content; it asks its followers to have faith in God's design and obey God's orders as, of course, enunciated by his self-appointed representatives on earth. Christianity and Islam in particular claim that all actions taken by man are part of God's will, even when one agonizes over his decisions and actions. Max Weber called this religious attitude "the height of ethical irresponsibility,"[30] arguing that it absolves man of ethical responsibility for his own actions. In fact, when one claims that whatever he does cannot be done without God's will, he says in effect that if he cheats or steals or commits a crime, he would be doing what God wanted him to do.

The chaos theory of history is thus the only theory that gives people the opportunity to shape their own lives and destinies. But in return, it demands that they be held responsible for their actions. Max Weber wrote that it was "the fate of a cultural epoch which has eaten of the tree of knowledge to be aware that however we may investigate history we cannot read its real meaning, and that we must be content to create our own sense of

104   GLOBAL ECONOMIC AND CULTURAL TRANSFORMATION

history."[31] As man is able to build dams, divert rivers, and create lakes, man is able to influence the making of history by consciously acting to plan for the future and shape his destiny.

Comparative Review

Hegel's conception of history seems to suggest that the establishment of a liberal democratic state creates the necessary conditions for freedom, equality, and social justice; and thus it causes social conflict as well as history to end. But looking at life conditions and production relations in the United States after more than two centuries of democracy, one must wonder if the liberal democratic state is able to guarantee freedom or equality or social justice, or even commit itself to achieving such goals. And while Marx articulates an elegant theory of world history based on class conflict and social change, he seems to suggest that history is incapable by itself of reaching its final destination without human intervention. In fact, Marx's call for the workers of the world to unite is a call for action, making his historical conception not just a theory of societal development, but also a plan for forced change. And so is Toynbee who feels that a divine intervention is capable of saving the West from a predetermined fate ordained by history.

On the other hand, while Marx was able to foresee the decline of the middle class in the capitalist society, he failed to foresee the near-destruction of the working class. So if this class is the vehicle that is supposed to carry history to its final destination, then what will happen to history in its absence? And while Toynbee was able to foresee the revival of religion as nations approach the end of their productive lives to comfort the dying, he failed to foresee that the dying would recover from their coma with their recent memories lost. As a consequence, instead of resuming the life they experienced before going into coma, they go back to the way of life experienced by their tribal ancestors—a life colored by suspicion, conflict, enmity, and fear of change, as the behavior of both Muslim and Jewish fundamentalists' clearly demonstrates. These are people who oppose individual freedoms in general, and reject equality of rights that include women's rights as well as the rights of minorities that adhere to different religions and ideologies and cultures and schools of thought.

Despite the merits of each conception of history, I believe that none of them is able to explain the making of world history and how civilizations developed over time, and therefore none provides the lessons we seek to learn from past history. However, I see all theories as complementary components of a comprehensive theory to be articulated in the following chapter. Since none of these theories is descriptive of the past or predictive of the future, dependence on either one is destined to mislead people rather than help them understand the past or comprehend the complexity of the present. Moreover, all conceptions fail to see transitional periods that separate civilizations from each other as different historical epochs having their own nature and forces, as well as their destructive transformational characters. Therefore, all conceptions reviewed in this chapter are incapable of explaining the meaning or the consequences of transitional periods, and thus unable to predict the future or help us plan to meet its many challenges.

John Locke argued in his *Essay on Human Understanding* that reason founded on experience is the only path to understanding the world in which we live. However, he said that experience could only be personal, never collective. Since history is the story of societies and nations and cultures and states and civilizations, not just individuals, history, according to Locke, becomes inconceivable. While experience in life is very important to understanding the world and navigating its turbulent seas, experience is both individual and collective. Individual experience is more important to the development of one's mental capacity, reason, and basic convictions; collective experience is important to shaping nations' traditions, attitudes, values, consciousness, identities, and worldviews.

Human beings are instinctively social, and the social relations people normally forge tie individuals and groups and communities to each other through a web of traditions, customs, values, interests, economic entities, sociocultural organizations, and political and professional associations. Such ties, while making us human and conscious of our place and humanity, create communities and societies and group identities that hold people together. We cannot, therefore, be fully human without collective experience, and collective experience is not possible without society made of individuals and groups and cultures and economies.

Ever since the appearance of the most primitive form of human society, some 100,000 years ago, people have continued to form larger societies, more intricate social and political relationships, more specialized sociocultural and economic organizations, and more complex societal systems. Throughout history, people have been motivated by self-interest to preserve their race, to ensure food and physical security, to gain more freedom, to accumulate wealth, and to improve life conditions in general. Collective historical experience, or human history, clearly indicates that we have achieved a great deal of what we wanted and sought. But the process through which we traveled to reach our goals has not proceeded in either a linear or a cyclical manner. It has also been far from being chaotic.

History, as will be explained in the next chapter, has moved along a largely linear path, going through both cyclical and chaotic periods of change. But linear conceptions of history are mistaken in arguing that history has a destination or a final station to which it moves with diligence. In other words, neither the linear, cyclical, nor chaotic conception explains the historical process by itself; all conceptions and a little more are needed to explain it. Each theory therefore is only one component of a larger theory of history, the *Train of Time* theory that incorporates and integrates the three nonreligious conceptions of history into one theory.

7

The Train of Time

This chapter introduces a new theory of world history that differs substantially from the theories reviewed in the last chapter. The *Train of Time* theory acknowledges the contributions of the linear, cyclical, and chaotic conceptions of world history but finds them insufficient. It sees each conception as describing one aspect or one stage of a history in the making, and therefore, neither conception is able to tell the entire story of world history, which continues to unfold. The train of time integrates the three conceptions, constructing a comprehensive theory able to tell the story of the development of human societies, describe the process of historical change, and identify the forces that drive history and keep it going. However, to understand this theory and appreciate its way of reasoning, history must be viewed as a virtual space that contains the entire world with its peoples, animals, plants, and all other things.

History begins with the train of time standing at the edge of a vast lake, ready to move but unsure how to start its engine and which way to go. As the train wonders how to start and where to go, a small group of able people embodying the forces of the sociocultural process step forward and assume leadership, driving the train slowly and cautiously around the lake. After circling the lake hundreds of times and countless generations of leaders succeed each other in driving the train, some people find a new way to organize their lives, and develop a new method to produce food to meet their needs, farm the land, and use its produce for different purposes, making life more secure and less stressful. As a consequence, the people who developed this method are able to distinguish themselves from the rest of the train's population, construct a new, more comfortable wagon to live in, and move forward to assume the leadership duties of the train. But as the new society assumes the leadership role, it begins to pull the old wagon with its entire populations, giving those populations an opportunity to learn from the passengers of the first wagon, experience change, and improve the quality of their lives.

After some 5,000 years of a history dominated by farmers and leaders having the same mentality and following the same way of life, a new type of leadership with authority emerges to embody the forces of the political process and assume societal leadership. The moment the new leadership assumed power, it turned its attention to consolidating its powers, creating new organizations, writing new laws and regulations, facilitating trade, and imposing law and order on the train's entire population. As a consequence, the train was able to discover a new, more suitable path to follow and a new way to navigate the world and enjoy some of its wonders. In the process, however, the train was partially freed from the circular movement around the lake, which gave it the opportunity to adjust its speed and direction. After another 5,000 years of farming the land and trading and making incremental material and cultural progress, merchants and political leaders joined hands to lead the train of time and chart a new course.

The new leadership moved immediately to expand trade and manufacturing, encourage some people to explore the world, motivate others to produce new tradable goods, and place the train on a rather solid road going forward along a largely straight line. But before moving too far, the train encountered an earthquake that caused floods and tsunamis that engulfed the entire living space. As a consequence, the train got confused and its population got scared, forcing everyone to seek cover in a safe place. To find such a place, the train was led to move in many directions and try several paths, while the skies were getting darker and the nights getting longer and colder. Soon, out of the ashes of the earthquake, a new society with a new leadership that embodied the forces of the economic process emerged, constructing a new wagon, building a new way of life, developing a new economic system, and causing the train of time to accelerate its pace and move forward with confidence in the land of the unknown.

Now, after nearly 250 years of the industrial revolution, the train of time finds itself faced with a new tsunami, causing it to get disoriented and lose its sense of direction. But again, from the thick clouds of confusion and apprehension, a new society, led by a new leadership that embodies the forces of the infomedia process, is emerging slowly to construct a new wagon, build a new way of life, develop a new economy, and assume global leadership. But unlike previous societies, the new knowledge society, using the bulk of knowledge developed by humankind over thousands of years, is moving to open all wagons, creating an open space for people of the world to move around, explore different ways of living, learn from each other, and improve the quality of his lives.

Cooperation and Competition

The dialectical method of conflict and change developed by Hegel and advanced by Marx gives us an idea of what happens in society as it experiences social transformation. However, the human experience does not give us a single case where contradictions within a society or culture or civilization were allowed to reach the point of explosion and cause the demise of an entire social order. Societal change throughout history and in every land has never been sudden or total; on the contrary, it has often been subtle and gradual. "Change is inescapable and the more gradual and hidden the more decisive; the great shifts in fortune for ancient empires were usually not apparent to those living at the time."[1] In fact, the most important ideas that contributed to building the foundations of modern science, technology, and economies were small ones, arising primarily from actual needs to solve real problems and exploit new opportunities. Such ideas have worked in each field as clusters of competing and cooperating forces interacting with one another and with other clusters of ideas to cause societal change and make history.

Even the concept of discontinuity developed by Foucault is not in reality a discontinuity in a particular process; it is rather a phase in an unseen process of transformation that is forced to uncover its face as it reaches a major station on its journey. A breakthrough in science is not an accident or an isolated incident, no matter how it is viewed, but a culmination of years or decades of research trying to solve a fundamental problem or find a cure for a serious disease. Breakthroughs usually come as a result of having exhausted most options, which forces concerned scientists to try something out of the ordinary; it may also come as a consequence of being able to recognize the significance of an accidental discovery due to the accumulated knowledge and unique work experience of the person who makes the discovery.

Social orders, systems of thought, and organizations are usually driven by two major blocks of forces that cooperate and compete with each other continuously, while unconsciously complementing one another. Cooperation is what gives a social order its form and enables it to exhibit stability and functionality; competition is what gives the order a sense of purpose and enables it to change and be flexible and dynamic. And while the forces of cooperation strive to maintain stability and continuity, the forces of competition strive to cause change and be innovative. Meanwhile, working together, the forces of cooperation and competition give each social order its unique structure and character and enable it to meet the needs of the society it is meant to serve.

110 GLOBAL ECONOMIC AND CULTURAL TRANSFORMATION

During the early stages of systemic formation, the forces of cooperation usually prevail, enabling the social order to grow normally but slowly without serious challenges from the inside or the outside. Though the forces of competition are weak and largely ineffective at this stage, they are alive and active under the surface. But as social orders mature, the forces of stability become more conservative and less innovative, causing the order to become less able to meet the changing and often growing needs of society. As a consequence, the competing forces of change feel progressively more confident to expose the shortcomings of the conservative forces that are in control and challenge them to change. This, in turn, pushes both forces to engage in a serious blaming game that causes the order to become largely stagnant, unstable, and unproductive. While the conservative forces of cooperation usually become more reactive trying to protect their statuses and defend their record, the progressive forces of change become more vocal and proactive trying to advance their causes at the expense of the conservative ones.

As stagnation endures, the conservative forces begin to lose their credibility and self-confidence, giving the progressive forces an opportunity to promote their views openly and highlight the need for change. As a consequence, conflict between the weakened conservative forces and the emboldened progressive ones erupts, causing the need to restructure the social order or replace it to become apparent, at times urgent. If conflict is moderate, the major systems and organizations of society would be restructured in ways that reconcile the views of both parties and enable the new reformed order to restore stability and regain functionality. However, no change of this nature satisfies all forces on both sides, leading the more progressive elements of change as well as the more conservative elements of continuity to abandon the newly created systems and establish new ones more compatible with their views and objectives. If the restructured social order fails to meet the needs of society as expected, life conditions would continue to deteriorate and the order would ultimately die unless outside forces intervene to hasten its demise or keep it alive on a special life support system. The failure of the social order may lead to a revolution to replace the entire order and cause profound change and social transformation. But no matter what happens, it is unlikely to create a totally new social order, because neither the conservative forces nor the progressive ones will disappear or be prevented completely from playing a role, supporting the new order or opposing it.

Nevertheless, before a social order dies a natural death, the conservative forces, particularly in nondemocratic states, are more likely to launch a coercive campaign to suppress the progressive forces, discredit them, and deny them their legitimate rights. If the conservative forces prevail and manage to silence the progressive ones, the order would continue to lose functionality and relevance, causing the situation to deteriorate further and the pace of societal decline to accelerate. If the progressive forces succeed in defending their views and maintaining their social position, new systems and organizations would be born in the womb of the existing social order to totally or partially replace the old ones and lead change. However, as time passes and the new systems mature, the same process repeats itself; the forces controlling each system and organization would become gradually conservative, forcing the more progressive forces inside each system to renew the call for change and transformation.

The way conflict plays itself out at this stage may lead to a short period of social and political chaos or revolution, or to a prolonged period of sociopolitical, sociocultural, and socioeconomic stagnation, Both states of stagnation and chaos would ultimately cause the demise of the social order and the establishment of a new one on the basis of the ideas of the progressive forces or the vision of the conservative ones. In the process, however, more systems and organizations are born, causing social systems to multiply, and the social order to become more complex and less manageable. Complexity and multiplicity of systems, meanwhile, enable the social order to achieve some balance and change incrementally without much challenge, giving birth to new, largely special systems to quietly meet the needs of different segments and classes of society. As a consequence, the need for profound change becomes less urgent, and the call for genuine transformation becomes less popular.

Since each idea, social system, social organization is a product of a particular time, place, and stage of societal development, it has a life of its own. And just like people, animals, and plants, some systems live longer than others and are more resistant to adverse environmental changes. Therefore, the capacity of each system to perform and defend itself against new ideas and existential challenges varies from one system to another. This capacity is a function of the structure of the system itself and the nature and weight of the inside and outside challenges it usually faces during its life. Each system is also influenced by the dynamic relationships that tie the forces of continuity to the forces of change inside the system and within the larger society. Depending on such factors, some systems could stagnate for a long time without a meaningful change before they fade away into irrelevance; others may live their entire lives in a state of perpetual imbalance and change. However, no change can be implemented in society without causing conflict, and no conflict is resolved without change.

Social orders that manage the lives of traditional agricultural societies in general tend to be stable and largely stagnant. In contrast, social orders that manage the lives of industrial societies tend to be largely unstable but dynamic. The first orders tend to be stagnant because life conditions in traditional agricultural societies are simple, and social change is usually governed by traditions and values and convictions that seldom change. Social orders that manage life conditions in industrial societies tend to be dynamic because life conditions in such societies are complex, and social change is usually governed by interests that never stop changing. Nevertheless, all social orders encounter difficulties during their lives due primarily to changed circumstances, causing the need to restructure or replace the orders to become apparent. However, some systems, such as capitalism and democracy, possess an incredible capacity to rejuvenate themselves and respond to changing economic and political conditions and changed environmental settings, which gives them the ability to adapt to the new situations and prolong their productive lives. In contrast, systems like dictatorships are born sterile and live largely unproductive lives until their often violent death.

Most social orders, however, do neither die nor rejuvenate themselves but give birth to nontraditional systems that live and function next to them without disturbing their largely peaceful lives. The new systems are usually established by certain elements of the conservative forces that consider the breadth and depth of cooperation less than satisfactory, or by certain elements of the progressive forces that perceive the pace of change as less than desired and needed. The creation of such systems serve to stabilize the social order by helping it get rid of serious internal challenges, while making it less amenable to change and thus less productive. As a consequence, the larger social order becomes less vulnerable to the many internal as well as external contradictions. In the meantime, however, people become a collection of sociocultural groups that are more inclined to seek different paths and live separate lives.

Both Hegel and Marx consider stability, balance, and progress in society the result of a social process that leads to replacing complex social orders containing major contradictions with simpler ones that contain less severe contradictions. In contrast, the ideas outlined above see balance and progress in society as a result of a social process that leads to the multiplication of systems and causes the deepening of the complexity of the prevailing social order. While Hegel views the process he describes as a political process leading to freedom, Marx views the process he describes as a socioeconomic process leading to equality and social justice. But the simplicity that characterizes the final orders that are supposed to emerge at the end of the Hegelian and Marxist processes makes the new social order less dynamic, particularly when it comes to economics, and this in turn makes society less able to make further progress. Competition, as has been argued earlier, represents one of the major forces that drive history and enable societies to make more material and cultural progress.

Nevertheless, the social order that the train of time describes is a tentative one that lives a life of continuous change and transformation; it is, therefore, never complete or stable. And while it guarantees balance and progress in all fields of human endeavor, it does not guarantee stability because progress requires creativity and creativity needs a good amount of chaos to flourish. Therefore, complex social orders live, develop, change, and die without seeing stability or achieving freedom, equality, or social justice; in fact they may lead to restricting freedoms of peoples and undermining social justice in society.

The Context of Change

Each society, regardless of its size and structure, has many traditional and nontraditional systems, as well as formal and informal arrangements and organizations, all of which can be grouped into the four societal processes of change and transformation articulated in Chapter 3: the sociocultural, political, economic, and infomedia processes. While all processes exist in every society, the role each process plays in societal life differs from one society to another, depending on the stage of societal development in which society lives. As a consequence, the relationships that tie these processes to each other differ from one society to another. While the relationship between any two processes may be characterized as cooperative in one society, it may be characterized as competitive in another. The nature of systemic relationships and the degree of cooperation and competition between the different processes are what determines the course, pace, and extent of social transformation in each society. The following is a summation of the roles these processes play in facilitating change and influencing the making history.

The sociocultural process came into existence with the formation of the first human society; it continued to evolve slowly and freely, concentrating primarily on maintaining social unity and harmony. The assignment of individual roles in family and society in older times, and the definition of mutual obligations and norms of behavior, and the transfer of knowledge from one generation to another were regulated by customs and enforced by traditions, the two pillars of the culture of those times. But with the emergence of the political process around the middle of the agricultural age, things began to change slowly, causing the fortunes of the sociocultural process to decline steadily.

The development of agriculture changed the tribal society and transformed its culture and economy, and thus it changed its social and economic structures. The transition from forager to farmer required so many changes in human life that the adjustment is called the agricultural revolution. By changing the mode of production, agriculture changed the economic conditions of life and the way of life of the old society. The greatest impact of agriculture on society, however, was related not to the production of food but to the fundamental transformation of the social and political and economic organization of society.

"The division of the world between farmers and foragers created permanent tension between two types of subsistence with very different needs."[2] Because of that tension, people were divided into two different societies having different outlooks and largely contradictory goals. Each society saw itself and was perceived by the other as different, causing suspicion and conflict to dominate their relationship. In fact, "from the beginning of the division between farmer and forager, the relationship was never equal or just,"[3] or peaceful. And while the forager continued to live a primitive life that knew no noticeable change, the farmer began to live a life of slow change and see his life conditions improve gradually, causing the socioeconomic gap between the two societies to widen.

Late in the life of the agricultural age organized religion appeared as a body of knowledge to explain what man had failed to explain, matters related to life and death, to nature and meteorology. Due to its mysterious nature and absolutist claims, religion became sacred, forming a system of values and beliefs at the heart of culture; it actually became the core of agricultural culture everywhere. Since traditions and customs and religious beliefs tend to be stable over time, the agricultural society managed to change very little over thousands of years. In the absence of economic and technological change, ideas became the only force to challenge the forces of the sociocultural process from within and introduce smaller doses of change in societal life. The European experience of the Renaissance proves this point. New philosophical and political ideas and scientific discoveries and technological devices emerged slowly, challenging the conventional wisdom and its religious foundation. As a consequence, the sociocultural process was weakened causing its influence in society and role in initiating change and maintaining stability to weaken as well.

The political process was born in the womb of the sociocultural process as an extension to it, not as a replacement for it. The political process evolved in response to the growing needs of a larger agricultural society of many communities, particularly the law and order functions. Since such functions could also be performed informally by customs and traditions, competition and at later times conflict became a characteristic of the relationship between the political and sociocultural processes. Competition between these two processes and expansion of trade were instrumental in introducing a modest, but effective dose of dynamism into the life of agricultural society, causing the pace of change to accelerate. Private and collective property ownership, taxation, tools, trade, and financial transactions appeared later as components of the economic process and indispensable activities to a properly functioning agrarian economy.

Trade was followed by conquest and empire building, which necessitated the production of new tradable goods and the manufacturing of arms and ships to fight wars and secure trade routes. Consequently, new conditions were created that facilitated cross-cultural interactions and caused new challenges in the form of interest-related relationships and nonconventional social and economic organizations to be born. Nevertheless, the basic life conditions, the state of technology, culture, and the mode of economic production remained largely the same throughout the agricultural age. But as soon as the economic process became more active around the end of that age, and the pace of technology development and manufacturing accelerated, change began to be systematic and systemic and transformational.

Agricultural communities were able to produce a surplus of food and thus free some people to engage in other, largely noneconomic activities. These activities were dictated by the growing needs of the new society and covered all aspects of human life, causing all societies to be transformed, some more than others. The consequences of such transformations produced important changes that included:

1. The emergence of social classes, or, to put it more accurately, the segmentation of agricultural society into farm workers, landlords, rulers, religious men, and others;
2. The division of labor according to economic activity, which gave rise to farmers, merchants, craftsmen, money handlers, and others;
3. The development of new technologies and products in response to the expansion of trade and population growth, and in order to increase land productivity, improve the quality of life, and enhance the efficiency of arms; and
4. The birth of other, nonmaterial activities such as the arts, teaching, writing, acts of magic, and entertainment.

The last group of activities was instrumental in introducing the idea of individual freedom in societal life. These are creative activities that nonfree and insecure people are less able to engage in than are people who enjoy security and have more freedom and a better quality of life. And because of their importance and visibility, these activities became trademarks distinguishing one state from another or one civilization from

116 GLOBAL ECONOMIC AND CULTURAL TRANSFORMATION

another. In fact, advancements made in this area led to the evolvement of the great civilizations of the past and differentiated one nation, such as the Egyptian, from most other nations.

The economic process began to evolve as a distinctive societal process due to trade expansion and the creation of large states and empires. By the middle of the fifteenth century, the pace of change in certain parts of Europe began to gain momentum and impact the lives of neighboring communities and states. After some 300 years of slow but chaotic change led primarily by the forces of the economic process, the Industrial Revolution occurred, first in England and later on in other European countries and North America. As a consequence, the sociocultural and political processes were forced to endure great, often painful changes that led to conflict, war, and loss of direction in many parts of Europe. Describing the German scene as Germany was in labor trying to give birth to the Industrial Revolution, Hegel wrote, "All the mass of previous representations, concepts, and bonds linking our world together are dissolving and collapsing like a dream picture."[4] A chaotic conception of world history at the time would have been very appropriate indeed.

The Industrial Revolution, which was carried out by the economic process, could not have happened without the trials and tribulations of the transitional period that lasted about 300 years and separated the age of agriculture from the age of industry. Societies that went through that period had to endure the transformation of their value systems, social, political, and economic structures, as well as their sense of identity, even their relationships to one another. Nations that did not experience such transformations, such as China, Egypt, India, Iran, Vietnam, and all other African, Asian, and South American nations, were unable to enter the industrial age at the time. The sociocultural and political forces of continuity and stability in those countries were able to meet the challenges posed by the rather weak economic and technological forces of change and suppress them, limiting their contributions to society.

While cooperation has characterized the relationship between the forces of the economic process on the one hand and science and technology on the other, conflict has almost always characterized the relationship between the sociocultural and economic forces. Because of such conflict, the progress of economics, science, technology, and industry has always come at the expense of established traditions, values, magic, and mythical convictions. In fact, as science, technology, and industry advance, traditional attitudes and relationships as well as belief systems undergo drastic changes that weaken them and undermine their influence in society. And as traditions, values, belief systems, and conventional ways of thinking remain in control, science, technology, and economics usually fail to make adequate progress.

The need to expand trade and legitimize financial transactions in Europe during the transitional period could not be met without the support of the state. Because of that need, the economic process was forced to forge a cooperative relationship with the political process, while its relationship with the sociocultural process grew more competitive and conflictual. This cooperative relationship between the economic and political processes was also dictated by the need of rulers for financial support, which only the merchants were able to provide at the time. European rulers needed money to build national armies, rally people around them, and challenge Church authority and teachings. Yet, as the economic process expanded and its men grew richer, it became more powerful and assertive, leading it to exert increasing influence over the political process. By the middle of the twentieth century, the economic process emerged in the Western industrial states as the most powerful and influential process, forcing the other two processes to adopt defensive postures.

The infomedia process, unlike the other societal processes, was the product of scientific research and technological developments that produced the information and communications revolutions. Because the economic process supports and partially finances research and development activities, the infomedia process evolved as an extension of the economic process, causing the ties between these two processes to be strong. Since science and technology are themselves products of universal efforts to improve life conditions and facilitate communications between people, the infomedia was born as a universal process. As a consequence, it is able to reach every person in the world at all times, regardless of race, color, culture, religion, nationality, and geographical location, and influence every human activity.

Because economy and culture remained largely the same during the tribal age, as well as throughout the agricultural age, history's movement was cyclical: all wars and conquests and migrations have failed to change the economy, culture, or life conditions of either society. However, during the transitional period from the tribal to the agricultural age and from the agricultural to the industrial age, history's movement was definitely chaotic; no one knew at the time the direction of change or its manifestations, causing the connection between the past and present to be severed. In the mid-1990s, the most advanced industrial societies began to enter a new transitional period, with its pain, problems, and loss of direction. History, as a result, began to move again in a chaotic manner and lose its connection to the past, and with that loss, past history lost its relevance and wisdom.

The first transitional period from the age of the hunter-gatherer to the age of agriculture lasted about 3,000 years. The second transitional period separating the agricultural from the industrial age lasted about 300 years. The latest transitional period separating the industrial from the knowledge

118 GLOBAL ECONOMIC AND CULTURAL TRANSFORMATION

age is expected to last about 30 years only. This seems to suggest that each successive transitional period lasts about 10 percent of the preceding one. If this suggestion could be used as a general rule of thumb, the age of knowledge should become a reality around the year 2025. As a consequence, the age of knowledge is expected to become an age in transition, or an age of perpetual change and transformation, causing knowledge societies to experience successive revolutions that transform the near-totality of life conditions on a continuous basis, as they invalidate existing ideas, systems, institutions, and most theories and replace them with new ones.

One might correctly argue that all societal processes were born at the same time that the first human society was formed. While no society could be formed without a system to obtain food, no society could be held together without a value system and a system of authority. In addition, no society could function and last without a language that enables its members to communicate with one another. But there is no doubt also that one of the four societal processes has always played the lead role in society during each stage of societal development, and that that role was taken away from it by another process at a later stage.

In other words, history has always been led by the forces of one societal process, not by a culture or state or nation or leader, with the sociocultural process being the first to lead. It provided and continues to provide the social glue that holds members of each society together. When the political process emerged, its union with the sociocultural process led initially to the strengthening of the sociocultural forces in society; but slowly and gradually the sociocultural forces were subordinated to the authority and rationale of politics. And when the economic process emerged, its union with the political process led initially to the strengthening of the political forces, but slowly and gradually the political forces were subordinated to the power and rationale of economics. Today, the infomedia process is cooperating more and competing less with the economic process. But if the current merger trends continue and the commercializing of the media intensifies as expected, the economic and infomedia processes would eventually merge together forming a powerful societal process beyond serious challenge.

If the level of industrial and military technology were to remain constant, which was largely the case throughout the pre-industrial times, conflict and change would be a zero-sum game, and history would be rather cyclical, moving much in place but very little in time. But if conflict and change were to produce too many winners and too many losers, and if a winner in one respect could be at the same time a loser in another, history would be chaotic, moving in place, in time, and in all directions simultaneously. But if the number of winners produced by change were to be large and on the rise, and continued change gives the losers an opportunity to become future winners, history would be linear, moving in place but more in time, and making progress as it proceeds forward.

Before concluding this section, it must be noted that all revolutions that caused history to move from one civilization to another had come as a result of small advances in knowledge that accumulated over time causing history to take giant leaps forward. Since the first transitional period lasted about 3,000 years, no tribal generation could feel the magnitude of change in its culture or life conditions. And what is true of the tribal society is largely true of the agricultural society, which went through the transitional period leading to the industrial age. Nevertheless, the entire continent of Europe had to live in turmoil for roughly 300 years because the industrial revolution spread relatively fast from one society to another causing tremendous transformations in the ways of life and the conditions of life of every industrializing society. Today, not only every society, but almost every individual in the world is feeling the impact of change in his life regardless of his place of residence and the stage of societal development in which he lives, because change is blowing from all directions at the same time.

Dynamics of Change

Throughout pre-agricultural and agricultural times, the state of technology was primitive and more or less the same everywhere. Ideas, belief systems, leadership qualities, and the collective will to fight wars were the decisive factors that enabled the few to distinguish themselves from the many. Tribal societies, though very weak economically, were able to fight and win wars because they had more of the decisive factors of power at the time, and consequently they were able to defeat their agricultural neighbors. In fact, most empires of the past, such as the Roman and Islamic empires were destroyed by tribal forces that were culturally unsophisticated and militarily poorly armed.

The strength of the sociocultural process, the clarity of authority in society, and superior military mobility explain the stunning success of the Arabs under Islam in their wars against the more advanced and larger Persian and Roman empires in the seventh century. The nomadic barbarians in Europe were also able to win wars against European states in pre-industrial and early industrial times. But despite their successes, no victorious tribal society was able to replace an agricultural one, and no defeated agricultural society was forced to regress back into tribalism. On the contrary, almost all victorious tribes were ultimately absorbed by the defeated agricultural societies who were more culturally sophisticated and economically developed.

Generally speaking, a tribesman is a person who fights to live and lives to fight, while an agricultural man is a person who eats to live and lives to eat. Therefore, a man whose primary goal in life is to cultivate the land and enjoy consuming its products cannot defeat a man whose primary goal is to fight, especially since fighting was not only a necessity for tribesman to survive but also the major entertainment activity.

The formation of the state system in the agricultural age involved new elements of power that included political organization and armies and leadership qualities and moral convictions that motivated people to act. Due to this multiplicity of the elements of power, many states were able to gain substantial power at different times, build empires, and dominate other, less powerful states, only to be weakened and defeated later by the vanquished peoples or by similar powers. History, under the leadership of the political process in pre-industrial times, was therefore forced to behave in a largely, but not entirely, cyclical manner, allowing new powers to emerge as others decline, but without causing much change to the ways of life or conditions of life or the social and economic structures of society.

The formation of the modern nation state in the industrial age involved even more of the decisive elements of power that included ideology, advanced military systems and technology, as well as economic power. Fewer states consequently were able to gain enough power to distinguish themselves and project influence beyond their borders. Due to the cumulative nature of technology and economic power, history during the industrial age was forced to abandon its cyclical behavior and move in a rather linear fashion. And this in turn caused the relationship between the agricultural society and the industrial one to become unequal and unjust, causing the former to become dependent on the latter. No agricultural society was able to defeat and replace an industrial one, and no defeated industrial society was forced to regress back to the agricultural age. Even when the Allied forces destroyed the German industrial base and many of Germany's universities and research institutions during WWII, it took the defeated and demoralized Germans less than two decades to recover and create the "German Economic Miracle" and rebuild their economic and technological power; Germany did not need political or military power to attain international prominence because the economic process had by then replaced the political one as the leading societal process.

In traditional agricultural society, the sociocultural process is largely communal and particular, not national. It works to strengthen ties within communities on the bases of faith and ethnicity, and because of that it tends to deepen cultural differences and cause societies to be divided along sociocultural lines. In more developed, largely industrial societies, the sociocultural process tends to be national, not communal; it works to unify people and give them a sense of belonging to one nation and one state. The political process, on the other hand, tends to be strong but despotic in agrarian societies, and to work closely with the sociocultural process to legitimize its domination of societal life. In industrial societies, the political process tends to be democratic and stable, and to work closely with the economic process to acquire more economic and military power to advance the national interest. And due to its interest in power, the political process cooperation with the economic process enables the latter to enrich itself and function as a regional process.

In more developed, largely knowledge-based societies, the political process tends to be weak and to lack focus, causing power to be scattered among a few centers. In contrast, the economic process is strong and able to enjoy freedom; it works closely with the infomedia process to gain more power and become international, integrating national economies into the larger global economy. As for the infomedia process, it tends to be hyperactive, confiscating some of the traditional functions of the sociocultural and political processes, including the role of traditional political party. And as it expands globally, it helps the economic process expand its reach and exploit new investment and trade opportunities. In addition, the infomedia process works to synthesize the cultures of the knowledge people around the world, helping them to form a unique global culture. And due to its advanced means of communications, the infomedia facilitates the creation of subcultures that help religious and ethnic minorities form *cultural ghettos* where their members mentally live in isolation from all other cultures and communities.

The sociocultural and political processes are responsible for change within civilizational lines—change that is primarily in place, not in time. In contrast, the economic and infomedia processes are responsible for change across civilizational lines—change that is primarily in time, not in place. A movement in place leaves peoples and their cultures and economies largely unchanged, living in the same civilization; a movement in time causes peoples and their cultures and economies to move to more advanced civilizations, fundamentally transforming their life conditions and social and economic structures and ways of living. While moving in place makes history largely cyclical, moving in time makes history largely linear, and moving across civilizational lines makes history largely chaotic.

Traditional agricultural societies fit the first model. While the sociocultural process is busy dividing people and creating and fighting wars and

122 GLOBAL ECONOMIC AND CULTURAL TRANSFORMATION

conflicts, the political process is busy consolidating power and building the state's institutions of control and repression. Meanwhile, the economic process is still in its childhood relying primarily on trade and traditional industries, and the infomedia process is still in its infancy, being shaped by a manipulative political elite determined to monopolize political power and stay in power.

Industrializing and largely industrialized societies fit the second model. While the sociocultural process is busy developing a national culture, the political process is in control of its destiny, building strong armies and national economies and defining and defending the national interest. Meanwhile, the economic process is maturing and gaining more power and independence, and the infomedia process is growing and strengthening its links to the economic process and fighting to free itself from the hegemony of the political process.

Mature industrial and post-industrial societies fit the third model. While the sociocultural process is weak and busy reviving minority cultures and developing them into viable subcultures and cultural ghettos, the political process is getting weaker and losing focus and sense of purpose. Meanwhile, the economic process is mature and in control of its destiny, and the infomedia process is free, influential, and fast becoming the supreme power in society, assisted by and allied with a dynamic globalizing economic process.

When the sociocultural process dominated societal life in tribal and early agricultural times, its forces represented the engine of the train of time or the spirit of history and charted its course, moving exclusively in place rather than in time. When the political process, represented by the state, dominated societal life in maturing agricultural and early industrial societies, its forces replaced the sociocultural ones, assuming their role in driving history and influencing its pace and course, causing history to move in place and in time simultaneously. Wherever the economic process dominates societal life in mature industrial and post-industrial societies, its forces represent the engine that drives history and influences the pace and nature of change and charts its course.

The dominant process in society always overshadows the other processes, forcing them to accommodate themselves to its rationale and objectives. Today, the infomedia process is fast becoming dominant in all post-industrial, knowledge societies, causing immense sociocultural, sociopolitical, and socioeconomic transformations that affect the lives of all peoples. And because this process was born as a global process, the people most involved in shaping its activities and defining its objectives are fast becoming dominant as a national socioeconomic class and a global sociocultural group.

The state where the dominant societal process is also the most developed process in the world assumes global leadership, forcing all other states to follow its lead and accommodate themselves to its interests and cultural values and lifestyles. For example, when the economic process was the most developed and dynamic in England in the nineteenth century, England was able to lead the world and dominate more than half of its population for almost 150 years. And since the economic and infomedia processes emerged in the United States in the post-WWII era as the most developed and dynamic processes in the world, the United States was able to foster its world leadership and strengthen its global economic and military dominance ever since.

Being the engine of history, the most developed society pulls the other, less developed societies along the path it travels. In other words, the most developed society helps other societies change and reach higher levels of civilization, always showing them a realistic image of their future. No societal process, however, has been able to establish itself and attain power without first forging a cooperative relationship with the preceding one. And no process has been able to continue to develop and make further progress and lead without freeing itself from the cooperative relationship it had previously forged. Because of this fact, cooperation has always been replaced by competition, leading to more dynamism and change and causing history to never repeat itself. Cooperation, no matter how strong it is and how long it may last, represents a passing phenomenon, while competition is more of a permanent aspect of process relationships and therefore societal life.

The conception of history presented in this chapter views history as a train with a powerful engine that pulls a number of civilizational wagons or societies behind as it travels. As the train started its movement in older times, it started slowly, circled around a huge lake many times before it could locate a convenient path and move forward. But as it began to accelerate, it encountered one obstacle after another, causing it to slow down and, at times, to lose its sense of direction for a while. Every time the train of time encounters formidable obstacle that must be crossed, it finds itself forced to move in all directions until it finds a convenient path to establish and resume its forward movement.

The sociocultural process was the first engine of history that led the pre-agricultural and early agricultural societies. It caused those societies to move very slowly in place while making no noticeable movement in time. The political process gave history a more efficient engine suited for an agricultural society of many communities, causing society to move slowly in place and in time, with the latter being less noticeable. In both cases, however, the dynamic nature of life in traditional agricultural society caused history to behave in a largely cyclical manner.

The economic process gave the train of time a more efficient engine, enabling history to increase its speed, pull all previous civilizational wagons and less developed peoples and move in place and in time simultaneously, with the second being more pronounced and consequential. As a consequence, the small number of societies driven by the economic process is able to lead the entire world and dominate the major activities that count in the industrial age. The dominance of the economic process and its global reach, while causing progress to be made and benefit all peoples in varying degrees, they empowered the rich and powerful segments of each society only, causing the rest of society to feel either cheated or unfairly treated.

As we advance into the twenty-first century, the infomedia process is fast becoming the new engine of history; it represents a more sophisticated and efficient engine that only few can drive and fully utilize. And while the infomedia process drives the knowledge society, it pulls all other industrial and agricultural and pre-agricultural civilizational wagons forward, enabling them to move faster in time while moving in place. However, people inside the knowledge wagon seem to be moving exclusively in time rather than in place. Due to this development, the knowledge wagon has become more like an open space in which the knowledge elite drive at full speed in all directions, believing that there are no limits to what they can achieve and have, and enjoy having.

As explained earlier, the transformation of society from the pre-agricultural to the agricultural state of living passed through a difficult transitional period. Since transitional periods are times of chaotic change, they confuse history and cause it to experience a discontinuity that ends its connection to the past. But the moment the transitional period ends, it becomes a bridge connecting two banks of a wide river and enabling people living on both sides to establish links with one another and learn from each other, with the less developed societies learning more from the developed ones. The transformation from the agricultural civilization to the industrial one had also to pass through a difficult transitional period, during which history experienced a new phase of discontinuity, causing the history of the agricultural era to end. As the history of an era ends, it loses its ability to lead, causing its logic and wisdom to lose their influence and relevance. As a consequence, the new era or civilization is forced to develop its own history and detect that history's unique logic.

Inside each civilizational wagon, the movement of history is more or less cyclical moving in place rather than in time, particularly inside the pre-agricultural and agricultural wagons. During transitional periods that tie two civilizations together, the movement of history is primarily chaotic, where change moves in all directions searching for a logical direction. But viewed from a wide historical perspective, the movement of human history has definitely been largely linear. And with every new historical engine, the lead civilizational wagon got smaller, while the preceding one got larger, as more societies learn from the new civilization, borrow some of its knowledge, apply it, and move forward, causing the last wagon to shrink further. And this clearly signifies progress over time.

The train of time theory makes it clear that there is no ultimate destination or station to which history aims; it also gives all peoples the opportunity to learn from one another and make progress by bringing them closer to each other and enabling the less developed societies to borrow from the more advanced ones. Nevertheless, the theory shows that dependency is an inevitable consequence of change associated with the historical process.

After so many centuries of human progress in all fields of knowledge, the cumulative change that history has caused looks today like a giant, colorful spring based in sand. While everyone is able to see the spring standing tall, and appreciate its imposing presence, no one can see its base or know how deep it is in the ground, or understand how it started. However, everyone can see its head pointing upward. Optimists, whose conception of history is linear, are more likely to focus on the spring's head and appreciate its upward-looking trend. In contrast, pessimists, whose conception of history is cyclical, are almost certain to focus on its bottom and appreciate its downward-looking movement. Others, whose conception of history is rather chaotic, are more likely to see in the spring's chain an upward–downward trend that signifies a largely motionless, meaningless movement. Yet, the rational view of history is the one that sees how the three conceptions coexist, and appreciates the interlocking relationships they forge with one another to make history and move it forward despite all odds.

8

Ideology and History

An ideology is a grand idea around which people cluster, and on the basis of its ideas and ideals and promises coalitions are built and activated. Ideology functions as a social system to organize and educate people, motivating them to develop certain attitudes, adopt certain worldviews, and seek, through collective action, certain objectives. As such, ideology tends to govern a broad range of human relationships and influence the course of change in society. Since culture represents the social glue that holds society together, ideology has become the core of many cultures and the organizing principle of societies in distress.

Ideology is either particular concerned with only one people, such as nationalism, or universal concerned with humanity, such as communism, Christianity, and Islam. Since ideology represents the core of many cultures, it tends to shape the attitudes of people, causing them to feel different from others, sometimes superior to them, and sharpen their collective sense of identity. As a consequence, ideology makes its followers more committed to the welfare of their own group or nation, and less tolerant of other groups' beliefs and convictions, giving them an excuse to be prejudiced, belittle others, and often discriminate against them.

Throughout modern history, progress has been closely associated with the ideas of freedom and social justice, which provide an environment conducive to change. Freedom facilitates individual initiative, political participation, liberal education, scientific research, and technological innovations; it also protects people's rights, allowing them to pursue personal goals, be creative, and engage in new activities and relationships that encourage them to welcome cultural and political plurality and participate in shaping their individual and collective destinies. Social justice, meanwhile, motivates people to fight for their rights, be compassionate, and care for others and the common good.

Transformations in society are made at all times, at every level through a social process that has two sides, conflict and change. Change, by its very nature, undermines the balance of power that governs relationships between the major social actors, creating winners and losers and causing conflict. Conflict, which tends often to be initiated by losers, causes relationships to become unstable, at times dysfunctional, thus creating a need to restructure them, which only change can do. But for change to succeed, it has to take into consideration the new reality created by the previous round of change and conflict. Therefore, the way conflict is managed tends to influence the nature and magnitude of change, and the way change is introduced and pursued in society tends to influence the magnitude and ramifications of conflict.

Because ideology is a worldview with its own values and goals, change instigated by ideology tends to influence most aspects of life. As a result, change driven by ideology tends to be predictable; the path it follows is often revolutionary, and attitudes it nurtures are often radical. Violence is sometimes promoted by ideology and accepted by its followers as a legitimate means to effect change. Societies dominated by ideology often lack the social tools to deal with conflict and manage change peacefully. Germany under Nazism, the Soviet Union under communism, Serbia under religious nationalism, and Afghanistan under religious fanaticism are examples of societies that were dominated by ideology and where violence and coercion were used widely to deal with conflict and manage change. In such societies, every deviation from the basic tenets of ideology is usually defined in extreme terms that demand swift, uncompromising action.

In contrast, open societies, where ideology is weak and political and cultural plurality exist and tolerated, tend to have flexible rules and pragmatic tools to deal with conflict and manage change. Such societies view conflict and change as social mechanisms to restructure fractured relationships and achieve desired goals. Consequently, change is encouraged, conflict is managed, and compromise solutions are sought to maximize the number of winners and minimize the number of losers. However, if compromise solutions are invented to appease a growing ideology, they usually limit the number of winners, increase the number of losers, and cause the situation to deteriorate over time.

Issues of conflict are normally divided into two general categories, value-related and interest-related. Because values are closely associated with deeply held convictions, value-related issues, such as religious convictions and collective identities, are usually viewed as existential, and therefore they are less amenable to compromise solutions. In contrast, interest-related issues, such as trade and labor disputes are normally viewed as circumstantial, and therefore they are more amenable to compromise solutions.[1] Ideology tends to view all issues of conflict as value-related, and thus existential, making violence and coercion, not compromises, the means often used to deal with conflict. In fact, the history of societies dominated by ideology, regardless of their place and time, has been shaped by war and colored by blood. No ideology has ever been able to perceive another ideology as legitimate, and no ideological state has willingly accepted a neighboring ideological state as equal. Ideologies were and still are viewed by their followers as mutually exclusive and inherently antagonistic: "Competing self-interests allow for compromise, whereas rigid moral arguments lead to war."[2]

Every relationship in society has at least two components that are interlinked and mutually reinforcing. One represents cooperation, the other competition. Relationships having only one component reflect either dependency or antagonism. Relationships that have too much cooperation due to sharing an ideology tend to be dull and mostly stagnant, and thus largely unproductive. Relationships characterized by too much competition due to lack of shared interests and concerns tend to be unstable and largely conflictive. For a relationship to be viable and productive the level of cooperation must be perceived by most people as good or satisfactory; the level of competition ought to be perceived as desirable or tolerable.

Relationships among individuals and organized groups are based either on interests or on values, but mostly on both. Interest-related relationships encourage people to compete to maximize their gains when winning is possible, and cooperate to minimize losses when losing is unavoidable. Acts to maximize gain and fame, and minimize loss and pain, are both causes of conflict and forces of change. However, because such relationships stem primarily from desires, and deal largely with material things, the change they usually cause and the conflict they precipitate tend to be tolerable and often beneficial. In contrast, value-related relationships and ideologically inspired ones tend to induce people and organizations to cooperate more and compete less and advance their shared causes at the expense of others. As a consequence, change that value-related and ideologically inspired relationships usually cause tends to be structural, and the conflict these relationships often precipitate tends to be long and painful.

Ideologies can be divided into three general categories: sociocultural or religious, sociopolitical or national and ethnic, and socioeconomic or materialistic. The ascendance of either one in society leads usually to the suppression of the others and undermining their role in shaping society's culture and future. Since the dominant ideology opts almost always for continuity and stability, the subdued ideologies opt almost always for subversion and change. Nevertheless, it is possible to incorporate two ideologies into one state system. China and Cuba are cases where a state system based on nationalism and socialism has dominated society for decades.

130 GLOBAL ECONOMIC AND CULTURAL TRANSFORMATION

And Iran and Israel are other cases where religion and nationalism have been incorporated into one state system, causing conflict to be lodged in the consciousness of society, and discrimination against the other to become a state policy. In both cases, the ideological superstructure limits the ability of society to see the contradictions inherent in its system, recognize the other, and deal with it rationally and fairly.

When asked about the reasons for Iran's lack of economic development, former Iranian president Mohammed Khatemi said, "It is impossible to have economic development in a socially and politically underdeveloped society."[3] While correctly linking lack of economic development to lack of social and political development, the Iranian president failed to link the failure of economic, social, and political development to the ideological superstructure of the Iranian state. As a consequence, he failed to identify the actual forces responsible for creating and perpetuating the sad state of socioeconomic and sociopolitical affairs in his country.

Ideology, be it sociocultural, sociopolitical, or socioeconomic, tends to be deterministic. Because of this characteristic, ideology tends to belittle people in general, depreciate their ideas and potentials, and ignore their feelings. Ideology considers the individual a tool to be used to achieve lofty ideological objectives; an expendable piece of wood to light the fireplace of history. To every ideology and ideological leader, history glows only when it burns people, leaving their ashes behind to remind us of the fire, not of the tragic fates of the people who produced it and how they produced it.

Before talking about specific ideologies, their natures, objectives, and the roles they play in individual and group life, there is an important point that needs to be made and emphasized. Ideologies are in essence social philosophies, or grand ideas, transformed by able, ambitious men into mass movements to change reality on the ground. As leaders transform philosophical ideas into plans of action to change life conditions, the transformed philosophy becomes an ideology. To achieve their objectives, ideological leaders try always to control politics, the media, and the state. And to guarantee popular support, they create mass movements by changing people's perceptions, falsifying their consciousness, and convincing them to subordinate their passions for the sake of what they are told to believe in. While philosophies concentrate on studying human behavior and world history with the aim of explaining reality and providing guidance for a better life, ideologies are political movements meant to change reality by using the power of persuasion, deception and coercion, the spread of fear, and oftentimes violence as well.

Religion, for example, is a grand idea meant to prescribe a way for man to reach God. If religion remains as such and concentrates on developing man's consciousness to do good deeds and stay away from bad ones, religion would render a valuable service to man and society and therefore to humanity. But if religion concentrates on convincing its followers that it is the only true path to God, and tries to convert them into missionaries and worriers, it would become a mass political movement with ideological zeal. All social philosophies acquire zeal as they are transformed into ideologies meant to change reality to correspond to the ideological visions articulated by their ideological leaders.

Marxism is a philosophy to explain history and the role of social conflict in making history; it criticizes capitalism and free markets, condemns exploitation, and calls for social justice. If Marxism were to stay as such, it would render a valuable service to man, society, and humanity. But as an ideology, Marxism has caused the killing of millions of people, denied entire nations their rights, and led to creating dictatorships that paved the way for the spread of corruption and fear. And if nationalism were to remain an idea to unite people and convince them to feel and act as free people with equal rights and responsibilities, and motivate them to help each other and work for a common good, it would become a humanist idea serving the interests of all human beings. But nationalism has committed many massacres, ethnic cleansing of millions of people, and untold tragedies throughout the last three centuries.

Every noble idea acquires a negative, at times evil aspect in the process of being transformed into an ideology; it adopts an attitude that rejects competing ideas and systems, as well as peoples and cultures viewed as different. And since the feeling of rejecting something is often stronger than the feeling of liking something else, all ideologies have become more negative than positive, which led them to foster hatred and enmity, and undermine the human spirit of man. In fact, all rejectionist movements, throughout history, have demonstrated a great capacity to define with clarity what they stand against, but have failed to define with the same degree of clarity what they stand for, making them less able to do good and more able to do harm.

Religion

Religion is a system of beliefs and rituals based on a conviction that a supernatural power or a god exists and has control over the world and its inhabitants. Most religions also believe that god is the only power that can and does intervene occasionally to change the course of history and the fate of people. Believers, to reach their god and gain his blessing, are called upon to believe in certain myths, follow certain rules, adopt certain attitudes, and perform certain rituals; all of which are meant to strengthen

132 GLOBAL ECONOMIC AND CULTURAL TRANSFORMATION

their unity and deepen their belief. As a consequence, religions create distinct faith-based communities whose faithful members help each other as a matter of duty, and view followers of other religions with suspicion or disgust.

When human societies first appeared, people were able to use only their instincts to meet their basic needs of survival and security. Lack of knowledge regarding their environment and the absence of tools made people a product of their environments rather than masters of them. Meanwhile, people's apparent helplessness led them to discover the ideas of god and religion. Gods were the power that created the universe, and religion is the system that regulates man's relationship with the gods and with his fellow men. People of ancient times constructed religion to suit their needs and calm their fears and give meaning to their lives.

Religion is a social system invented by man to establish a channel of communications with an imagined god; religious leaders are mediators to connect man to god, represent god on earth, and ensure that man obeys gods' orders as prescribed by the same leaders. To do so, all religions imposed certain practices of worship and asked their followers to make certain sacrifices deemed necessary to please and appease the gods. People were willing to do whatever religion asked of them to gain the approval of their gods and avoid their wrath. And depending on the particular characteristics of the environment, people assigned different roles to the gods they invented and worshipped.

Due to such a relationship, God became a power to be feared and obeyed, not loved or challenged, and man's unconditional surrender to God's will became the only path to attain happiness. As a consequence, religious practices, rituals, and symbols became sacred, unifying the believers while ensuring their submissiveness, and religion became the system that defined the path to happiness and enforced its laws. "Ancient societies were held together primarily by religion," which shaped people's attitudes and worldviews, and regulated their relationships to one another and to their gods.[4]

Gradually, religion emerged as the institution representing the most sacred and feared force in life, and the only power entitled to speak in the name of the highest authority in the universe. It promised good life to believers and salvation to those who surrender their freedoms to it and accept its teachings. Consequently, religion became the core of every living culture, particularly cultures of pre-industrial times. Even cultures whose core has been reduced to a set of basic values and religious traditions, like the Chinese and Arabic cultures, they have continued to be influenced by religious beliefs and rituals and religious men.

Before the dawn of the age of agriculture, every tribe had its own god and religion and rituals. As a result, "religion and race went together," leading everyone to believe in one's own people's god.[5] And despite the appearance of the monotheistic religions of Christianity and Islam as universal faiths in the latter part of the agricultural age, religion has continued to be associated with race. Judaism, which is the oldest monotheistic religion, was born as a religion for the Israelites who used it as a faith around which they built an exclusive culture. Jewish resistance to accepting converts has kept the number of Jews very small compared to the numbers of Christians and Muslims. In July 2012, the *Economist* reported that the number of Jews in the world was in 2010 about 13.5 million, of which about 5.7 million lived in Israel and 5.3 million lived in the United States.[6] With the exception of Christianity and Islam, all major religions are primarily race-related or region-related; expansion to other races and regions has come with population migrations, not active promotion and conversion. Because Christianity and Islam claim universality, they have continued to expand and recruit converts.

The major world religions, namely Buddhism, Christianity, Confucianism, Hinduism, Islam, Judaism, and Taoism were born during the later part of the agricultural age. While Judaism is the oldest, having been born around 1200 BC, Islam is the youngest; it arose in the seventh century AD.[7] This means that all of the great religions of the world were born within less than 2,000 years, signifying that the same social and economic conditions were able to travel and transform most societies in the world in the same manner during a relatively short period. In fact, the Asian religions of Buddhism, Confucianism, Hinduism, and Taoism, as well as Islam, were born within 200–300 years of each other.

Karen Armstrong says, "Religious systems reflected the changed economic and social conditions. For reasons that we do not entirely understand, all the chief civilizations developed along parallel lines, even when there was no commercial contact."[8] Judaism, for example, seems to have come in response to economic and social conditions that tolerated slavery in Egypt after that country had reached an advanced stage of the agricultural age. And when the Roman Empire arrived, about 1,200 years later, at roughly the same level of development, Christianity emerged in Palestine to fight for equality and social justice. Within the next 600 years, other parts of the world, particularly China, India, and Arabia, arrived at the same stage, giving birth to new religions, the most important of which are Islam, Hinduism, and Buddhism.

With the appearance of cities, states, and empires in the agricultural age, the number of tribal gods and religions decreased; gods that belonged to individuals and families were demoted and forgotten. Nevertheless, all peoples seemed at the time to have accepted religion as a faith and a set of values and customs to organize their lives around them, leading religions to play similar roles in the lives of all societies. But since no one could prove

134 GLOBAL ECONOMIC AND CULTURAL TRANSFORMATION

or disprove claims made by religion, magic and myth became part of all religious beliefs: "The priest as well as the magician has a role to play: to provide a systematic procedure of sanctification in order to accommodate the needs of believers with a meaningful worldview."[9]

While almost every religion believes that it is the true path to God, Hinduism believes that each religion is a path to God. It claims, "God has made different religions to suit different aspirants, times and countries. One can reach God if one follows any of the paths with whole hearted devotion."[10] Hinduism, therefore, urges each person to follow the religion of his or her people, thus reinforcing the unifying role of religion in society and its affiliation with race. Hinduism claims that the Savior, be it Jesus, Muhammad, or Krishna, is one and the same; he appears in different places at different times but for the same purpose.

Religion and Agriculture

Religious teachings and rituals were meant to help individuals find the meaning of their lives and suffering. And since religion was a product of the age of agriculture, it had to "adapt itself to the demands and timetables of agriculture."[11] It accepted agriculture as a worthy way of life, adopted most of its values and traditions, and promoted the notion of life after death. The life cycle of plants, by demonstrating continuous renewal, and other preexisting myths as discussed below, apparently convinced the followers of Christianity and Islam of the existence of a life after death, an idea not much different from that of reincarnation widely believed by the followers of Asian religions. But by adapting itself to the culture of agricultural society, religion tied its fate to that of the agricultural civilization. Judaism did not originally adopt the concept of life after death; however, some Jewish scholars developed the concept centuries later but failed to convince all believers to embrace it.

Long before the birth of Judaism, the Babylonians believed in an afterlife, as did the Egyptians of the Pharoanic era, who used mummification to preserve the bodies of the dead in order to enable them to resume life later on. The ancient Egyptians believed that "as long as the corpse, or at least a material image of it, subsisted, life continued."[12] Friedrich Hegel cites Herodotus as having said, "The Egyptians were the first to express the thought that the soul of man is immortal."[13] They even believed that the soul goes first through a system of justice before the afterlife is resumed, and therefore they wrote the "*Book of the Dead*" instructing the soul how to defend itself in the Day of Judgment. And from that book, Jews copied a few things that came to represent the "Ten Commandments." Similarly, the Chinese talk about ancestors being living spirits, and about the need to keep them happy. Even the Aztec, Inca, and Mayan peoples believed in an immortal soul, with the dead passing from one phase of life to another while becoming invisible.

Peoples of the past, just like peoples of the present, feared death and wanted to deny it, which led them to believe in immortality. Religions could do nothing but to reinforce this belief through the idea of the continued life of the soul. However, religions in general claim that life after death would not treat people equally—there would be heaven for the good and hell for the bad. Being the path to both God and heaven, religion became the only institution capable of helping its followers prepare themselves for the heavenly eternal life by doing good deeds and avoiding evil ones, and thinking more about the promise of heaven than of the material attractions of life on earth. But to care less about life on earth for the sake of a promised life beyond it is to ignore life's complexity and accept being subject to its whims.

Social stability maintained by agriculture, sustained by religion, and enforced by an authoritarian state, made life seem motionless for countless generations. "However agriculture was organized, no serious change in the way of living occurred till after 1700."[14] Meanwhile, lack of advanced technologies to transform economic conditions made ideas and charismatic leaders the major forces of change in society. Religion, despite having accepted the way of life of agricultural society and sanctioned most of its values, was the idea of change in older times. It introduced new values that called for equality and social justice and new rules for relationships among its followers. But once established at the core of culture, religion became a formidable obstacle to social and cultural change. No real change was possible at the time, and no idea had a fighting chance unless sanctioned by the religious establishment.

As agricultural society entered the transitional period leading to the industrial age, the emerging society began to adopt different, less traditional and religious values and attitudes. But neither the culture nor religion at the time was willing to accept change; they instead waged war against all ideas they perceived as threatening to their entrenched statuses. Even after the Industrial Revolution began to transform the European landscape, primitive, semi-tribal enclaves sustained by religion, persisted for generations in every part of Europe. "Hundreds of dialects and equally numerous local semi-barbaric religious cults sustained these [enclaves] of the past in the midst of modern centralized states."[15] Nonetheless, science, technology, reason, geographical discoveries, and industrialization managed to expose the fallacies of many religious claims and create doubt in the minds of enlightened people.

By the time the transitional period had been completed, the old culture and its religious core had lost the battle. A new culture with its own ideological core appeared to compete with the old one. Nationalism, which emerged as a sociopolitical ideology, began to transform state cultures and shape individual and group consciousness, causing the political process to win its last battle against the sociocultural one around the middle of the seventeenth century.

Since no religion can prove its claims scientifically, the only way for religion to convince its followers of its claims is by resorting to the purported experiences of some faithful individuals whose deep convictions led them to live unique spiritual experiences. However, no claimed experience could be corroborated or objectively validated, and no religion can provide an explanation for how and why these claimed experiences happened to the people who claim to have experienced them. Thus the new age of industry, anchored in science, technology, and reason, drove both magic and religion out of the cultural core, vastly reducing their role and influence in the industrial society.[16]

Societies that failed to embrace science and reason have continued to value magic and organize themselves around religion. Claimed miracles, as a result, have continued to perform in many societies some of the roles that technology and medicine perform in advanced societies. In the developing states where the traditional role of religion is preserved and revered, old values and relationships have survived the great transformations of our times with little change. Traditional elites in such societies, being exposed to both science and reason through travel and study abroad, are often forced to live a life of hypocrisy, pretensions, and contradictions. And this has made genuine transformation less likely, while making sociocultural stratification and political polarization more likely.

The decline of religion as a body of thought and a sacred set of values at the core of culture is due primarily to the transformations experienced by Europe over the last 600 years that cover the Renaissance and Enlightenment ages. Among those developments are the following:

1. The increasing tendency of the Catholic Church hierarchy to live a worldly, affluent life and ignore the predicament of the poor. In the thirteenth century, the behavior of the popes was harshly criticized, and in the fifteenth century the corruption of the Church was exposed as the popes began to do everything for money and nothing without money.

2. The expansion of trade and financial transactions that violated the Church's teaching led those who were benefiting from

such activities to question the Church's authority and work to undermine its power.

3. The development of printing, which facilitated the spread of ideas and education, revolutionized intellectual interaction, and allowed critical voices to be heard.

4. The increasing collaboration between the emerging merchant class, city dwellers, and kings who formed an alliance to challenge the Church's political authority and economic doctrine and free themselves from its hegemony.

5. The discovery of the New World, which fascinated people and exposed the fallacy of some convictions such as the idea that Earth was flat, and opened new frontiers for the adventurers and the oppressed.

6. Increased competition among the major European states, which flooded some states with wealth causing interests and leisure to overshadow values and convictions.

7. The dawn of the age of reason and science, which served to undermine the logic of many religious ideas, forcing the Church to move forcefully and act irrationally to impede scientific and philosophical inquiry, causing its reputation to be tarnished beyond repair.

8. The triumph of the Reformation movement, which refuted certain Church teachings, split the Church into several denominations, and promoted new work and business ethics. The Reformation started in the sixteenth century with Martin Luther protesting the sale of indulgences by the Church, precipitating one of the bloodiest and longest wars in European history.

9. "The growth of new tastes, desire for comfort, and even love of ostentation among the rich. Medieval man had devoted much of his spare income and labor to building cathedrals, churches, abbeys, and castles. Early modern man has felt other possible attractive uses for his wealth";[17] uses he could not pursue without abandoning strict adherence to Church teachings.

10. The involvement of the Church in war and its use of religion as a pretext to wage war against its enemies. The religious wars of the seventeenth century, for example, caused great destruction and untold human suffering; they ended in 1648 with the Westphalia Treaty, which called for the separation of state and religion, and thus ended the Church's role in the political life of most European states forever.

In the age of agriculture, and among all traditionally less developed societies, life was one of religion—religion was, and to a great extent still is, a

138 GLOBAL ECONOMIC AND CULTURAL TRANSFORMATION

lofty ideal to live for and, if necessary, to die for as well. In the age of industry, religion was reduced to a mere social system whose primary goal is to create and sustain communities of faith. In other words, the industrial age transformed religion into a social organization whose sole role is to meet the spiritual needs of its members. In the knowledge age, religion is rapidly becoming personal rather than communal. The church has become a place for those who lack spirituality and for others who need moral support to find comfort, as well as for people marginalized by the breathtaking pace of scientific and technological developments. And while most believers still give money to churches, they seldom live or die for them or for what they represent any more; people also expect their personal needs to be fulfilled in return for what they give. The Church, as a result, is forced to tailor its services to the particular needs of its clientele, not to enforce God's orders.

Nationalism

Nationalism, like religion, is a social philosophy that espouses certain values, attitudes, and relationships meant to strengthen the unity of peoples and shape their cultures, particularly their political culture. Nationalism believes that peoples form nations, and nations have their own cultures, languages, histories, and, above all, homelands. But unlike religion, nationalism is concerned with political organization, military and economic power, and foreign affairs, not with issues of life and death. Although tension has dominated the relationship between religion and nationalism in modern times, both ideologies can coexist peacefully and even merge to form one state system. The affiliation of race and religion makes such a merger not only possible but also probable. And while the merger has made several societies more cohesive, it led them to become more aggressive and often racist as well.

Authority, which comes down from either God or state, has traditionally been used to convince people or force them to subdue their passions and interests for the sake of either God or country. However, the affiliation of race and religion makes it quite possible to subordinate man's passions and interests to both God and country at the same time. In fact, nationalism has been able to marshal the forces of religion to serve political ends, and religion has been able to marshal the political aspirations of people to serve religious ends. The history of religion and nationalism indicates that both ideologies were used by religious and political leaders to control people, mislead them, and stay in power.

The origins of nationalism can be traced back to the Spanish war against Spain's Arabs around the end of the fifteenth century. The Spanish leadership was able to marshal the forces of nationalism and Catholicism, unite Spaniards, and motivate them to fight Arabs and Jews, Islam and Judaism, and evict them from Spain. Following their victory, the Spaniards carried out atrocities that included the killing, expulsion, and forced conversion of Muslims and Jews to Catholicism. Nationalism therefore was born as a racist idea believing in the superiority of one race and the righteousness of one religion.

As a nationalist consciousness develops among people, it makes them feel different from other peoples. A feeling of cultural superiority, more than anything else, is what makes people feel different, convinces them that they are entitled to special things, and encourages them to act, often aggressively, to attain envisioned means of superiority. Armies are built, taxes are imposed, and people are asked to serve the homeland. New history books are written, and older ones are rewritten to glorify the past, belittle the historical legacy of others, and make claims, often unwarranted, on other people's land. As a consequence, cultural, ethnic, and religious minorities are discriminated against, denigrated, and often denied their legitimate rights.

Nations usually claim that they need to be independent and have their own states to develop their economies and cultures and protect their identities. That is, they need to live their own experiences, nurture their own dreams, develop their own languages, and build their own economies and armies to defend their homelands. Consequently, the nation-state appeared in Europe as the embodiment of nationalism and the highest authority in the land, demanding that people subdue their individual passions and interests for the sake of their country, as dictated, of course, by the nation's political leadership. Meanwhile, developments that caused the decline of religion served to enhance the appeal of nationalism as an alternative ideology.

The Reformation, which weakened the Catholic Church and caused its splintering into several factions, was instrumental in reviving different European languages. The development of printing was also helpful; it enabled intellectuals to write and publish in their native languages, and criticize Church teachings. And with the Church's influence on the wane, the Latin language began to lose its appeal and constituency. This loss was exacerbated by the 1648 Westphalia Treaty, which gave the head of each state the right to determine the religion of his people. Consequently, the head of the state, often an absolute king, acquired religious as well as political authority and used it to consolidate his powers.

The nation-state, aided by economic mercantilism, began to practice colonialism. And because nationalism was the ideology of choice, all classes in society were happy to participate in the colonial enterprise. "From the

140   GLOBAL ECONOMIC AND CULTURAL TRANSFORMATION

mid-seventeenth century to the French Revolution late in the eighteenth, the idea that each state should seek its own economic independence by founding colonies and controlling large supplies of gold and silver shaped European policies and caused a series of imperial conflicts."[18] Writing around the middle of the nineteenth century, Karl Marx criticized the colonial enterprise harshly and predicted that the working class in the European industrial states would not support imperialism, and that it would revolt against it. Max Weber, in contrast, argued 50 years later that imperialism could not succeed without the industrial workers being a part of it, and that they would not rise against it. Karl Marx underestimated the emotional power of nationalism and the lure of economic benefits generated by colonialism, and overestimated the impact of class conflict on the consciousness of the industrial workers. A racist attitude toward the other nourished by nationalism, and economic opportunity created by owning colonies and controlling other peoples had served to justify popular participation in imperialism. But for the colonized nations, imperialism was a catastrophe of immense consequences.

Spain and France were the first powerful states to emerge in Europe with centralized authoritarian regimes built around nationalism, ready to wage war and compete for influence within and outside Europe: "victory in war took precedence over all else. The common strategy was total offense."[19] The new European monarchies were happy to practice colonialism, repress their national and religious minorities, and ignore the legitimate rights of their own peoples. The hallmark of a great monarchy at the time was to humble the proudest of its people. Nevertheless, the absolute monarchy of those times did not possess the means of power of the twentieth-century totalitarian state, and thus it could not carry out large-scale atrocities or even total suppression of opinion. Although nationalism "sanctioned the monarch's interference in every aspect of the national life, most of the kings lacked both the temperament and the actual power to dominate their subjects totally or crush out racial and cultural minorities like a Hitler or a Mussolini or a Stalin."[20] The modern state's institutions of control and repression were still in their early formative stages.

Philosopher Thomas Hobbes wrote, "Violence was the natural result when nations either sought to conquer other nations or feared being themselves overrun. In the early seventeenth century every country of Europe fell into one or another of these categories, if not into both."[21] In fact, one can easily argue that most of the history of the nation-state was dominated by violence and colored with blood. Nevertheless, the nation-state idea has continued to gain support and be realized, largely because of its call for political and economic independence. By the end of the nineteenth century, most nations of Europe had claimed independence and achieved sovereignty over the claimed lands of their fathers. In the meantime, the collapse of each empire led to the formation of new nation-states.

World War I was supposed to be "the war to end all wars," but instead it turned out to be a European civil war, in which the seeds of future wars were planted. The treaty that concluded the war in 1918 sanctioned all of the claimed prerogatives of the nation-state. It acknowledged, either explicitly or implicitly, the right of each state to independence and sovereignty over the territories and peoples under its control, but failed to repudiate the state's colonial enterprise.

One of the most famous points of the treaty, introduced by President Woodrow Wilson, was to recognize self-determination of nations as an internationally sanctioned right. This right, which was reaffirmed by the United Nations following World War II, was interpreted as the right of nations to political independence and the establishment of states. Nonetheless, national and racial minorities living within the borders of established states were not recognized as nations entitled to the same right; their grievances were considered domestic issues, not international ones. Consequently, minorities and peoples living under the hegemony of European states were denied their political, human, and economic rights; some were even subjected to persecution and deportation. By sanctioning the idea and the prerogatives of the nation-state, the treaty to end all wars created conditions that allowed the extremes of nationalism to dominate some states and transform them into military machines committing war crimes and crimes against humanity.

Following the conclusion of World War II, the United Nations was established as an international forum for states to meet, discuss issues of common concern, resolve conflict, and manage peace. The new organization, by reaffirming the inalienable right of national self-determination on the one hand, and calling for an end to colonialism on the other, was able to strengthen the nation-state while moderating its behavior. The atrocities committed by Nazism, Fascism, Communism, and Japanese nationalism were apparently not convincing enough to declare nationalism a bad idea and an inhumane experiment. The nation-state is the major actor on the international stage, and no replacement for it has been sought or emerged, leaving the right to national self-determination the only framework through which smaller nations and colonized peoples could seek independence and freedom. The gradual termination of colonialism in Asia and Africa, and the disintegration of the Soviet Union led to increasing the number of nation-states while enhancing the appeal of self-determination.

As the nation-state was enjoying its golden age between the two world wars, new conditions and changed circumstances were undermining its

142   GLOBAL ECONOMIC AND CULTURAL TRANSFORMATION

political legitimacy and economic rationale. The atrocities it committed against European Jews and Gypsies and the colonized peoples of Africa, Asia, and the Middle East were too much for many European intellectuals to accept. In the meanwhile, the imperialist enterprise was being exposed as less economically rewarding than had previously believed, especially in light of the revolutions launched by the colonized peoples in the name of self-determination. On the other hand, the rapid expansion of international trade, the deepening of economic interdependence, and new economic thought promoting free market were steadily undermining the economic rationale and political power of the nation-state.

Losing control of the national economy is probably the most significant damage the nation-state has so far sustained. The mobility of investment capital, the broad dissemination of information and knowledge, and growing economic and cultural globalization have weakened the ability of every state to manage its economy and deal successfully with domestic issues, such as unemployment and inflation on its own. Multinational corporations no longer need permission from their states to do business in foreign countries. And because the management of such corporations has become separate from ownership and largely unanswerable to stockholders, most corporations no longer feel an obligation to an ideology, constituency, or community. As a consequence, the ability of the nation-state to protect claimed political and economic prerogatives has been substantially eroded. And with that erosion, its capacity to care for its own people declined, causing citizens' attachment to nationalism to wane. A state that cannot provide opportunity and security for its people cannot demand, and is not entitled to demanding, their allegiance.

Nationalism, by positioning itself as the organizing principle of the nation-state, has unconsciously tied its fate to that of the state. Since this state is on the decline, as its economic power falters and its political prerogatives face challenges, nationalism is facing an uncertain future. In today's world of globalization, "the nation-state [has] become an unnatural—even dysfunctional—organizational unit for thinking about economic activity."[22] In the United States, Congress has practically made US foreign policy an extension of domestic policy, which makes it nearly impossible to formulate a foreign policy without inference from business, lobbies, and other special interest groups, causing the national interest to become a big loser.

Because of its very nature and structure and ideological underpinnings, the nation-state tends to think of economic decisions and choices in light of their political consequences, while globalization dictates that political decisions should be made on the bases of their economic ramifications. Instead of thinking globally and acting locally as multinational corporations do, nation-states in general still think locally and act globally. As more societies move into the age of knowledge, nationalism will face the same fate that religion faced when society moved from the agricultural age to the industrial age.

Marxism

As explained earlier, Hegel and Marx were responsible for advancing the idea that contradictions exist as an inherent characteristic of societal life, and that contradictions cause conflict, and conflict causes new social formations or syntheses to emerge where old contradictions are resolved and new, less severe ones are born. Both Hegel and Marx saw the continuous search for syntheses as a process reflecting the spirit of history and charting its course. This process would eventually lead to solving all contradictions and creating conditions for a life without conflict.

Hegel argued that systems of thought and sociopolitical systems fall apart and disintegrate under the pressure of their own internal contradictions; they are then replaced by new, more complex systems that contain less fundamental contradictions. This seemingly unending process of systemic change explains the notion of historical dialectics developed by the Hegelian and Marxist philosophies of history. However, the basic contradictions in society, according to Hegel, are related to human freedom, and, therefore, the conflict they cause and the syntheses they produce are of a political nature.[23] But for Marx, the basic contradictions in society are related to the private ownership of the means of production, and therefore, the conflict they cause and the syntheses they produce are of a socioeconomic nature.

The mode of production, according to Marxist thought, includes two components: the social forces of production and the relations of production. While the social forces of production represent man's relationship with nature, the relations of production represent man's relationship with other men in the workplace. However, the forces of production do not include all people; they include only the proletariat, or the laborers who do the actual work. Relations of production, on the other hand, are the social ties that develop among people during the production process, as workers and capitalists perform their tasks, and this makes production relations a function of the ownership of the means of production at any given time. Property ownership, in other words, determines the nature of the relationships that tie the forces of production to the relations of production.

Marx argues further that when property ownership of the means of production is communal as it used to be in primitive societies and is

144 GLOBAL ECONOMIC AND CULTURAL TRANSFORMATION

supposed to be in communist ones, society is classless, and therefore no basic contradictions exist within its borders. But when property ownership of the means of production is private, social classes appear and contradictions and antagonisms between them arise, causing conflict. Resolving the basic contradictions requires economic change that leads to new syntheses or new societies. But since the new syntheses contain within themselves their own contradictions, economic change would have to continue to create new social formations until all basic contradictions are resolved and private ownership of the means of production is abolished and a classless, communist society emerges.

According to Marxism, the identity of each social class is determined by its relationship to the means of production, which creates the conditions that enable capitalists who own the means of production to exploit the poverty-stricken working class. Marx identified the major classes in capitalist society as follows.

1. The proletariat, which represents the industrial workers who sell their labor to the owners of the means of production or the bourgeoisie to earn a living.
2. The Bourgeoisie, which owns the means of production and hires the proletariat to work for it. Members of this class exploit the proletariat by paying them less than what their work is worth and confiscating the difference. Marx divides this class into two subclasses: the bourgeoisie and the petit bourgeoisie.
3. The petit bourgeoisie or the middle class in industrial capitalist society represents the small employers, such as merchants and small business owners, who hire members of the proletariat to work for them but also work alongside their employees. Marxism argues that as the means of production advance and become more productive, they cause this class to lose its production base and be destroyed, forcing its members to join the ranks of the proletariat.
4. The landlords, which represents the remnants of the old land aristocracy, who still have a good deal of wealth and power in society.
5. The farmers, who represent the small landholders. Since farmers live in transition, they are unable to form a distinct social class; therefore, some farmers would eventually join the landlords' class, and others would lose their land and join the proletariat.

In fact, with the exception of the petit bourgeoisie and the proletariat, no group of people in society has been able to develop class consciousness and become aware of its interests and social role, and without such awareness, no group could be called social class and gain enough power to cause change in its favor. On the other hand, the social class that owns the means of production usually rules society, and whoever rules society, his ideas influence policy and shape social change. As explained in Chapter 2, the forces of the dominant societal process always claim most of the talent in society and employ them to serve their interests.

Due to the appalling life and work conditions of the proletariat, Marx predicted that it would revolt against its capitalist masters and eventually take ownership of the means of production. The revolution to settle class conflict and resolve the basic contradiction in society will, therefore, be carried out by the industrial working class. Because this class represents the most exploited people in the capitalist society, its exploitation makes revolt against the existing relations of production inevitable, argues Marxism.

Exploitation of workers is realized when the amount of labor one invests is larger than what one receives in compensation. Since all societies, starting with the agriculture one, have produced surpluses, exploitation has been a feature of every society since the dawn of the agricultural age. In capitalism, the labor theory of value considers the value of any good equals to the value of labor required to produce it. The difference between the value of labor needed to produce a certain good and the value of labor the worker is required to invest in work represents surplus value. While capitalism calls this profit, Marxism considers it exploitation.

In pre-capitalist economies, exploitation of workers was achieved via physical coercion or slavery. In the capitalist system, exploitation is achieved through legal arrangements between the capitalists who own the means of production and the workers who need to work to survive. Because workers have the opportunity to choose which capitalist to work for, the arrangement is considered voluntary and thus legal. However, the worker in reality has no choice; he has to work or starve to death. Thus, exploitation under capitalism is inevitable, regardless of the nature of the arrangement between capitalist and worker.

As explained in Chapter 6, progress in history according to Hegel, is made as people gain more freedom, which is supposed to be "embodied in the modern liberal state." The end of history would, therefore, come when freedom is universal and the liberal democratic state is established to represent its people and implement their desired principles of liberty and equality. Marx, in contrast, rejects the vision of a liberal democratic state as the embodiment of liberty and equality, as well as the notion that the establishment of such a state causes history to end. For Marx, the liberal state had failed to resolve the fundamental contradiction in society, and the freedom it brought was only freedom for the bourgeoisie. Democracy, Marx argued, is the tool used by the bourgeoisies to protect

146 GLOBAL ECONOMIC AND CULTURAL TRANSFORMATION

its interests, which are at odds with those of the proletariat. Therefore, he envisioned the historical process coming to an end with the establishment of a classless society, in which class struggle ends and the state withers away. Marx maintains that class conflict, which dominated life throughout history, has manifested itself in different stages with distinct characteristics; it started with primitive communism, and is supposed to end with classless communist. Marx defines these stages as follows:

1. Primitive Communist society, which tribal societies represent.
2. Slave Society, which emerged in the wake of the transformation of tribal societies into urban and rural societies.
3. Capitalism, where capitalists form the ruling class and own the means of production and create and employ the proletariat.
4. Socialism, where the industrial workers gain class consciousness and revolt against the dictatorship of the bourgeoisie, replacing it with a dictatorship of the proletariat that carries out the socialization of the means of production.
5. Communism, where a classless, stateless society free of contradictions emerges and endures.

In view of the above, Marxism could be defined as a social philosophy or worldview that considers economics the major force driving history and causing societal transformations. In other words, Marxism is a theory to describe the development of societal life, identify the forces that cause conflict and change, and explain the mechanism through which change is made. And due to its revolutionary nature and sweeping analysis of historical change, Marxist ideas have influenced economic as well as social, cultural, and political thinking everywhere, leading many theorists and political figures like Vladimir Lenin and Mao Zedong to play major roles in developing Marxist thought and influencing its applications. Consequently, Marxism became, just like Christianity and to some extent Islam as well, one religion with several factions.

The failure of the socialist states and the disintegration of the Soviet Union in 1991 raised questions concerning the validity of Marxist ideas. While some thought that Marxism is not a practical economic system, diehard Marxists claim that the failure is due to people's inability to understand and implement Marxism correctly. Still others claim that Marxism cannot succeed at the national level and that a world revolution is needed for Marxism to succeed. Critics of Marxism, however, say that the Marxist ideology itself is to blame for its failure. And with the end of the Cold War, radical Marxism ceased to be a political force in global politics.

Capitalism and Free Markets

The concepts of capitalism and free markets are products of the same economic thinking. However, while the capitalist system has historically concentrated on the production of manufactured goods, the free market system concentrates on the production of services and information and nontangible things like financial products. Because early capitalism practiced exploitation of workers and monopoly of markets, Western governments were forced to regulate markets to facilitate competition, undermine efforts to create monopolies, limit the excesses of capitalism and capitalists, raise workers' minimum wages, and protect consumers and the environment. Nonetheless, regulations were not strong enough to protect workers from exploitation, or national economies from business cycles, recessions, or inflation. Nevertheless, capitalism was able to create jobs and facilitate social mobility and the creation of a middle class in every industrial state.

In the wake of the collapse of communism and the disintegration of the Soviet Union in 1991, democracy and capitalism emerged as the most promising political and economic systems, if not the only legitimate ones. As a consequence, the proponents of free markets declared victory, and moved forcefully to convince, at times coerce, most other nations to follow their lead: "This triumph has inaugurated—for the first time in the history of humankind—the reign of a single, acceptable way of viewing things in the area of economics, which is considered by its proponents as being universally valid, in both its premises and applications."[24] Harvey Cox sees the market system through the eyes of its promoters as god; he says, "The market is becoming . . . the only true God, whose reign must now be universally accepted and who allows for no rivals."[25]

Globalization and the Internet, which followed the collapse of communism, have helped the forces of free markets to transform the concepts of democracy and free markets into an ideology. And though confidence in the major institutions of democracy and free markets has declined substantially since the early days of the twenty-first century, the American people's attachment to both systems remains strong; no Western state seems to imagine keeping one system and abandoning the other. And though the housing bubble of 2007 and the financial crisis of 2008, or the Great Recession, have exposed the shortcomings of the free market system and the serious excesses of the people who manage it, lack of an alternative economic system leaves the American people trapped and largely helpless, if not hopeless; they are unable to free themselves from either an increasingly dysfunctional democratic system or a largely inhumane free market system.

148 GLOBAL ECONOMIC AND CULTURAL TRANSFORMATION

While religion, nationalism, and communism pursue their objectives usually by means of coercion, discrimination, war, and fear, free markets pursue their objectives by corrupting politics and politicians, manipulating people's fears and needs, and falsifying their consciousness. Because corrupting politics and politicians leads to corrupting the political system, keeping a functioning democracy requires the abandonment of the free market system; no state can protect the rights of its people, enable them to feel and act as free people and pursue their dreams, while free markets work to corrupt politics and politicians. And while making money is the gold standard by which the value of everything in life is measured, the free market forces work diligently to confiscate people's economic and political rights and thus their freedom. Contrary to what most people think, freedom in society is limited: the more markets have of it, the less people are able to have, and the less freedom people have, the less democratic the system will be. Since history indicates that every ideology has failed to protect people's basic rights, the free market system is destined to fail and cause people to lose trust in both capitalism and democracy.

High unemployment rates in Europe and the United States and many African, Asian, and Latin American countries suggest that the free market system is not fit for the knowledge age. To renew the viability of most economies and make them fair and equitable, drastic changes are needed in the spheres of politics and economics and social policy. The popular uprisings in the Arab Middle East and North Africa, dissent in China and India, and demonstrations in several European states are signs that the economic and political arrangements associated with free markets are unfair and inefficient and therefore no longer acceptable.

The Future of Ideology

Ideologies, regardless of their nature and intentions, have had a poor record of delivering on their promises. One of the major promises of religion, for example, is to free slaves as well as masters from the chains of slavery and prejudice. Instead, religion imposes on people rigid values, rituals, and worldviews that engender discrimination and prejudice toward those who do not accept its dogma. "Every religion," as Sigmund Freud once remarked, "is a religion of love for those it embraces, and each is disposed towards cruelty and intolerance against those who do not belong to it."[26] Men and women of religion tend to judge nonbelievers harshly, impose rigid rules on themselves and on others they control, and forego liberating ideas and knowledge. "God in his overweening love for man is destructive of man's creative energy," says Charles Van Doren.[27]

Religion tells man that there is an unseen order that is the order of all orders, or the order of the master of the universe, and that adjusting to that order and behaving according to its rules will make man happy. But "the means to realize such things as happiness are irrational in that there is no scientific basis of producing what is promised through prayer and ritual," argues John Patrick Diggens.[28] A belief in fate, which religion emphasizes, is an acceptance of submission to certain invisible forces whose very existence is doubtful and whose designs diminish the humanity of men and women. Blind belief in fate makes man less free, less creative, less able to think and act to shape his destiny, and often less optimistic. Religion, in fact, tends to crush the power of imagination and lead man to accept subordination to people who claim to speak the word of God. And while religion in principle permits and sometimes invites people to negotiate with God, God's self-appointed representatives on earth usually refuse to be questioned.

Religions in general and Christianity and Islam in particular are dedicated more to life after death than to life before death. They promise heaven to true believers in exchange for accepting the word of God as conveyed to them by his self-appointed representative and doing what is asked of them to do. But promising followers everything later and almost nothing today absolves religion of its responsibilities on earth, while leading people to mortgage the present for the sake of after-death rewards no one can guarantee. Religion, therefore, cannot fail; it will continue to make claims that cannot be proven and promises that cannot be tested without being challenged by its believers. In the process, however, religion makes committed believers less able to relate to reality in a meaningful way, because to do so means to sacrifice faith for the sake of science, life, and rational thinking.

The advancement of science, technology, and reason since the fifteenth century has led to the demystification of many things that were once sacred, causing an ideological vacuum to be created. This vacuum has facilitated the birth of new philosophical ideas such as nationalism, democracy, capitalism, communism, secularism, and atheism. Yet despite this development, the ultimate question regarding the meaning of life and death has remained unanswered, enabling religion to continue its role as a social institution with enough authority to calm people's fears, and a heavenly promise to claim the allegiance of billions of people around the world.

Societies that are still socially, politically, and economically underdeveloped have become more dependent on the developed ones but estranged from them. Estrangement has caused the less developed nations in general to become suspicious and feel insecure. And to deal with their insecurities and preserve their traditional identities and ways of life, these nations have moved toward religious conservatism and cultural nationalism. This suggests that ideology has developed two lives, one in the industrialized and

150 GLOBAL ECONOMIC AND CULTURAL TRANSFORMATION

knowledge societies, where it is dying of old age and loss of relevance, and the other in traditional societies and among alienated minorities, where it is being revived and pushed sometimes to its extremes.

Since religion grew out of a deeply felt need of agricultural society in the distant past, religion is expected to meet the same fate as that of the agricultural civilization. As the agricultural way of life is transformed and the logic of its history is terminated, its culture and religious core will be transformed as well. For religion to survive and remain viable, it has to transform itself to reflect the needs of the civilization it lives in. Otherwise, it will become an obstacle impeding economic and cultural transformation and human freedom and progress: "The part of religion in the transformation is the most important element concerned. Religion has often been, and is still often, an impediment rather than an encouragement to independent inquiry."[29]

Societal transformations precipitated by economic and cultural globalization and the information and telecommunications revolutions have weakened the rationale of nationalism. But the collapse of communism and the failure of Third World socialism have given both religion and nationalism a new life, enabling them to reemerge and claim the future. Small nations, as well as ethnic, religious, and cultural minorities that lived under communism for generations, and others that lived under authoritarian dictators for long, saw in religion and nationalism an opportunity to revive old identities and free themselves from oppression.

However, the introduction of new ideologies and the revival of old ones usually create mass movements to effect change, and, in the process, enable certain individuals and groups to dominate society. This in turn creates super-leaders and national heroes that widen the gap between those at the top of the sociopolitical ladder and the rest of the population, causing the new relationships to reduce the humanity of everyone involved. People at the top tend to develop a sense of superiority and divine inspiration that drives them to denigrate the value of those at the bottom. But sadly enough, most people at the bottom tend to feel that their lives are only worth what they can do in the service of their ideology and their largely deranged leaders. The bulk of the masses are thus led to accept the unacceptable like embracing death for the sake of mysterious causes, and to believe the unbelievable like the power of miracles and prayer in healing the sick. Critics and free thinkers are treated as liabilities whose exclusion becomes necessary to maintaining social harmony, ideological purity, and popular commitment to the ideological zeal.

Since history is irreversible, neither a traditional religious institution can reclaim lost social or political influence, nor can a much weakened nation-state recover lost economic power; therefore, the revival of both ideologies will be temporary. Nonetheless, before they resume their impending decline, religion, nationalism, and cultural particularism are expected to cause poorer nations and religious and ethnic minorities to suffer needlessly. History records seem to suggest that the power of ideology is a function of its political utility rather than its ability to help people who believe in it to free themselves from oppression and need and regain dignity.

When people are helplessly trying to deal with the unknown, understand the invisible, and rationalize the irrational, they are most vulnerable to the work of magic, the seduction of myth, and the false promises of miracles and ideology. But when people are free and in control of their life conditions, they are less vulnerable to such forces and more able to deal with the irrational, appreciate the invisible, and plan for the unknown. Wherever ideology dominates, people tend to develop a mindless mind and a false consciousness unrelated to reality; helplessness and ignorance tend to invite ideology, while ideology tends to perpetuate ignorance and helplessness.

Scientific research and philosophical inquiry, by their very nature, present a challenge to the conventional wisdom based on history, tradition, myth, and ideology. Therefore, science, reason, and philosophy cannot thrive in a society burdened by ideology, because people cannot discover or develop their potentialities under authoritarian rule, be it national or theocratic or military. The system authoritarianism imposes on society, and the obedience it demands of people, tends to suffocate freedom and limit individual initiative and human imagination.

Being rigid and dogmatic, ideology is incapable of practicing the art of politics, which requires negotiating with adversaries and making compromises. And since we live in a dynamic world where reality is changing every day in front of our own eyes, thinking in purely abstract terms inspired by ideology causes politics to lose touch with reality. Total commitment to a religious or national cause is no longer compatible with global economic activity, political and intellectual freedom, human rights, cultural plurality, or scientific and philosophical inquiry. On the other hand, total commitment by the rich to creating and accumulating personal wealth has never been compatible with justice, fairness, economic progress, freedom, or democracy.

Centuries ago, change in the state of mind inspired by grand ideas represented a great motivational force that united people and shaped the consciousness of nations. Religion and nationalism were probably the most effective of all such ideas. But by uniting individuals and tribes to create nations, nationalism and religion have widened the gaps separating nations and accentuated the real and perceived differences among them, causing

152   GLOBAL ECONOMIC AND CULTURAL TRANSFORMATION

countless conflicts and wars and lives. In fact, one can easily argue that probably 90 percent of all wars and victims of war throughout history were caused by religion, nationalism, colonialism, and communism.

Globalization, in contrast, is gradually erasing the old political, cultural, and ideological divides, and tying individuals, rather than states or nations, together, creating a new reality that reduces the causes of conflict. George F. Kennan remarked in the early 1990s that the "ideologies of the early decades of [the twentieth] century have today, in any case, largely lost their reality... The fact is that we live, at the moment, in an un-ideological age."[30] The judgment was made perhaps too early; transitional periods from one civilization to another, as explained throughout this book, cause many people to become more conservative and seek refuge in the shadows of religious fundamentalism and old-fashioned nationalism.

Social systems, regardless of their ideological nature and objectives, are creatures of life conditions that are themselves products of their own times. As times change, life conditions change causing social systems to change as well. Every system has a life of its own that could be short, long, stagnant, dynamic, dull, or interesting, but never perpetual. Since continuous change is the only unchangeable fact of life, change is destined to cause all systems to reach sooner rather than later their limits, forcing them to restructure or lose relevance.

When life is largely static, convictions can and often do change conditions; but when life is dynamic, conditions can and often do change convictions. In the knowledge age, where change is unstoppable, changing conditions are destined to shape and reshape convictions without interruption. Ideology and its absolute values and belief systems are destined to change and, in the process, end the reign of ideology and the terror of ideological leaders.

Looking at the history of ideology, it is easy to conclude that all ideologies have produced more pain than gain and caused more harm than good; they narrow man's choices to one choice only, limit man's freedom and independence, and suffocate man's power of imagination. Ideologies encourage man to discriminate against his fellow men and women, and at times, hate them, because ideologies cannot survive without violence, and hate is needed to justify the use of violence. And above all, all ideologies have failed to change any nation to correspond to their visions and died often violent deaths. Because religions tend to promise everything later and nothing today, religious ideologies have survived the great transformations of our times, and therefore they continue to undermine rationality and destroy the human spirit.

Since ideology has served the interests of countless individuals and deranged leaders over the centuries, ideological thinkers, whose ideas were invalidated by the great transformations of recent years, felt the need to invent a new ideology to preserve their fame. *Cultural determinism,* as a result, was invented as a philosophy to claim that culture stands behind all good and bad things in life, and that bad cultures and the peoples who belong to them present an existential threat to the West. The writings of Samuel Huntington and Francis Fukuyama give full exposure to this rather inhumane ideology. Huntington in particular says directly and indirectly that Western nations need to protect themselves and preserve their values and way of life; and to do so, they have to hate other cultures and their followers and do whatever they can to undermine their capacities to develop their economies and gain enough power to become competitors. Because cultural determinism gives the national and religious ideologies a new life to resume their efforts to destroy the human spirit, it deserves more attention. Therefore, the next chapter will be devoted to explaining cultural determinism and highlighting its mission.

9

Cultural Determinism

The end of the Cold War and the collapse of communism were two major developments that contributed to moving the world toward a new transitional period. They created a fluid, largely unstable state of political, social, economic, security, and cultural affairs, causing the old balance of power to end. Chester A. Crocker wrote in 1992 that the "historic changes since 1989 have profoundly destabilized the previously existing [world] order without replacing it with any recognizable or legitimate system. New vacuums are setting off new conflicts. The result of this is a global law-and-order deficit that is straining the capacity of existing and emerging security institutions."[1]

Since "old habits die hard and the habits of power die hardest of all,"[2] the sociopolitical and security thinkers of the waning era could not accept the invalidation of the ideas they helped develop, nor could they reformulate old ideas to suit the new reality and trends of global change. The old guard could only claim victory for free markets and democracy, unaware that both systems have already entered a new era that threatens their relevance and legitimacy. The United States, wrote Chester A. Crocker further, "wants to preach to the rest of the world the post-cold war litany of U.S. goals and hopes: democracy and human rights, free markets and peaceful settlement of disputes. This sermon is fine as far as it goes, but it is a hopelessly inadequate answer to our era of change."[3]

Yet, the leading American thinkers have continued to repeat the same sermon, hindering the development of new ideas to deal with the emerging situation. And in order to explain the failure of most nations to adopt Western ideals and ideas of democracy, human rights, and free markets, some Western thinkers moved to develop a new model based on culture, claiming that culture is responsible for progress as well as backwardness, success as well as failure, peace as well as violence. And since cultures, as they claim, do not change meaningfully, many developing nations

156 GLOBAL ECONOMIC AND CULTURAL TRANSFORMATION

are destined to languish in a state of perpetual backwardness, as other Western and Eastern nations make further progress. Consequently, a new philosophical view emerged that considers culture the decisive factor determining the fate of nations, giving credence to what might be called *cultural determinism*.

When several Asian nations entered a period of rapid and sustained economic growth in the 1980s, questions were raised regarding the secret of the Asian economic success. The answer, several American political philosophers and economists were quick to claim, was the Asian culture and its Confucian ethics. Francis Fukuyama said, "The important variable [in the Asian economic experience] is not industrial policy per se but culture."[4] As for the role of Confucian ethics, Fukuyama wrote, "Confucianism has defined the character of social relations within the Chinese society over the last two and a half millennia. It consists of a series of ethical principles that are said to undergird a properly functioning society."[5] Alan Greenspan, the former chairman of the US Federal Reserve, said in a congressional testimony in 1997, "Much of what we took for granted in our free market system to be human nature was not nature at all, but culture."[6]

But if culture is the determining factor behind the economic success of China and the other industrializing Asian nations, then why did those nations had to wait until the second half of the twentieth century to industrialize? And if Confucian ethics have been embedded in the social fabric of the Asian society for 2,500 years, as Fukuyama claims, then why did such ethics fail to cause the industrialization of China centuries or even decades earlier? Why did it take the Asian nations more than 200 years after the Industrial Revolution had transformed the economic and sociocultural and political landscape of Europe to enter the industrial age? And why did North Korea, which shares with its southern neighbor the same culture and supposedly the same Confucian ethics, has failed to replicate the experiment of the south and industrialize? And if culture is the true force behind the Asian success story and the source of the social trust that is supposed to prevail in Asian societies, then why did most of those nations face a deep social and economic crisis in the late 1990s? Although culture is an important factor influencing the fate of nations and the course of their economic and social development, it is not the only factor.

China, in fact, was the most advanced nation in the world during the European Middle Ages. The art of printing, for example, was discovered and used in China at least a century before Europe developed it. China also had the best and most complete records regarding its past, and it is said that its bureaucratic system had been the most sophisticated of any state in older times. "Consider China at the outset of the fifteenth century. Its curiosity, its instinct for exploration, and its drive to build and create all the technologies necessary to launch the industrial revolution—something that would not actually occur for another 400 years, wrote Lester Thurow."[7] What happened to China had also happened to other great nations of the past, particularly the Arab and Indian nations.

Although some 250 years have passed since the Industrial Revolution occurred, historians are yet to reach a consensus regarding the social forces that instigated the revolution and describe the role each force had played in making it happen. In contrast, the promoters of Asia, and particularly the believers in cultural determinism, were quick to declare that Confucian culture is the force behind Asia's economic success. But as tribute was being paid to Asian cultures and Confucian ethics, values and relationships built around them were rapidly crumbling and replaced by the ethics of the free market and consumerism. Nevertheless, Western political strategists who believe in cultural determinism have continued to ignore these facts and blame the cultures of other nations, particularly Muslim nations, for their failure to industrialize and liberalize. Even after Malaysia and Turkey entered the industrial age and began to industrialize and liberalize without abandoning their allegiance to Islam and its culture, cultural determinism continued to deepen its roots and gain more followers in America and other European states.

Culture and Politics

After winning World War II, Western nations decided to forge a strategic relationship among themselves to foster cooperation, rebuild shattered economies, enhance military power, and contain the Soviet military threat and its communist ideology. While security considerations were the major force behind the alliance, Western culture and its Christian ethics were given credit for sustaining the alliance and making cooperation possible. Democracy and human rights were also found to be traits of Western culture and its Judeo-Christian ethos. In contrast, most other cultures whose core is neither Jewish nor Christian were degraded and often called "barbaric," their peoples "uncivilized." And when ethnic conflict spread in non-Western states in the 1990s, culture was identified as the villain causing trouble and committing atrocities.

Samuel Huntington wrote, "Cultural identity is the central factor shaping a country's associations and antagonisms."[8] While culture plays a major role in shaping every group's identity, it does not necessarily shape state identity, because less than 10 percent of all states in the world have homogeneous populations identifying with one race and one culture only.

158 GLOBAL ECONOMIC AND CULTURAL TRANSFORMATION

In fact, the identity of every national group is influenced by history, geography culture, ideology, education, interests, as well as the outside world. An individual in society is usually a member of several groups that have different and sometimes contradictory goals. Every citizen is a member of a family tied to it by blood, a member of a residential community tied to it by shared concerns, often a member of a professional organization tied to it by shared goals, a member of an economic entity tied to it by interests, and a member of a nation tied to it by history, culture, and symbols. All of these associations seek different goals and thus affect the attitudes of individuals and groups in more contradictory than complementary ways.

Huntington also says that "global politics is being reconfigured along cultural lines. Peoples and countries with similar cultures are coming together. Peoples and countries with different cultures are coming apart."[9] He asserts that cultures, or as he says, civilizations, are destined to clash, and that their inevitable clash will determine the nature and intensity of conflict in the world. Huntington, it ought to be noted, employs the concepts of "culture," "civilization," and "religion" alternately to mean the same thing, while their meanings and roles in society are different. Francis Fukuyama, in contrast, does not see cultural competition as a major source of conflict. "On the contrary," he writes, "the rivalry arising from the interaction of different cultures can frequently lead to creative change, and there are numerous cases of such cultural cross-stimulation."[10] Thomas Sowell echoes the same thing; he says, "Cross-cultural experiences have been associated with cultural achievements."[11]

If the claims of Huntington were to be correct, and that "peoples and countries with similar cultures are coming together and peoples and countries with different cultures are coming apart," then the European nations should have never fought each other; they should have always worked together because they have had similar cultures since the times of the Roman Empire, and have had democratic systems for almost two centuries. Yet, most European states fought each other and committed atrocities against one another and against their citizens who were members of racial and religious minorities. They also allied themselves with non-Europeans having different cultures, particularly the Japanese, the Turks, and the Arabs, against other Europeans having similar cultures. But if the correct assumption is that Europeans have different cultures and, because of that, they fought each other, then how could they unite after World War II and cooperate to achieve shared goals and even form a European Union?

In contrast to the Europeans, Arabs claim to have and do have the same culture, not just similar cultures, the same history, the same language, and the majority of them have the same religion. Yet Arabs have failed to unite and ally themselves against non-Arabs; all attempts to unite Arabs have failed. Most Latin Americans also share similar cultures and the same religion and language, but are unable to unite. Moreover, the central Asian countries, which were freed from the yoke of communism, were quick to rediscover their Turkish cultural roots and Islamic heritage, yet they are unable to unite. Even African tribes having similar cultures, languages, and religions and very little to fight over seem to have found fighting and killing each other easier than uniting with one another. The examples of Somalia, Rwanda, and Liberia are cases that prove beyond doubt that culture is incapable by itself of uniting peoples separated by ethnicity and living in pre-industrial times.

"People separated by ideology but united by culture come together, as the two Germanys did and as the two Koreas and the several Chinas are beginning to,"[12] wrote Huntington. This claim is very far from the truth. The two Germanys did not come together and could not have come together while separated by ideology; they came together in 1989 after the collapse of the Marxist ideology and the failure of East Germany's economy. The people of East Germany moved en masse toward the west, destroying the Berlin Wall and forcing open all borders. Race, common history, and need were the real forces that incited the East Germans to move west and encouraged the West Germans to embrace their blood brothers and save them from economic catastrophe. As for the Koreas, the only thing uniting them today is not culture but mutual antagonism and enmity nurtured by ideology and fostered by a cynical American policy. The return of Hong Kong to China in 1997 was not the result of choice; it occurred because Hong Kong was an occupied territory whose return to China was agreed upon between the occupied and the British occupier a long time ago.

The United States' relationships with other countries also make the point that culture is not the major force shaping interstate relationships. The United States, despite sharing a similar culture with Western European nations, cooperates more with Mexico that has a different culture than with France. It also allies itself with nations such as Israel, Saudi Arabia, South Korea, Pakistan, and Turkey, with which it does not share culture, language, religion, or borders. In 1991, shared security concerns, not culture or religion, compelled a few Arab states to join the United States to fight Iraqi Arabs with whom they shared not only culture, but religion and family and tribal ties as well.

Unity of peoples and countries in the past was accomplished by force, not by choice. Unity of peoples and countries in the age of globalization that is dominated by interests and security considerations is accomplished by choice, not by force. Mutual economic interests and shared security concerns are strong justifications for unity among different states with

160 GLOBAL ECONOMIC AND CULTURAL TRANSFORMATION

different cultures; cultural similarities are helpful but not sufficient to provide by themselves a rationale for political unity or even security coordination.

Culture and Conflict

When a few groups of Muslim radicals began to engage in terrorism, Islam and its values and Arab culture were blamed for the terrible acts. Many voices were raised in the West, particularly in the United States, condemning Islam, its followers, and its legacy, warning against the impending Islamic mortal threat to the West. One such voice called Islam a "killer culture," its followers "barbarians."[13] Christianity, in contrast, was hailed as a culture of tolerance and peace.

Samuel Huntington saw Islam, not only Islamic fanatics, as a serious problem facing the West and threatening its way of life. He wrote, "The underlying problem for the West is not Islamic fundamentalism. It is Islam; a different civilization whose people are convinced of the superiority of their culture and are obsessed with the inferiority of their power."[14] He also considered other non-Western nations a threat to the West, especially Asians in general and China in particular: "At the micro level, the most violent fault lines are between Islam and its [Christian] Orthodox, Hindu, African and Western Christian neighbors. At the macro level, the dominant division is between the West and the rest, with the most intense conflicts occurring between Muslim and Asian societies on the one hand, and the West on the other."[15]

While Islam and its followers are seen as the West's eternal enemy, China is seen as Islam's natural ally in its fight against the West. As a consequence, both Howard Bloom and Samuel Huntington implore the West to divide other nations and use its superior power to suppress, weaken, and dominate non-Western nations. Huntington wrote, "To minimize its losses requires the West to wield skillfully its economic resources as carrots and sticks in dealing with other societies, to bolster its unity and coordinate its policies so as to . . . promote and exploit differences among non-Western nations."[16] He further calls, although implicitly, for ethnic cleansing, accusing non-Western immigrants of promoting values and traditions that undermine Western culture: "Western culture is challenged by groups within Western societies. One such challenge comes from immigrants from other civilizations who reject assimilation and continue to adhere to and to propagate the values, customs, and cultures of their home societies."[17]

Huntington even sees economic progress in China as a serious threat to America: "If the Chinese economic development continues, this could be the single most serious security issue American policy-makers confront in the early twenty-first century."[18] Bloom warns the West against the impending danger posed by other cultures and religions: "It is important that the societies which cherish pluralism survive. It is critical that they spread their values. It is imperative that they not allow their position in the pecking order of nations to slip and that they not cave in to the onrush of barbarians."[19]

It is clear that the neoconservative forces in America are unwilling to accept anything less than total control of world affairs and other nations. They seem to have learned nothing from their misguided economic and financial policies at home that weakened the American economy, or from their military adventures in Iraq and other places that undermined American credibility abroad. No one seems to be willing to admit, not even President Barak Obama, that America cannot maintain its only superpower status forever, and that America needs to make the necessary mental and actual adjustments accordingly. Nevertheless, the US intelligence community seems to have realized this impending eventuality. A report issued by the National Intelligence Council December, 16, 2012, stated that "the United States government cannot remain the world's only super power past the year 2030."[20]

But are other peoples really barbarians and Christians and Jews are angels, as Huntington and Bloom and other cultural determinists insinuate? Let us look at history and review some of its records. For a fair comparison, actions, reactions, and interactions of peoples and states must be placed within the same historical contexts; they also have to be chosen to represent the same or very close times and events. Otherwise, actions and reactions would be unrelated, and the progress in all human endeavors throughout history would be rendered meaningless.

For example, the predecessors of most "civilized" Americans of today are the barbarians who massacred the indigenous peoples of America, confiscated their property, and destroyed their cultures and lives. And the forefathers of the "cultured" Europeans of today are people who never took a bath in their lives when peoples in the East had known bathing for centuries. They are also the people who invented the colonial enterprise and justified the killing of other peoples and the confiscation of their land and the exploitation of their resources. The aristocrats of today, in both the East and the West, are mostly the descendants of people who used violence at will and robbed, exploited, and enslaved others. In fact, social position in almost every society is little more than the residue of robbery and murder throughout the ages. A few encounters between Muslims on the one hand, and Christians and Jews on the other shall be briefly examined.

162 GLOBAL ECONOMIC AND CULTURAL TRANSFORMATION

In AD 638, the Muslim forces entered Jerusalem after its Christian inhabitants surrendered. But Sophronius, the patriarch of the city, refused to deliver the Holy City to anyone but to Caliph Umar bin Al-Khattab. "Once the Christians had surrendered," writes Karen Armstrong, "there was no killing, no destruction of property, no burning of rival religious symbols, no expulsions or expropriations, and no attempts to force the inhabitants to embrace Islam."[21] When Caliph Umar arrived, he was invited to tour the city, and while visiting the holy places, the time for Muslim prayer came around. "Sophronius invited the caliph to pray where he was," beside the tomb. "Umar courteously refused; neither would he pray in Constantine's Martyrium. Instead he went outside and prayed on the steps beside the busy thoroughfare of the Cardo Maximums."[22] The reason for refusing the invitation of the patriarch was, as Umar explained later, "that had he prayed inside the Christian shrines, the Muslims would have confiscated them and converted them into an Islamic place of worship ... Umar immediately wrote a charter forbidding Muslims to pray on the steps of the Martyrium or build a mosque there."[23]

In contrast, when the Christian Crusaders entered the holy city of Jerusalem in 1099, more than 450 years later, they committed unimaginable massacres against its Muslim and Jewish inhabitants. "For three days the Crusaders systematically slaughtered about thirty thousand of the inhabitants of Jerusalem ... Ten thousand Muslims who had sought sanctuary on the roof of the Aqsa [the third holiest place in Islam] were brutally massacred, and Jews were rounded up into their synagogues and put to the sword,"[24] writes Armstrong.

Muslim Arabs governed parts of Spain for almost eight centuries; neither Christians nor Jews during that period suffered persecution or even intentional hardship. Historians, Jewish historians included, seem to agree that Jews enjoyed their golden age in Spain under the Arabic-Islamic rule. But when Spain returned to Christian rule around the end of the fifteenth century in the wake of the Arabs' defeat, no Muslim or Jew escaped persecution. All non-Christians were massacred, expelled, or forced to convert to Catholicism.

When Jewish Zionism began its quest to establish a Jewish state in Palestine, its plans included the forced deportation of Palestine's people, both Muslim Arabs and Christian Arabs. Terrorist acts were committed against Palestinian Arabs before and after the declaration of Israeli independence in 1948. Jewish gangs and the state's army killed innocent people and carried out terrorist acts to frighten the Muslim and Christian inhabitants of Palestine and force them to flee their homes and towns and homeland. Nathan Ghofshi, describing the actions of his fellow Jews, said, "Zionists forced the Arabs to leave cities and villages which they did not want to leave of their free will."[25] Yigal Alon, a former Deputy Prime Minister in Israel, wrote in his memoirs that he used psychological warfare "to cause the tens of thousands of Arabs who remained in Galilee to flee."[26] Almost all of the Galilee people who were forced to flee their homes were Christian Arabs, not Muslim Arabs.

A case from contemporary history may be even more instructive. In Bosnia, Serbs, who are Orthodox Christians, Croats, who are Catholics, and Muslims, came into conflict. All of them had lived at the time in the same country, under the same political and legal system, adhered to the same ideology, and had the same ethnic background; in other words, all had the same culture and the same life experience. But when the ideological bind fractured and the political process of nationalism was reactivated, the three communities were divided and numerous massacres were committed. Accounts of human rights groups, the UN, and other American and European government agencies indicate that the crimes committed by the Muslims of Bosnia were less vicious compared to the atrocities committed by the Serbs and Croats. Muslims were also more willing to coexist with the others peacefully in one state.

To explain the causes of mutual enmity, Huntington claims that the three peoples of Bosnia belonged to three different civilizations. Bogdan Denitch, a political activist who, unlike Huntington, is a son of former Yugoslavia and a witness to its tragedy, says that all Bosnians are ethnically and linguistically identical. "Both Serbian and Croatian national myths emphasize the centuries of wars against the Ottoman Turks. Muslim Slavs, though ethnically and linguistically identical to the Croats and Serbs, are somehow transformed into the legendary Turkish enemy and made to pay for the years of Turkish dominance."[27] Denitch explains how this perception was created and used to justify the killing of the other and the expropriation of their property and humanity.

> For the Serbian nationalists, it is self-evident that the Albanians and Bosnian Muslims are in cahoots with the world conspiracy of Islamic fundamentalism. The Croats are obviously an extension of the permanent plot of the Vatican against Orthodox Christianity. For the Croat nationalists, the Serbs represent the barbarian non-European hordes of treacherous Byzantine out to destroy Western civilization and Christian culture.[28]

Since cultures are products of civilizations, cultures acquire their major traits from the civilizations that produce them. People, regardless of their cultural backgrounds and religious beliefs and histories, adopt the attitudes and values dictated by the civilization in which they live. Muslims living in Western countries such as Sweden, Germany, and the United States are generally more tolerant and less inclined toward violence than Muslims living in Egypt, who are in turn more tolerant than Muslims living in Saudi Arabia. On the other hand, Christians living in the same Western states are generally more tolerant and less inclined toward violence than Christians living in Ireland, who are in turn more tolerant than those living in Serbia and Nigeria. And what is true for Muslims and Christians is also true for followers of other religions.

People who live in industrial and post-industrial societies are generally more tolerant than those living in pre-industrial and agricultural societies. A German Muslim, for example, is likely to be more respectful of human rights than a Lebanese Christian. The culture of the German Muslim is in essence Western whose civilizational context is industrial, while the culture of the Lebanese Christian is in essence Eastern whose civilizational context is agricultural. Because of such cultural affiliations, many American Muslims with children tend to have Christmas trees during the holidays, and many Christian Arabs "fast" during the holy month of Ramadan, or refrain from eating and drinking in public places while Muslims fast. Democracy, respect for human rights, the rule of law, and religious tolerance as we know them today, are products of mature industrial and post-industrial societies. Therefore, no Christian or non-Christian society living in pre-industrial times is capable of adopting the same attitudes and values dictated by democracy and the rule of law, or have the same respect for human rights.

Every civilization, its peoples and economies and cultures are dependent on the civilization that follows. All nations and states living in pre-industrial times are less advanced, less powerful, less culturally sophisticated, and less self-confident than nations living in the industrial and post-industrial times. And because the political process dominates the lives of peoples living in pre-industrial times, they are less free and generally bound by religion and nationalism, two ideologies that seldom tolerate political dissent or cultural diversity.

While religion is the core of all agricultural cultures, nationalism is the core of all early industrial cultures. Democracy on the other hand, is the core of all mature industrial cultures. Individualism, meanwhile, is fast becoming the core of the culture of the knowledge age, to which the emerging global elite belong. It is elite that, while increasingly assuming world leadership, is helplessly losing attachment to traditional ideology and social responsibility. It lives in an age where continuous change is the only unchanging fact of life, and where the culture of individualism is built around two major pillars: the maximization of personal gain, and the minimization of personal pain, nothing more and nothing less.

CULTURAL DETERMINISM **165**

All Third World peoples, regardless of their nationality and religion, may seek to enhance their military power, may condemn Western values, may talk passionately about that part of their collective memory that deals with Western colonialism; they may also complain bitterly about American policies and the dictates of the International Monetary Fund (IMF). However, they cannot challenge the West or undermine its military superiority, nor can they destroy its civilization upon which they are very much dependent. The West, therefore, has no reason to worry; its nations as a group are more than one full civilization ahead of all Third World nations. The frustration of Third World peoples should not be used as a warning shot to invoke age-old hatreds in the hearts of Christians in general and Western peoples in particular. Helping Third World peoples get the right education, industrialize, and move beyond the age of agriculture and its self-centered culture is the shortest, fastest, safest, and certainly most morally rewarding way to spread democracy, promote human rights, foster world peace, and ensure prosperity for all.

Culture and the World Order

As the Cold War ended and the Soviet Union disintegrated, the then existing world order, which regulated international relations for the previous half a century, came to an end. The "balance of power," which governed East–West relations and kept the peace in Europe for decades, suddenly collapsed, creating a security vacuum in its wake. States and nations that suffered under the old order were happy to witness its demise. Other states and nations that were able to benefit from it or violate international law with impunity under its umbrella, felt the need to resurrect it or replace it with a similar order. Henry Kissinger, for example, still argues that the bipolar balance of power system is the only workable one.

The United States, being the only superpower left, claimed victory and assumed, without challenge, world leadership. And while the world was looking for a new just order to end the controversial legacy of the past and restructure international relations on fairer bases, the United States moved to assert its dominance and ensure American economic, political, and military hegemony. As a consequence, the grievances and legitimate demands of most nations that longed for freedom and economic development were not met, leaving the old problems to fester and become endemic.

Since the political philosophers who represent the heart and mind of Western culture are themselves products of the Cold War era, they could not find an alternative concept to the balance of power. They could only reinvent it, using culture and hatred to replace ideological antagonism and

166 GLOBAL ECONOMIC AND CULTURAL TRANSFORMATION

military power. Consequently, "hatred" and "mutuality of enmity" were advanced as principles that govern the relationship between "the West and the rest." Huntington wrote, "There can be no true friends without true enemies. Unless we hate what we are not, we cannot love what we are."[29] Such enemies, he implies, are all non-Western, non-Christian peoples in general, and Muslims and Chinese in particular: "Islamic and Sinic civilizations differ fundamentally in terms of their religion, culture, social structure, traditions, politics and basic assumptions about the root of their way of life." He goes on to urge the West to hate the East as a way to maintain its unity. "It is human to hate. For self-definition and motivation people need enemies,"[30] he asserts.

Such arguments and assertions and the message they carry simply say that the West must hate the East, especially and profoundly the Islamic and Chinese peoples. They also say that the West must do everything it can to limit the potentialities of non-Western nations, divide them, and keep them weak and on the defensive at all times. Without such a plan of action, he seems to suggest, the West would not be able to sustain its unity, preserve its supremacy, protect its interests and way of life, and promote its values. A new balance of power based on mutual hatred and perpetual enmity is thus advocated.

Despite the flashiness of the slogan, "The Clash of Civilizations," the basic assumptions of Huntington's thesis are flawed, making it neither realistic nor helpful. It, for example, ignores the role of economics in global politics as well as the role of globalization in unifying the world's business and political elites and spreading the West's culture of consumerism everywhere. It also ignores the negative impact of such developments on each state's power base, social and cultural cohesiveness, national sovereignty, and claimed political prerogatives. In fact, the rise of China on the one hand, and the Great Recession on the other prove that the West is unable to maintain its dominant global position forever, and that the world's economic and knowledge elites have every reason to work together and no reason to hate each other.

While all violence is bad and must be condemned, there is no violence as dangerous as the one committed in words. It poisons the soul, destroys the mind, and transforms good, innocent people into criminals. What we need is not more hatred, enmity, and violence but compassion, understanding, and tolerance. The only true path to peaceful coexistence that enhances the humanity of all people lies in building bridges across cultural divides, recognizing and accepting ethnic, national, and religious diversity, and helping poorer nations and suppressed minorities free themselves from need and oppression and climb the civilizational ladder.

Social Trust

Trust in society is without doubt an aspect of culture and changed circumstances. However, since cultures differ from one another, expressions of trust also differ from one culture to another, and therefore from one society to another. Where trust is a shared habit, society acquires "social capital," whose presence is important to economic development. Francis Fukuyama defines social capital as "a capability that arises from the prevalence of trust in society or in certain parts of it."[31] Fukuyama argues further that there are societies with more social trust than others (high-trust societies) and that there are societies with less social trust (low-trust societies), that societies with more social trust produce more social capital and, therefore, they are better prepared to make progress and achieve prosperity.

Social capital, which is a function of social trust, facilitates the creation of certain associations in society whose presence is indispensable to economic growth. However, "social capital, the crucible of trust and critical to the health of an economy, rests on cultural roots,"[32] Fukuyama adds. This simply means that culture determines the depth and breadth of trust in society, and trust determines the proclivity of society to acquire social capital, which, in turn, determines the capacity of society to create the organizations and associations needed to facilitate economic development and progress.

"High-trust" societies, which are supposed to enjoy substantial social capital, are capable of building competitive, vibrant economies. And since "trust is culturally determined," as Fukuyama claims, culture becomes the most important factor determining the economic performance of society. David Landes says, "If we learn anything from the history of economic development, it is that culture makes all the difference."[33] The arguments made by Fukuyama and Landes support the one advanced by Max Weber about a century ago; however, they contradict the argument made by Karl Marx half a century earlier. To Karl Marx, economic conditions and structures shape cultures, but to Weber and Fukuyama, cultural forces shape economic conditions. This simply means that there are people who think that economic circumstances and production relations are the forces that shape peoples' cultures and determine their destiny, while others believe that cultural habits and values are the forces that shape economic conditions and determine people's future. In fact, there are still others who claim that culture is genetically determined and, therefore, it is incapable of change. In other words, such people claim that there are peoples who are destined to succeed due to their cultural genes, that there are others who are destined to fail due to their cultural genes, and that there is little that can be done to change this fact.

168 GLOBAL ECONOMIC AND CULTURAL TRANSFORMATION

Max Weber, observing the different economic achievements of religious communities in America, was correct to argue that different religious beliefs and values are largely responsible for different economic outcomes. Different attitudes, work ethics, and outlooks were capable of generating different economic accomplishments. Karl Marx, observing the disruptive and corrosive influence of capitalism on people's way of life and social relations, was also correct to argue that changed material conditions and economic structures are largely responsible for changing people's ways of living, attitudes, and values. Nevertheless, I believe that neither culture alone nor economic conditions by themselves are capable of causing or even explaining the profound sociocultural and socioeconomic and sociopolitical transformations of society.

Cultures, which "involve attitudes as well as skills, languages, and customs,"[34] appeared in the early stages of human development as tools and views to deal with the environment, tie people together, and help them form communities. Therefore, culture evolved in reaction to changing life conditions and was developed to enhance humans' ability to deal with their physical and social environments. For example, the development of agriculture, which changed society's economic conditions profoundly, led to changing the culture of people who adopted agriculture. The practice of farming the land transformed the old society, creating a new society, a new way of life, and a new civilization. This simply means that the economic aspects of life influence the development of cultures. But once established and accepted the new culture becomes the organizing principle of society, the basis of social relationships, the framework of thinking, and the social tool to deal with life challenges and changed circumstances. Culture, consequently, shapes people's attitudes toward both man and nature, making the economic aspects of life subject to the influence of culture.

Trust, being a cultural habit, exists in all societies, in the poor as well as in the rich ones, in the traditional as well as in the modern. No relationship can be forged or sustained without a degree of trust large enough to enable all participants to feel comfortable working with each other. The form and role of trust, however, differ from one society to another because of differences in social structures and civilizational settings. In traditional societies living in pre-industrial times, trust is more of a habit that reflects traditional values embedded in the social fabric of society. In nontraditional societies living in the industrial and post-industrial ages, however, trust is more of an attitude that reflects rational thinking. The former tends to be concerned primarily with relationships shaped by values; the latter tends to be concerned primarily with economic interests and relationships shaped by laws and ethical codes of conduct.

Traditional Trust and Social Trust

Traditional trust prevails within largely closed circles such as families and communities of faith. Nontraditional trust, or social trust, prevails in largely open circles, particularly in organizations and relationships built around interests. And since relationships within smaller circles tend to be stable, traditional trust tends to be stable as well, playing similar roles in all such relationships. Social trust, in contrast, tends to change as business interests change; it thus plays different roles in the lives of different societies and organizations. The first is a function of culture, which seldom changes within one's lifetime; the latter is a function of economic interests that normally live a life of continuous change.

In an increasingly complex world, where global transactions are numbered in the billions every minute, no system can function without social trust. Traditional trust would certainly make things easier and life less stressful, but trusting people who place different values on the same things is not possible. Only social trust based on enforceable laws and contractual agreements will do. However, as societies move from the agricultural to the industrial age, life becomes more complex, relationships multifaceted, and interests more prevalent and relevant, causing old traditions and values to fracture. Since cultures change slowly and have always resisted change, all societies in transition experience cultural chaos and a *trust deficit*.

During transitional periods, while traditional trust loses ground as its space shrinks, social trust is still weak because its legal base is yet to be developed and accepted. A trust deficit is created, allowing an environment of corruption, hypocrisy, opportunism, and nepotism to grow and prevail. Nevertheless, some people could still be trustworthy in the traditional sense, yet untrustworthy in the social sense. Nepotism is only one example of a behavior exhibiting commitment to traditional family ties and blood relationships and, at the same time, disregard for the law, the public interest, and the interests of strangers. While personal and familial loyalty may continue and even strengthen in an environment characterized by political corruption, national loyalty and social responsibility are always weakened in such circumstances.

If you were driving a car in a Third World town where you know most people, you are likely to have little trust in drivers facing you on the road, even drivers you know personally. In contrast, if you were driving in a large American or European city where you do not know anyone personally, you are more likely to trust drivers facing you on the road, even drivers you do not know at all. Generally speaking, drivers in underdeveloped countries tend to ignore traffic regulations and disregard the law, making it less safe to drive in such countries. In contrast, drivers in Western societies in general tend to respect traffic regulations and abide by the law, making it safer to drive in such countries. So, in the first case, you have little or no trust in the driving habits of other drivers because you know they often ignore the law. However, in the second case, you trust the driving habits of other drivers because you know they seldom violate the law. Trust in the first case is traditional based on personal knowledge of established habits; in the second case, trust is social based on enforceable laws and regulations. Social trust emanates from trusting that others respect the same laws and agreements we respect and abide by.

The so-called "low-trust" societies have plenty of traditional trust, but little social trust; the so-called "high-trust" societies have plenty of social trust, but little traditional trust. Since social trust is more important in industrial and post-industrial societies, traditional trust alone is not enough because it lacks the capacity to manage complicated transactions that characterize life in such societies. Traditional societies lacking adequate social trust are unable to manage complicated systems and institutions and organizations that characterize industrial societies, and therefore they are less able to develop their economies and make progress. Yet, they are better equipped to define their identities and maintain the integrity of their families and cultural communities. Minorities whose members are tied to one another by faith and age-old values, tend to exhibit strong allegiance to their traditions and identities, but lack what it takes to make enough scientific and economic progress to live the age and enjoy what it has to offer. In fact, there is no faith-based and religiously conservative minority anywhere in the world, be it Muslim or Jewish or Christian or Hindu, that enjoys high standards of living and can relate to the modern world in a rational manner.

The Great Recession is an indication of a trust deficit caused by the transition of the American society from the industrial age to the knowledge age. People in banking and finance, mortgage lending and insurance, driven by greed and lack of social responsibility, were able to exploit the outdated old laws and regulations to create new, highly complicated financial products, manipulate their clients, and take unwarranted risks that caused a mortgage bubble that led to the 2008 financial crisis. The health reform bill passed by the US congress in 2009 and the financial reform bill passed in 2010 are attempts to unconsciously close that trust deficit. But since the trust deficit in my view is very large and deep, the reform bills are unlikely to prevent by themselves another financial crisis and a deeper recession from happening in the near future. In fact, most people do not understand the meaning and importance of trust deficits, and therefore they do not know where and when they occur and how to deal with them.

According to Fukuyama, Japan is a high-trust society, with plenty of social trust. As such it is supposed to be more capable of organizing its economy and economic relationships in ways that improve the productivity of workers and increase the efficiency of business operations. And because of its "propensity for spontaneous sociability," as Fukuyama claims, Japan is supposed to be more innovative in creating and managing new systems and relationships. In other words, the high-trust societies are supposed to have more dynamic economies and innovative business communities and more efficient wealth-generating institutions. But at the end of the twentieth century, Japan appeared to have a stagnant economy, a largely conservative business elite, and a slowly wealth generating society.

In an open society with a dynamic economy, people are more concerned with interests than with values, causing social trust to be more important than traditional trust. In such a society, which the United States represents, contractual arrangements become the norm, and winning, just like losing, becomes an ordinary occurrence with minimal social consequences. In a rather conservative Japanese society, some business managers committed suicide in the 1990s because of business failures and due to the social stigma that goes with failure. In the United States about 1.6 million people declared bankruptcy in 2011 with no Americans committing suicide because of failure. Meanwhile, many Americans who were convicted of stealing public money, defrauding investors, and committing sexual and other crimes became celebrities. The United States today is a country where an infamous person has a good chance of becoming rich and famous, while an honest person has a better chance of dying without either money or fame.

The Chinese society, says Fukuyama, "is regulated not by a constitution and system of laws flowing from it but by the internalization of Confucian ethical principles on the part of each individual as a process of socialization."[35] The same socialization process of ethical principles pervades in most Islamic countries such as Iran, Egypt, and Saudi Arabia as well as in most Catholic countries such as Bolivia, Croatia, Ireland, and Mexico. The fact that Chinese societies were able to achieve genuine economic development in the last 30 years, while most Islamic and Latin American countries are still unable to do the same, has little to do with either Islam, Confucianism, or Catholicism. Only when China did what Japan had done a century earlier, departed from its traditional value system and communist ideology, and launched a plan to transform its culture, that it was able to make meaningful progress. So, the key to societal change and economic development is not reviving old cultural values and traditions but transforming existing cultural values and attitudes.

172　GLOBAL ECONOMIC AND CULTURAL TRANSFORMATION

The old Chinese ethics to which much credit is being given by Fukuyama and others were described by Hegel about 150 years ago as deceptive and fraudulent. Hegel wrote, "No honor exists and no one has an individual right in respect of others, the consciousness of debasement predominates. [The Chinese] are notorious for deceiving whenever they can. Friend deceives friend and no one resents the attempt at deception. Their frauds are most astutely and craftily performed."[36] Such a judgment, while clearly racist, describes ethics that could not engender social trust or be responsible for the rise of any nation. No one at the time asked Hegel if he had lived in China long enough to understand the Chinese culture or if he had interacted with a Chinese farmer. Large Third World cities like Cairo, Lagos, and Mexico City are places where traditional trust is dying, and social trust is still unable to be born; large cities in industrial states like London, New York, and Rome are places where social trust is in a coma, and on one is aware of what is happening to it. The micro-credit enterprise that was started in Bangladesh decades ago and has become a global phenomenon, could not have happened without trust because loans are made without collateral. And though poor women are the major recipients of these loans, the rate of default is near-zero, not because of social trust but due to the prevalence of traditional trust.

Plans to organize societies in ways that promote economic development can only succeed if sociocultural incentives and hindrances are flexible enough to facilitate social and economic change. In southeast Asia, the plan to transform the economy was introduced in conjunction with a program to transform the sociocultural context. In Egypt, Venezuela, and Nigeria, the economic plans failed because they did not include similar programs to transform the sociocultural contexts. And when the industrializing Asian nations decided in the mid-1990s to preserve traditions and rely on traditional relationships, both the economy and society suffered a serious setback. Relying on traditional trust, while failing to further develop social trust, had encouraged cronyism and led to the spread of corruption and unaccountability, causing crisis to engulf society.

Cultural values, traditions, and attitudes are generally valid within their own civilizational contexts, and more so within their societal contexts. Therefore, values, traditions, and attitudes are relative and should not be judged outside their particular societal contexts. For example, while it is possible and largely fair to compare certain Indian traditions with similar ones in Egypt, it is neither possible nor fair to compare aspects of Indian or Egyptian cultural values with those of Germany or the United States. For example, an attitude that tolerates casual sex in America is considered immoral by cultures rooted in the agricultural age. And while, punishing political dissent in Egypt is normal, it is unlawful in America.

The high-trust/low-trust model articulated by Fukuyama is an attempt to explain the differences in economic achievements among nations. However, it ignores three important facts that make its assumptions largely unrealistic and its conclusions highly unreliable, if not harmful.

1. It ignores the fact that cultures are products of civilizations that change greatly and profoundly as society moves from one civilization to another.
2. It ignores the fact that all industrial societies have similar cultures because they live in the same industrial civilization and that their economic and technological achievements are at roughly the same level.
3. It fails to realize that the impact of economy on culture is nearly as great as Marx had argued when society is industrializing, and that the impact of culture on economy is nearly as great as Weber had argued when society is in a largely stable civilizational stage. Therefore, to base the analysis on one view only and dismiss the other is to distort reality and produce unreliable conclusions.

Every person has a need to belong to a group in which he can seek and receive recognition. Yet, while seeking social recognition, most individuals find themselves belonging to several groups starting with the family and moving outwards to larger circles that usually end with the state. As one moves from the smaller, more intimate circles to the larger, less personal ones, his sense of belonging and loyalty weaken progressively. The rules of belonging and competition within smaller circles are usually well defined and strictly observed, but loose and flexible within larger circles. As a consequence, trust, honesty, and collective responsibility tend to be very strong within family circles, good within clans, weak and shadowy within organizations, and largely nonexistent between estranged communities. Social trust in pre-industrial societies, therefore, is very weak not because of culture or religion but because of social and economic structures. Association in such societies is largely vertical, not horizontal, and this limits individual social mobility as well as opportunities for socialization. Traditional trust and social trust are largely incompatible; where traditional trust is strong, social trust tends to be week, and where social trust is strong, traditional trust tends to be week.

While the prevalence of traditional trust deepens mutual obligations within smaller circles, it weakens social trust and social responsibility within larger circles. Members of each circle or group, while trusting each other, tend to vest little trust in members of other groups, especially competing ethnic and religious ones. On the other hand, the prevalence of

174 GLOBAL ECONOMIC AND CULTURAL TRANSFORMATION

traditional trust and the mutual obligations it engenders within such circles serve to strengthen families and ethnic communities as well as communities of faith, helping them control crime and social vice. They also provide a strong social support system to help the poor and the elderly, preventing them from drifting in large numbers into drug addiction, poverty, homelessness, and despair. For example, the 21 Arab states have a population of about 360 million compared to 320 million for the United States, and a per capita income about 10 percent of that of the United States. However, while the United States has millions of homeless people, the homelessness phenomenon hardly exists in the Arab world. Yet mutual suspicion between different ethnic and religious groups on the one hand, and a general lack of social trust on the other, make conflict in traditional societies easy to ignite but difficult to contain. When conflict erupted in Sudan, Somalia, Lebanon, and Algeria, it was bloody and very costly in human as well as material terms.

Where vertical association is the norm, as is the case in traditional agricultural societies in general, authoritarianism normally thrives and democracy suffers, and where horizontal association is the norm, as is the case in industrial and post-industrial societies, democracy normally thrives and authoritarianism suffers. Where vertical association is the norm, no member of a small ethnic or religious group is usually able to get more recognition unless someone else gets less. The game in such societies is more of a zero-sum game that facilitates neither social change nor social mobility, nor encourages personal initiative. In contrast, where association in society is horizontal, most people are able to get more without necessarily causing others to get less, because the game in such societies often produces positive results. Historical records show that since the Industrial Revolution the relative number of losers in all post-agricultural societies has decreased as the relative number of winners has increased. For example, the United States created more billionaires in 15 years, from 1983 to 1998, than it did in its previous history. While the number of billionaires was only 13 in 1982, it reached 189 in 1999;[37] and due to the information and communications revolutions, the number approached 500 in 2010.

People living in pre-industrial times are less able to produce and accumulate wealth, even when money arrives without much effort; they are more able to spend it senselessly than invest it wisely as the Spaniards had demonstrated in the sixteenth century and the oil-exporting Arab, African, and Latin American states have demonstrated since the 1950s. While most Arab states were able to build their infrastructure, they have failed to develop their social infrastructure and human capital. Economic restructuring needs sociocultural transformation to cause societal development and facilitate progress that touches the lives of all people.

10

A World in Transition

A careful look at our world as the second decade of the twenty-first century advances reveals that we are getting closer to completing a historical transformational transition that promises to take us to a higher, more complex civilization. It is a period dominated by five major trends of change: economic integration across state lines; political fragmentation within state lines; sociocultural segmentation within national lines; a fast-changing balance of global economic power; and the creation of virtual communities of individuals across all national, cultural, and political lines.

While economic integration is moving fast, creating a global economy and weakening the state's ability to control its nation economy, political fragmentation is causing the division of nation states into smaller entities that compete more and cooperate less with each other; sociocultural segmentation is working, largely unnoticed, to divide all societies into groups rather than social classes that have little in common. On the other hand, economic integration and the rise of new world economic powers is changing the balance of power and causing the center of global economic power to shift rapidly from the West to the East. Meanwhile, the creation of virtual global communities of individuals is causing cultures, particularly traditional cultures, to gradually lose their major characteristics and capacities to hold communities together.

The first transitional period in human history, which moved most ancient societies form the pre-agricultural to the agricultural civilization, took about 3,000 years to complete, because change was incremental and traveled very slowly. As a consequence, the impact of the transformation on society and its culture could not be noticed or felt by any generation. The second transitional period, which enabled many societies to move from the agricultural to the industrial age, took about 300 years to complete. Because this period was relatively short, the transformations it caused were noticeable in many parts of Europe, causing the successive generations that

176 GLOBAL ECONOMIC AND CULTURAL TRANSFORMATION

went through that period to feel the depth of change and its impact on their cultures and life conditions. It also caused the number of societies that could complete the transition and experience the industrial revolution to be limited. The third major period of transition is the one we are living today. It is expected to last about 30 years, at the end of which, around 2025, a small number of societies will have moved from the industrial to the knowledge age. Because this period is very short, almost every person in the world is able to feel the impact of change on his life conditions, as well as on the lives of others.

The Nature of Transition

Transitional periods of civilizational change are troubling times; they create doubt and cause confusion and fear, leading some people to lose their sense of direction, while encouraging others to nurture guarded optimism. They also cause many more people to feel bewildered, and lead them to seek refuge in old traditions and traditional values and religious beliefs. In the short run, the ability of values to resist change enables conservative cultural and religious forces to score some gain, but rationality and history win in the long run, causing diehard conservatives to lose and be sidelined. However, resistance to change deepens the struggle between beliefs and rationality, science, and faith, and causes societies to be divided along sociocultural lines in addition to the old socioeconomic ones. As a consequence, change becomes more disruptive of all life conditions and relationships and thus more painful.

Radical nationalism, religious fundamentalism, and cultural particularism are the major forces that usually oppose change, and because they believe that history is capable of reversing itself, they usually call for the creation of a future in the image of an imagined past that may have never existed as imagined. Due to such convictions, the only connection such conservatives have to reality is a negative one; they reject it, see no hope in it, and express readiness to use whatever power they may have to hasten its demise. Though conservatives in general tend to express belief in history and claim to accept its judgment, they have repeatedly failed to learn history's most fundamental lesson, which says that history never repeats itself. As a consequence, conservative forces are always on a collision course with history, unable to understand its logic and accept that social, cultural, and economic transformations are inevitable and irreversible.

The reaction of nationalism, ethnicity, and religious fundamentalism to the sociocultural transformations that characterize our times has caused these ideologies to become less of a liberating force and more of a bind that ties people to an outdated past, more able to limit their horizon than expand it. Meanwhile, the economic and cultural transformations caused by globalization continue to weaken the nation-state, forcing it to lose its ability to manage its economy and become more of a liability than an asset. On the other hand, ethnic aspirations are emerging as ghosts haunting the memory of the nation state, threatening its integrity and sovereignty and undermining its moral and political authority. And as transformations proceed and create uncertainty and spread fear, they cause religion to become more popular as a sanctuary for the deprived, the weak, the ignorant, and the hopeless. The ascendance of money and interests at the expense of values and ethics have, moreover, caused democracy to lose its spirit and become less able to represent the masses and less capable of responding to their legitimate needs and changing life conditions.

Meanwhile, the media, by promoting a culture of individualism, pleasure, greed, envy, and unlimited consumption is undermining the social glue that ties members of society together. Through its various entertainment programs and commercials, the media is distorting reality and making vice, immorality, drugs, and violence, not just acceptable actions, but at times respectable virtues. It is gradually destroying the essence of community and the values that served people well for countless generations—values that enabled man through trials and tribulations to make progress toward liberty, freedom, tolerance, human rights, justice, cultural diversity, and the pursuit of happiness in a just society.[1]

The Culture of Individualism

Economic and cultural transformations of recent decades have made competition a characteristic of individual and group attitudes toward most things in life, transforming individualism into a culture of selfishness and greed. "So many of the rich want to turn their backs on the poor; selfish concerns seem to displace enlightened self interest."[2] Robert Theobald says that the standard by which individualism judges what is sacred in life "is money and the only thing more sacred than money is more money."[3] Individuals are being empowered by technology and laws that emphasize individual and corporate rights, but fail to emphasize individual and corporate responsibilities.

During tribal times, the tribe represented the unit of society as well as society itself. During agricultural times, the clan, or the extended family, became the unit of traditional agricultural community as well as society. While agricultural community usually consists of a few clans, agricultural

178 GLOBAL ECONOMIC AND CULTURAL TRANSFORMATION

society consists of many communities. In the industrial age, the family replaced the clan to become the unit of community as well as society. And as the knowledge age advances, the unit of society is fast becoming the individual. This clearly indicates that the unit of society has gotten smaller with every succeeding civilization.

Within tribal societies, loyalty and responsibility are collective: the cause of the tribe is the cause of every one of its members, and the cause of each member is a tribal cause. Within agricultural societies, both loyalty and responsibility are clannish: the cause of every individual is the cause of the clan to which he belongs, and the cause of the clan is the cause of every one of its members. As a consequence, any commitment made by an individual or a family or a clan to community or society is largely voluntary, not obligatory. Within industrial societies, loyalty and responsibility are familial; the cause of each individual is the cause of his or her family, and the cause of each family is the cause of every one of its members. Consequently, any commitment made by an individual or a family to community or society is voluntary, not obligatory. As the knowledge age advances, both loyalty and responsibility are fast becoming individualistic, causing any commitment made by an individual to family or community or society or national or international cause to become strictly voluntary.

The individual of our times has become like the nomadic man of the hunter-gatherer times a lonely creature; he has almost no loyalty or attachment to any place except to the individual social unit that he represents and to which he belongs. And while his predecessor spent his entire life roaming the fields and forests and deserts looking for vegetables and fruits to collect and animals to hunt, the nomadic man of the knowledge age is spending his time roaming our global village in search of an opportunity to exploit, even if his actions come at the expense of others. While the main goal of this man is to make as much money as possible and gain as much power as attainable, his lust for both money and power drives him to often disregard business ethics, social values, the rights and feelings of other people, as well as the interests of society. And since passion and love are collective feelings shared by more than one person, the new man is on the verge of losing most intangible things that make him truly human: a man who knows how to live and love and care for others.

A culture based on individualism is as dangerous and removed from reality as any ideology the world had witnessed in the past. Since all previous ideologies have caused more pain than gain, individualism is harming society and distorting its human image. Emphasis on individual rights without equal emphasis on individual social responsibilities is undermining the value systems that nurture decency, honesty, equality, and social justice in society. As a consequence, a need is created for new values, ethics, and laws to manage a world of individuals who feel no obligation to any cause except to themselves, and have no goal except accumulating more wealth and power. "Any serious quest for a just society," wrote Roger Conner, "starts with a recognition that the values represented by rights and responsibilities are morally equal."[4] The ascendance of the law in society and emphasis on its role in defining and protecting individual rights, though indispensable to a properly functioning society, have restricted the role of ethics and values in guiding human and community relations.

In an environment of individualism, lack of social responsibility, and money worship, inequality is widening and fast becoming structural in the rich and poor states, as well as in all other states in between. "We live in a world scared by inequality," said former World Bank president James D. Wolfensohn, "Something is wrong when the richest 20 percent of the global population receive more than 80 percent of the global income... and when 2.8 billion people still live on less than $2 a day."[5] In the United States, over 16 percent of the American people lived in 2010 under the poverty line. And while over 30 million tons of food is wasted every year, millions of people sleep hungry every night; many of them sleep on the streets and under the bridges of American cities. "Each year, Americans waste 33 million tons of food. Forty percent of the food in the U.S. today goes uneaten, which means Americans are throwing out the equivalent of 165 billion dollars worth of food each year."[6]

The Reality of the Middle Class

A nomadic life organized around hunting and grazing and regulated by strict traditions and tribal customs kept the tribal society classless for tens of thousands of years. But as man developed agriculture and began to build settlements, private property appeared causing social classes to emerge slowly. Throughout that age, people were either rich or poor; there was no middle class. Religion, which was the predominant social philosophy at the time, convinced the poor to accept their lot in life; the poor were made to believe that God ordained their fortunes and position in society. Meanwhile, the poor were seen by most religions, particularly Christianity and Islam, as being closer to God and morally and spiritually superior to the rich. Both the rich and poor, as a result, were largely satisfied, the first having money in their pockets and slaves to serve them at home and farm their land, the second having God on their side.

In the industrial age, both the economic conditions of life and the ways of living changed dramatically. While the position of religion in society was weakened and transformed into a social system with diminishing moral authority, new values and work ethics were introduced, enhancing labor productivity and enabling the industrious person to make and accumulate more wealth. And as science and technology advanced, and economic liberalization, freedom, and democracy spread, traditional and religious wisdom began to lose its role in society. The poor, consequently, were no longer considered closer to God, and could no longer claim moral superiority; their position eventually drifted to the point of being seen as liabilities and socially and morally inferior. But as the rich and poor were being separated by wealth and knowledge and even brick walls, a middle class emerged gradually to bridge the gap between them. However, as the economy expanded and diversified further, the socioeconomic gaps separating the three classes from one another began to widen rapidly.

While land ownership defined the line separating the rich from the poor in traditional agricultural society, income and the means to earn an income defined the lines separating all classes in the industrial society. As a consequence, the fortunes of all classes became a function of their ability to recognize and exploit the economic opportunities that industrial society was creating. However, the requirements to recognize and exploit such opportunities grew more complex, demanding capital, skills, experience, and formal and informal education. As a result, the traditional socioeconomic gaps began slowly but systematically to reflect sociocultural divides. And due to the adoption of the free market philosophy in the 1980s, the middle class began to lose income, lose power, and shrink in size. The economic shift from manufacturing to services and the changing nature of knowledge have caused opportunities open to members of the middle class to narrow drastically. A knowledge barrier, as a result, was added to the old capital and skill barriers causing upward mobility in all mature industrial Western societies to decline substantially.

People in the new knowledge age are fast becoming more materialistic and less ethical; they are no longer able to see lofty goals, except money. They fight largely on their own to win battles they often frame by themselves and target. Individuals have difficulty accepting reality; they are always on the move searching for new opportunities to exploit, new virtual relationships to forge, and new realities to shape. Most people today seek to maximize pleasure, wealth, and power, while minimizing worry, risk, and pain. As a consequence, a privileged class made up of the super-rich has emerged, poverty has increased, and the traditional middle class is being squeezed. And "out of that squeeze comes a moral crisis that makes us want to cut loose from those who are suffering,"[7] as if to say—in word and deed—every man is on his own.

Materialism, which has gradually and quietly been acquiring the role claimed by religion in agricultural society, has become the major driving force in life. People are rich and poor, not because God and religion had ordained it, but because economics and knowledge and culture have determined it. Man, consequently, is seen as the master of his own fate, and that neither God nor religion has anything to do with his lot in life. And because individualism has become the philosophy of the knowledge age, both poverty and community are no longer seen issues of particular concern to the elites that control society. Meanwhile, national cultures are being divided into subcultures, national societies are gradually disintegrating into sub-societies, and the "national interest" is fast becoming a vague concept that is hard to define or relate to.

The industrial society was the only society in history that could and did produce a credible middle class. The tribal society had one class, the agricultural society has two classes, and the knowledge society is clearly unable to sustain the middle class it has inherited from the industrial society. The middle class, therefore, must be considered an aberration in the history of societal development, hardly 150 years old. Since history never repeats itself, we need to adjust our assumptions to reflect this fact in order to understand the new reality and deal with it rationally. Even the industrializing Asian nations are not expected to emulate the Western experience and produce middle classes capable of holding society together and forcing social and political change in their favor as their European and American predecessors did. People who have middle-class incomes in a knowledge society are unable to form a middle class, because their associations and the nature of their work denies them the opportunity to develop a class consciousness; one of the major requirements for forming a social class.

People who are fortunate enough to climb the social ladder and reach a middle-class status in the new industrializing states are more likely to move to other, less developed countries where the general environment is conducive to foreign investment and join the ranks of the rich in those countries; countries they are less likely to adopt, but more likely to exploit. And since they represent foreign capital interested in making money, they are unlikely to feel an obligation to contribute to the well-being of societies they live in and benefit from. Unless economic structures and production relations within society and between societies are changed, and the rights and responsibilities of individuals and corporations and the state are reformulated to reflect justice and equality, the world is likely to witness the disappearance of the middle class by the middle of the twenty-first century.

In the fast emerging world community, the knowledge segment of the world society would, generally speaking, represent the world's upper class,

182 GLOBAL ECONOMIC AND CULTURAL TRANSFORMATION

while the industrial segment represents the world's middle class. The agricultural segment of all societies, meanwhile, would represent the world's poor, and the tribal society and the poverty-stricken people everywhere would represent the underclass of the world. The only class expected to be large enough and powerful enough to influence global change in its favor is the knowledge class, unless states intervene to ensure the well-being of the other classes. The rich are able today to use knowledge and wealth and the infomedia to falsify the consciousness of most people, corrupt politics, and buy politicians and dominate the world.

The Reality of Capitalism

Change associated with the advancement of the age of knowledge has exposed the limits of both capitalism and democracy, which form together the organizing principles of the Western industrial society. As explained earlier, capitalism was hijacked in the 1980s by the free market idea, and democracy was hijacked by money, causing capitalism to lose its capacity to build and sustain an economy capable of benefiting everyone, while leading democracy to become largely dysfunctional. The average person in the new society, especially the American society, has become subject to manipulation by the media, exploitation by the free market forces, and deception by politics and politicians. At times, one is also at the mercy of violence and the constant fear of losing his job to immigrant labor and foreign nations, which feeds racism and deepens sociocultural fragmentation of society.

The free market economy, which was advanced over the last three decades by the United States and the International Monetary Fund as the solution to every problem in society, has never been as free as claimed, and its impact on society has never been as positive and desired. Lack of adequate state regulations and oversight has caused the system to lose its efficiency and fairness. Monopoly and oligopoly practices, control of certain industries and technologies, mergers and the continuous threat of mergers, and control of credit have erected strong barriers to market entry, making the system less free and less competitive and thus unjust. Economic downsizing, consolidation, manipulation of consumers, greed and the relentless pursuit of profits make free markets dangerous and socially irresponsible. "The market economy," wrote John Kenneth Galbraith, "accords wealth and distributes income in a highly unequal, socially adverse and socially damaging fashion."[8] Financial institutions and investment banks, insurance companies, large and multinational corporations, media conglomerates, and the oil and food industries tend to escape social scrutiny, bypass ethical standards, and avoid paying their fair share of taxes.

On the other hand, corporate decisions to relocate production and service operations in foreign countries, or expand production where labor is cheap and submissive and environmental regulations are weak and permissive have fueled competition among states and workers. The desire of some states to attract as many companies as possible and be competitive has caused some of the problems produced by the early industrialization in Europe to reappear in many developed and developing states. Such problems include exploitation of child labor, trafficking in human beings, polluting the environment, wasting natural resources, and the spread of slums and ghettoes. In a poor though thriving country like India, labor has become largely disposable. Workers are often exploited until their utility is exhausted; then they are abandoned to live in filth and die of hunger and disease. Meanwhile, income inequality and sociocultural diversity are causing upward mobility to become difficult and often morally hazardous.

Equality of opportunity, which was promoted as an alternative to the utopian concept of total equality in society, can neither help the poor nor can it protect the needy. Michael Young argued in 1958 in *The Rise of the Meritocracy* that equal opportunity serves to divide society into two groups. One is capable of seizing the opportunity offered to it, the other is incapable of doing so. Because of its inability, the second group finds itself moving downward and forming a lower, largely poor and neglected class. But unlike any other lower class in history, this class is neither enslaved nor oppressed, nor exploited, not even officially excluded. It is rather free yet excluded, has opportunities yet poor, lives in an open society yet cannot move upward on the social ladder. It is, as a result, permanently left behind, deprived even of a cause to rally around.

Since the formation of this lower class is not the result of certain actions taken by the state, its conditions cannot be changed by state action only. Structural changes in the social and economic and political systems of society, as well as the culture of the poor themselves are needed to make it possible for members of this class to move upward and be included. The association of knowledge with wealth and wealth with power in the new society is probably the single most important factor contributing to keeping this class permanently poor and excluded.

People with knowledge, that is people with the right education and the right attitudes, have the capability to seize opportunities, make more money, and move upward; they even have the capability to create new opportunities for themselves and for others to exploit. Moreover, people with money have the resources to acquire the right knowledge and get access to the power centers and expand the range of opportunities open

GLOBAL ECONOMIC AND CULTURAL TRANSFORMATION

to them. In contrast, people with neither wealth nor the right education are left behind, with nothing to enable them to compete in an increasingly complex world, where knowledge has become very important for making a decent living and gaining social recognition. "During this period of increasing income inequality, the value of a four-year college degree has dramatically increased. Those with one have continued to move ahead; those without one have fallen further behind."[9] Since equality of opportunity is not enough to facilitate social mobility, democracy cannot claim that it leads to a just society. "Gross inequality in wealth is itself a social evil, which poisons life for millions,"[10] and causes them to lose faith in democracy and pushes them toward apathy and despair.

Intellectuals and the Poor

In most cases in the past, voices representing the poor and the dispossessed emerged and gained public recognition and led often to alleviating the suffering of poor people. This was possible because societies were small, ethics were strong, and the misery of the poor was noticeable and intolerable. But due to the growth of populations and urban centers, and the rising walls and social barriers separating the rich from the poor, reaching the poor and knowing their life conditions have become more difficult. Meanwhile, giving the poor the opportunity to explain their situation and needs and present their demands has become subject to getting access to the mass media. But access to such media is increasingly becoming more difficult due to the prohibitive cost of media time and the exclusive culture of the media's owners and managers, causing the poor to be neglected and largely forgotten.

On the other hand, the ideas of dissenting intellectuals who have traditionally defended the rights of the poor have largely been curtailed by the media, forcing them to move within closed circles. The ideas of the rich and powerful, in contrast, have become prominent, coloring every society's outlook and influencing everyone's views of life and the other. As a result, dissenting voices are being forced to adopt an attitude and develop a vocabulary that expresses more rejection than constructive engagement. In fact, forces of rejectionism everywhere, on the left and right, in the rich and poor countries, seem today, as they have been throughout history, to be more aware of what they stand against, but less sure of what they stand for.

Intellectuals are individuals who have enough knowledge to understand what is going on in society and enough awareness to know where society is heading and what are the major obstacles it is facing and problems it is creating. Because of this knowledge and awareness, intellectuals usually

A WORLD IN TRANSITION **185**

express commitment to defending the rights of the disadvantaged and the needs of future generations. Foucault says,

> For a long period, the 'left' intellectual spoke and was acknowledged the right of speaking in the capacity of master of truth and justice. He was heard, or purported to make himself heard, as the spokesman for the universal. To be an intellectual meant something like being the conscious of us all. So the intellectual, through his moral, theoretical and political choice, aspires to be the bearer of this universality in its conscious, elaborated form.[11]

Nevertheless, the ever-widening sociocultural gaps in society, along with the tendency of intellectuals to associate themselves with like-minded individuals who often belong to the middle and upper middle classes, have caused intellectuals to be separated from the poor and the majority of the masses by culture, lifestyle, and language. The life experiences of the two groups are growing increasingly divergent, making communications between them more difficult day by day. This causes miscommunications and mutual mistrust to spread and deepen, and allows demagogues and ideologues to exploit the fears and needs of the masses and the poor, radicalize some and convince others to accept their lot in life and be content. While the masses and the poor are increasingly getting more doubtful of the honesty of intellectuals in general, intellectuals are increasingly getting more suspicious of the rationality of the masses in particular. This leaves the masses and the poor with no enlightened leadership they can understand and trust, and leaves intellectuals without a big cause to fight for. Whatever intellectuals do for the world's poor today is done by largely marginalized intellectuals who have neither money nor power; only a tortured conscience that refuses to let them sleep comfortably.

Helping the poor in pre-industrial times was very useful to the rich; it enabled them to atone for their sins and feel closer to God in a deeply religious environment. Helping the poor in the industrial age was also useful to the rich, particularly to owners and managers of large businesses; it enabled them to show generosity and social responsibility, and gain recognition and popularity in a nationalistic environment. In knowledge society where individualism reigns supreme and ideology is dying, and where globalism and money is the new frame of reference, helping the poor has become of no particular use to the rich. And because the poor can be isolated and are being isolated everywhere, they are being ignored and largely forgotten; they no longer get the attention they deserve or the compassion they need. In the not-distant past, societies used to care and give, even when their abilities to do so were limited. Today, most societies ignore the poor, even rich societies that can give without financial pressure.

A Future Global Outlook

Social issues such as justice, freedom, human rights, and equality of opportunity are no longer domestic issues any state can address on its own. They are issues that can be addressed only through international cooperation and global institutions. Today, every national problem, every national goal, and every challenge facing a nation, or even a multinational corporation, has an international dimension to it. Therefore, every political, economic, and security actor needs to think globally as he plans and acts locally. Otherwise, all such actors will fail to find long-lasting solutions to problems facing their societies and the world and create a space in which people can pursue their goals and realize their aspirations.

Throughout history, knowledge has been more spiritual than materialistic, more liberal than conservative, more pluralistic than ideological. Because of such characteristics, knowledge has played a constructive role in helping the poor and the needy, solving social and economic problems, causing change and making progress, and predicting future challenges and preparing societies to face them. However, the bulk of knowledge in the new age is more materialistic than anything else; it is composed primarily of technological knowledge and information and computer programs. And while technological knowledge has high economic returns that reinforce materialism in the form of greed and consumerism, information is vulnerable to manipulation by the media and other social actors to suit every strain of thought and business concerns. As a consequence, knowledge and the knowledge elite are increasingly becoming less committed to causes that intellectuals and thinkers of the recent past had fought for. Intellectuals and thinkers need, therefore, to become more conscious of the changing nature of knowledge as well as the evolving socioeconomic circumstances in order to address the daunting challenges of tomorrow.

Non-governmental organizations promoting respect for human rights and the protection of the environment, and others struggling to empower the world's uneducated and often enslaved men and women will be under great pressure to keep up with the deteriorating conditions of the world's poor. The United States, despite being the only superpower, is unlikely to succeed in solving its major domestic and international problems because politics is controlled by money and money is concentrated in the hands of small and ruthless global elite out to enrich itself at the expense of everyone and every issue. As members of this elite gain more knowledge, they acquire extra wealth and power and become more class-conscious, more ruthless, and self-centered.

A WORLD IN TRANSITION **187**

For example, as most American corporations were reducing their labor forces following the 2008 financial crisis, compensations of executives were increasing at astronomical rates.

> Compensation for senior executives, especially CEOs, has climbed to levels that strike many as excessive under almost any circumstances, [causing] the gap between the boss and workers [to stretch] to levels that many find difficult to comprehend. The Institute for Policy Studies estimated that the average CEO earned about 319 times more than the average worker in 2008, compared to a multiple of 42 in 1980. The sums paid to executives on Wall Street are greater still.[12]

The New York Times reported in 2012 that "nearly half of all revenue on Wall Street is earmarked for [executive] compensation."[13]

The transition from the industrial to the knowledge age is causing the four processes of societal transformation to become more active and disruptive of all systems. Today, the sociocultural process is contributing more to social segmentation and competition than to harmony and cohesiveness; the political process is contributing more to political fragmentation and conflict than to unity and peace; the economic process is contributing more to concentrating wealth in fewer hands than to narrowing the income and wealth gaps in society ; and the infomedia process is contributing more to falsifying the consciousness of the masses than to informing and educating them. The change instigated by these processes and the way they are managing domestic and international affairs are creating countless reasons to provoke conflict and radicalism, and equally countless reasons to contain conflict and accommodate change. The new world, consequently, is expected to live, not only in a perpetual state of transition, but, strangely enough, in a largely constant state of balance.

Therefore, every society is expected to change but without being able to transform itself by itself or according to its wishes. Attempts to carry out social revolutions are unlikely to succeed because of the conflicting interests of the thousands of players participating in the global game. Sociocultural and socioeconomic transformations can no longer be initiated by individual leaders, groups, or political parties alone, and the state is increasingly becoming less able to do so. This simply means that change and conflict, peace and war, economic growth and stagnation have become global issues requiring cooperation at the international level.

Many developing states are expected to experience more conflict than peace because ethnicity, nationalism, religion, and authoritarianism are fighting for survival. However, future wars are expected to be short, unless foreign powers intervene to protect old interests or to promote new ones.

188 GLOBAL ECONOMIC AND CULTURAL TRANSFORMATION

Nevertheless, serious civil and regional wars are likely to be limited in scope and duration because the great powers and the global economic elite will not allow such wars to escalate beyond control or last very long. In addition, the changing nature and requirements of war is making it very difficult even for a superpower to fight a long, protracted war; the cost of such wars in human and economic terms and lost opportunities has become prohibitive, while the chances of success have become less probable.

The real war that will be waged in the coming years with passion is a war of ideas: a war between ideology and liberalism, between religion and science, and between alternative sociopolitical and socioeconomic systems. The nature and intensity of this war will determine the pace of transforming the old world order into a new one as well as which model of socioeconomic organization will win the hearts and minds of most peoples. The five major international organizations, the United Nations, the World Bank, the International Monetary Fund, the World Trade Organization, and NATO are expected to play a significant role in debating alternative economic and security systems and determining the choices to be made.

By the time the knowledge age becomes a reality around 2025, ten major players are expected to emerge as global powers to shape and manage the new world orders. Seven of these players are expected to be industrial and largely knowledge states sharing influence, power, and wealth. They are the United States, the European Union, China, Russia, Japan, India, and Brazil. As for the other three global players, they are expected to be nongovernmental organizations working in the public sphere and having conflicting interests and different goals to pursue; they are the United Nations and its affiliate organizations and agencies, the multinational corporation, and the global civil society organizations working to help the poor, empower the powerless, promote freedom, defend human rights, and protect the environment.

The world is witnessing today a shift of economic power from the West to the East, causing the global balance of power to change drastically and irreversibly. A new balance based more on economic power and less on military power is expected to emerge in the near future, giving the multinational corporation a lot of leverage to advance its interests at the expense of the nation state and most peoples. For example, more than half of the largest 100 economies today are corporations, not states; for example, the market value of Apple exceeds the combined GDPs of the North African Arab states of Algeria, Libya, Morocco, Mauritania, and Tunisia by more than $100 billion. So as the major economic powers compete for economic advantages, they will struggle to tame the multinational corporations and the global civil society organizations.

On the other hand, problems related to poverty and social justice, freedom and human rights, extremism and racism, conflict resolution and peacemaking, as well as environmental concerns are expected to persist, causing global civil society organizations to grow and become more active and assertive. Meanwhile, the relative decline of the state's ability to deal with the many issues and multifaceted challenges at home and abroad is expected to force the great powers to strengthen the UN, not only as a forum to present their views and air their grievances, but also as a mechanism to contain conflict and deal with failing and failed states. Therefore, the UN is expected to gain more powers and assume more responsibilities, causing it to become one of the major global players. This clearly suggests that until the new world order emerges, the coming years are expected to be rather chaotic, where ordinary people and corporations and nongovernmental organizations rather than states will lead change and unconsciously determine its course and ultimate outcome, and thus influence the making of history.

Global strategic competition is expected to intensify due to the rise of several Asian and Latin American economic powers and the revival of Russia on the one hand, and the continued relative decline of the old Western powers on the other. Due to these changes, the balance of power is expected to change, and the center of economic power to shift from the West to the East. The new balance will be based more on economic power and less on military power. Nonetheless, most of the old issues and pressing problems of poverty, terrorism, extremism, racism, ethnicity, and conflict will not disappear; they will continue to occupy the time of politicians and be exploited by radicals and the media and free markets. The following are some of the trends that are expected to accelerate in the future.

Decline of ideology

Ideology in general and nationalism in particular is expected to decline further as issues of fairness, justice, human rights, environmental concerns, women rights, and poverty become common knowledge and global. These are issues capable of galvanizing conscious intellectuals, social reformers, workers, and students worldwide and motivating them to view the world as one village and its people as one extended family with the same roots, needs, fears, feelings, and expectations. Their message will probably echo what Martin Luther King once said: "Injustice anywhere is a threat to justice everywhere."

The collapse of Marxism around the year 1990 ended the age of ideological determinism, but heightened ethnicity and religious fundamentalism. Ethnicity causes national identities of people to contract and their

190 GLOBAL ECONOMIC AND CULTURAL TRANSFORMATION

traditional allegiance to the nation-state to weaken. Most people living in knowledge societies and others belonging to global cultures are increasingly becoming less attached to the nation-state and less willing to defend its often misguided zeal. In addition, no state today, especially democratic states living in the post-industrial age, is able to define its "national interest" in terms that enjoy national or even elite consensus. All states have lost the organizing principles of their foreign policies and societies. Today every state policy is being challenged on social or security or economic grounds, or because of human rights or environmental considerations.

The world's global economic and knowledge elites in general are losing their national identities and the ideologies they inherited from their parents, and, with that, the desire to fight for causes that do not concern them anymore. For example, about 40 percent of young Americans and probably a higher percentage of young Europeans say that they do not belong to any particular religion. As a consequence, the new battles are fast becoming personal rather than communal or national, and the battle grounds are mostly confined to tables situated behind closed doors in comfortable rooms equipped with computers and networks where ideas are debated, goals are defined, and strategies to achieve them are drawn away from the public eye.

Expanding globalization

Globalization is expected to continue to expand and impact the lives and destinies of peoples everywhere. Expansion is expected to go beyond economics and culture to include knowledge and education and other aspects of life. Interests, which have triumphed over values, and universal values that are about to triumph over ideological ones are linking the world's elites and young in many different ways. Interests are linking business people and corporations and pushing them to close ranks to protect their entrenched interests against the state and the public. Meanwhile, human rights and environmental concerns, and the deteriorating conditions of the world's poor are slowly linking conscious intellectuals and scientists, educators, social activists, and students and encouraging them to work harder to make our world safer, more livable, and humane. On the other hand, young people are using the social media to link together and form virtual communities that nurture varied worldviews that separate and differentiate them from their countrymen.

International cooperation

Realizing the increasing importance of economic power, the world powers are expected to devise new frameworks to coordinate policies to manage financial and economic crises and enhance mutual interests. On the other hand, the realization that international trade and foreign aid are effective tools to advance national interests is expected to encourage such powers to compete to win the hearts of the peoples and states that matter most to them, causing international relations to become more dynamic. Nevertheless, the realization that economic growth and prosperity are functions of peace and cooperation, not conflict and ideological antagonism, should make such competition moderate and largely civilized. Goals sought traditionally by military means, such as access to natural resources and foreign markets, are likely to be sought through economic means such as trade, investment, and foreign aid.

The spread of democracy

Democracy is expected to spread further and affect the attitudes of individuals and groups and the behavior of states everywhere. This development, however, will not come as a result of the accomplishments of democracy only, but due to the utter failure of the competing sociopolitical systems. However, the apparent shortcomings of the American democratic model are dampening enthusiasm among Third World intellectuals for democracy as a political system, but encouraging them to unconsciously promote democracy as a sociocultural value that calls for equality, social justice, freedom of speech and worship, tolerance, and respect for human rights. The increasing international acceptance of the democratic idea, even in states where nationalism and religion still thrive, is expected to moderate extremism, facilitate cultural interaction, and help make our world more peaceful in the long run. Democracy complicates all national decisions, especially decisions related to war; it makes elite and public consensus very difficult to reach and impossible to sustain for a prolonged period of time. And this weakens the tendency of world powers to go to war and encourages them to seek peace and accept compromise solutions to whatever problems they may have to deal with. Nevertheless, by facilitating cultural diversity, democracy tends to implicitly legitimize racism and pave the way for the revival of extreme views calling for racial purity and denial of minority rights, as the new trends in several European states indicate.

Learning the lessons of war

While wars are horrible and painful, their consequences last for generations and poison the spirits and destroy the lives of many people. Weapons that the world powers already own and others they are capable of producing can destroy our planet and all human life on it in days. Winning a war, moreover, has become easier and sometimes less expensive than winning the peace that is supposed to follow. In fact, wars seldom end, even after battles stop and troops go home. The American experience in Afghanistan and Iraq proves beyond doubt that fighting an easy war does not guarantee winning a difficult peace. Moreover, since the Korean War in the 1950s, the United States has not been able to win a major war, causing military power to lose its capacity to achieve strategic objectives on its own. The exposure of the limits of military power is expected to encourage states to use diplomacy and conflict resolution tools to deal with most problems, giving the many global civil society organizations and the United Nations new opportunities to become more active and influential.

Continued decline of the American Empire

The United States' influence, which has been declining since the late 1990s, is expected to continue declining in the future and bring an end to US hegemony. America is experiencing today all the problems that caused previous empires to retreat and slowly disintegrate: poverty, crime, homelessness, racism, widening income and wealth gaps, lack of business social responsibility, greed, materialism, and loss of economic competitiveness. Politically, America is experiencing ideological polarization, decline of the middle class and its societal role, and the hijacking of politics by money; it is also experiencing war fatigue and exhaustion due to fighting unwinnable long wars. Consequently, America is no longer able to dominate the world. What keeps the rest of the world listening to what America says are the fear of American military might and the absence of another world power capable of challenging the American power. The next 10–15 years are expected to witness the end of the American empire and the slow emergence of a new balance of power shared by seven economic powers and three non-state actors, as explained earlier.

The exposure of the spying scheme on Americans and foreigners by the National Security Agency is probably the last nail in the coffin of the American Empire. The criminal insider trading cases in stocks, which the 2008 financial crisis has exposed, are likely to be replicated by trading information that NSA employees and contractors have access to. Such trading will be used to blackmail and extort innocent and not-so-innocent individuals and corporations and, consequently, spread fear, mistrust, and loss of confidence in the American state and its major institutions. This suggests that the coming decade is expected to be rather chaotic, where political and economic and sociocultural change moves in all directions without a clear sense of direction, and where people rather than states will have to lead change and determine its ultimate outcome.

The rise of China

China's population size and potential military power make its rapid economic growth a unique geopolitical phenomenon of strategic importance. "When China was poor and introverted, it posed little threat to anyone but its own people. Now its expanding economy gives it more weight and the means to strengthen its military."[14] However, no one should expect China to use military force to attack its neighbors, because using such force would hurt China's image and trade relationship with other nations and consequently its future economic prospects. The Chinese leadership that dared to deviate from communism in favor of capitalism years before the Cold War ended is more likely to be flexible when it comes to territorial claims and economic interests.

China has managed within a generation to transform itself from a vastly underdeveloped, poor country to an industrially developed nation with the second largest economy in the world, and accumulate the largest foreign currency reserves, estimated to have exceeded $3 trillion at the end of 2012. The Chinese leadership seems to realize that rigid ideology and aggressive behavior produce nothing except enmity, and that the unprecedented economic achievements it has so far accomplished were made possible because of its willingness to play by international rules whose violation carries a price. The pronouncements made frequently by Chinese officials suggest that nothing besides economics really matters to them anymore. However, China's economic power and large population and location and history would not permit it to be a mere trading state like South Korea or Taiwan for long; it will have to behave as a superpower that cares for its long-term economic and security interests.

But as China builds and modernizes its economy, it will experience deep sociocultural, socioeconomic, and sociopolitical transformations, causing some people to feel rich and free, while others feel poor and denied their legitimate rights. As a consequence, subcultures and sub-societies will appear, creating a pluralistic society and complicating the decision-making process. And as the ideological leadership shaped by the Cold War legacy disappears, many Western-educated Chinese will assume leadership roles. Interest groups will eventually be formed, causing the economic process to be strengthened at the expense of the political one. Moreover, as China becomes an integral part of the global economy, the Chinese leadership will become an integral part of the global elite that is more interested in economic cooperation and personal gain than in competition and conflict. The Chinese society, meanwhile, will have become fragmented, with little power in the hands of the nationalistic class to contemplate waging war.

194 GLOBAL ECONOMIC AND CULTURAL TRANSFORMATION

There are two wild cards in this scenario, the United States and China; how they choose to behave and pursue their perceived national interests will largely determine the fate of peace, fairness, stability, economic change, international cooperation, and the world order. And how they view each other and the world, and how they manage their relationships will affect the future of all nations. If the United States acts like a wounded wolf and China acts like an opportunistic imperial power, the Cold War will be renewed with vengeance, and the Third World will be made to pay a heavy price again. But if leaders on both sides act as rational partners that care, not only about themselves, but also about the interests of future generations, things will be much better. Let us hope that they continue to conduct themselves in a responsible way and compete, as they pursue their legitimate objectives, to win the hearts and minds of the rich and poor, the powerful and powerless everywhere.

Concluding Remarks

Today, values and ideologies for which people fought and died in the past are dying, and interests and pleasures for which people live and strive are blossoming. However, when people are left alone to live in poverty and need, and feel oppressed and denied their legitimate rights, people will have no choice but to fight for justice and dignity, and die for liberty and freedom. The spirit of revolution that swept the Arab world in 2011 and beyond proves that no nation and no culture is incapable of transformation, no authoritarian regime is able to rule forever, and no ideology will die without a fight.

The transition from the twentieth-century industrial civilization to the twenty-first-century knowledge civilization is transforming people's life conditions and ways of living and changing them fundamentally and irreversibly, as well as the assumptions that form the foundations of political, economic, and social systems. And as assumptions change, they invalidate the theories to analyze, understand, and manage those systems. Due to this transition, states are losing the organizing principles of their politics, cultures, societies, and economies. Societies are being divided along sociocultural lines that are value-oriented and largely need-related, causing the fragmentation of all cultures and societies into subcultures and subsocieties. Generally speaking, national politics are becoming the politics of subcultures and special interests, while international politics are becoming the politics of economics, trade, finance, investment, and environmental concerns. A new world is fast emerging where interests and economic advantage count much more than cultural values, traditional relationships, and national identities and loyalties.

All issues related to national security, national interest, national sovereignty, national power, national industries, and national politics are being quietly redefined and placed in different historical and global contexts. The internationalization of the world's major trade, financial, and investment markets, and the consolidation of the world's major industries in fewer hands have substantially weakened the nation-state's control over its economy. No state is able today to manage its economy on its own and seek an economic destiny that differs substantially from that of its economic partners and political rivals. For example, when the cost of servicing Greece's public debt exceeded its ability to pay in 2010, its EU partners and the IMF intervened forcefully, forcing the Greek government to implement unpopular austerity programs as a condition for saving it from bankruptcy; practically ending Greece's claim to national political and economic sovereignty.

Political separation, sociocultural fragmentation, economic and cultural globalization, and the growing influence of global civil society organizations have caused the nation state to lose much of its self-confidence and sense of purpose. Chester A. Crocker wrote,

> Not since the Napoleonic upheavals if not the peace of Westphalia [1648] have the rights of states, people, and governments been so unclear . . . what sovereign rights, if any, do governments have to prevent outsiders from telling them how to treat their people, their economies, and their environments? And what about the rights of outsiders to come to the aid of peoples victimized by actions or inactions of local governments?[1]

This clearly means that the prerogatives of the nation-state and the foundations of the world order need to be redefined.

All notions to establish a new world order seem to be based on the idea of a military balance of power between two superpowers, and the assumption that the nation-state is the primary international actor. Since such ideas and assumptions are rooted in the past, they fail to capture the magnitude of global change and appreciate its political, economic, social, and strategic consequences. For example, Paul Kennedy bases his analysis regarding the future on the assumption that "the broad trends of the past five centuries are likely to continue."[2] This is a prediction that defies not only logic but recent experience as well. The transition from the industrial age to the knowledge age has caused the historical logic of the near past to change fundamentally and irreversibly. So to base a plan on a past experience is to base it on outdated assumptions, causing the intended plan to fail and cause more harm than good.

Kennedy's thinking, which reflects near-consensus among Western strategic thinkers, misrepresents reality, and therefore it cannot produce anything but misconceptions of the future. The fact that humanity is entering a new civilizational era does not seem to have occurred to those thinkers. Since the beginning of each civilization marks the end of its predecessor and its history, it invalidates the logic of the past, causing the forces and institutions and ideas that guided the past to become part of a largely irrelevant legacy. The current economic and cultural globalization, and the information and telecommunications revolutions are causing change like no other in human history; the consequences of this change represent the most serious challenges we face today. Yet, we have no choice but to face them—a task that cannot be done unless we understand the nature of change and depict the logic of the new history in the making.

Who makes history? We, the peoples of the world, are the major force that makes history. It is our passion, our needs and fears, our values and interests, our ambitions, our love for life and others, our power of imagination, our inventions, and the dreams we entertain for a better future that make and remake history. And on our way to making history, we created societies and states and identities, and developed cultures and economies and technologies to tame nature and make it more responsive to our needs and desires. And with the help of the environment, we invented religions and gods, ghosts and magic, ideologies and false promises, and built states and empires, allowing them to control our lives and limit our freedom to utilize our creativity and imagination to nourish our humanity. We also caused the evolvement of the societal processes of transformation to coordinate our activities and fulfill our desires and manage the many aspects of our lives.

The chaotic situation created by the transition from the industrial age to the knowledge age, while causing the state and other social actors to lose control, it creates a space for creativity, freedom, initiative, and innovation. As a consequence, the transition gives us, the people of the world, a historical opportunity to work together to make our own history and create a new peaceful, just, and prosperous future for all. Our national and global civil society organizations are challenged to guide us through this transition, because our cultures, states, and ideologies are unable to do so. In fact, old cultural values and traditions, outdated ideologies and ideas, and failed and failing states should not be allowed to shape our future; they are only able to create a future in the image of a dead past. But for national and global civil society organizations to do what they must do to help us create a better world for all, they need to commit themselves to the basic principles of honesty, decency, and humanity; they need to

1. Commit themselves to meeting the needs of all inhabitants of our global village, not just the needs of certain groups or states;
2. Realize that development is a comprehensive societal process that includes political and bureaucratic reform, social change, cultural transformation, economic restructuring, environmental protection, technological innovation, freedom, and social justice;

198 GLOBAL ECONOMIC AND CULTURAL TRANSFORMATION

3. Promote democracy, not just as a political system, but, more importantly, as a cultural value that acknowledges cultural diversity and strives to achieve equality of rights and responsibilities;
4. Stay away from all ideologies, because every ideology discriminates against people who do not adhere to its tenets and works unconsciously to deepen enmity and hatred; and
5. Commit themselves to denying cover to all spies, particularly great powers' spies, because every spy violates the rights of people he infiltrates and tends to hurt many of them to advance his and her often criminal career.

The life we live is the time we spend enjoying what we love doing in life; the rest is a waste of life. The past is the moment we just left behind dying of old age, while worrying about its legacy. The present is what we experience in everyday life, while trying to tame some challenges, enjoy others, and remake many more to meet our needs and fulfill our desires. The future is what we dream of having the next day in the morning. And history is what we make of our life as we live, love, cry, sing, dance, read, learn, think, work, build, destroy, imagine, and dream. Knowledge is the tool we have to have to transform reality and overcome the pain of failure and poverty, plant the seeds of success and enjoyment, and make all dreams come true. Transformation is the continuous process of questioning our traditions, attitudes, ideas, ways of thinking, convictions, and the wisdom of yesterday. And culture is what makes us human, able to live with one another and love each other, as we struggle together to transform our world and make history .

Notes

1 A View of History

1. Edward Hallett Car, *What Is History* (Vintage Books, 1961) 28
2. Gertrude Himmelfarb, *On Looking into the Abyss* (Vintage Books, 1994) 134
3. Himmelfarb, 134
4. William Dray, *Perspectives on History* (Routledge and Kegan Paul, 1980) 9
5. Dray, 11
6. Dray, 11
7. Michel Foucault, *The Foucault Reader*, Paul Rabinow, editor (Vintage Books, 2010) 54
8. Robert Reich, *The Washington Post*, April 5, 2000, E2
9. Richard Rubenstein, "Unanticipated Conflict and the Crisis of Social Theory," in John Burton and Frank Dukes, editors, *Conflict: Readings in Management and Resolution* (St. Martin's Press, 1990) 316–321
10. John A. Garraty and Peter Gay, editors, *The Columbia History of the World* (Harper & Row, 1972) 35–48
11. Hugh Thomas, *World History* (HarperCollins, 1979) 475
12. John A. Garraty and Peter Gay, *The Columbia History of the World,* 35–48
13. *Webster's Encyclopedic Unabridged Dictionary of the English Language,* 270
14. *Webster's Encyclopedic Dictionary*, 353
15. Constantine Zurayk, "Culture and the Transformation of Arab Society," in *The Arab Future: Critical Issues*, Michael Hudson, editor (Georgetown University, 1979) 17
16. Thomas Sowell, *Race and Culture* (Basic Books, 1994) 10
17. Michael Naumann, "A Dialogue of Culture," *Deutschland*, June/July 2000, 3
18. Jack Weatherford, *Savages and Civilization*; (Ballantine Books, 1994) 45
19. Howard Bloom, *The Lucifer Principle* (The Atlantic Monthly Press, 1995) 223–233

2 Stages of Societal Development

1. Jared Diamond, *Guns, Germs and Steel: The Fate of Human Societies*, (W.W. Norton, 1999) 92
2. Charles Van Doren, *A History of Knowledge* (Ballantine Books, 1991) 263

200 NOTES

3. Rogers and Teixeira, "America's Forgotten Majority," *The Atlantic Monthly,* June 2000, 68
4. John A. Garraty and Peter Gray, *The Columbia History of the World,* (Harper & Row, 1972) 23
5. Diamond, *Guns, Germs and Steel,* 92
6. Jack Weatherford, *Savages and Civilization* (Ballantine Books, 1994) 46
7. Weatherford, *Savages and Civilization,* 49
8. Garraty and Gay, *The Columbia History of the World,* 52
9. Weatherford, *Savages and Civilization* 50–51
10. Weatherford, *Savages and Civilization,* 26
11. Fukuyama, "The Great Disruption," *The Atlantic Monthly,* May 1999, 56
12. Marx and Engels, *The Communist Manifesto,* 51
13. David S. Landes, *The Wealth and Poverty of Nations* (W.W. Norton & Company, 1999) 328
14. Curt Suplee, "Imagine This," *The Washington Post,* January 2, 2000, B1
15. Quoted in Ohmae, *The End of the Nation State* (The Free Press, 1995) 10

3 Processes of Societal Transformation

1. Quoted by David Broder, "Frontline Exercise in Exaggeration," *The Washington Post,* January 31 , 1996, A23
2. Lester C. Thurow, "Building Wealth," *The Atlantic Monthly,* June 1999, p. 63
3. Broder, "Frontline Exercise in Exaggeration," *Washington Post,* January 31, 1996, p. A23
4. Hugh Thomas, *World History,* 232
5. Garraty and Gay, *The Columbia History of the World,* 729
6. Hugh Thomas, *World History,* 369
7. Richard Harwood, "Thinking Small," *The Washington Post,* March 25, 1994, A23
8. Richard Harwood, "A Loss of Nerve in the News Business," *The Washington Post,* November 2, 1995
9. Ariel Rosenblum, "Digital Knowledge," *Civilization,* April/May 2000, 54
10. Kenichi Ohmae, *The End of the Nation State,* 30
11. Ohmae, *The End of the Nation State,* 30
12. Lester Thurow, "Building Wealth," *The Atlantic Monthly,* June 1999, 46

4 Social Transformation

1. John A. Garraty and Peter Gay, editors, *The Columbia History of the World,* 40
2. John Kenneth Galbraith, *The Good Society* (Houghton Mifflin, 1996) 12
3. Curt Suplee, "Imagine This," *The Washington Post,* January 2, 2000, B1
4. Samuel P. Huntington, *The Clash of Civilizations and the Remaking of World Order* (Simon & Schuster, 1996) 51

NOTES **201**

5. Robert Lopez, cited by Norman Pounds, *An Economic History of Medieval Europe* (Longmans, 1974) 104
6. Garraty, *The Columbia History of the World,* 24–6
7. Hugh Thomas, *World History,* 121
8. Peter F. Drucker, "The Age of Social Transformation," *The Atlantic,* November 1998, 54
9. Drucker, 56
10. Drucker, 59
11. Thomas Hylland Eriksen, *Ethnicity and Nationalism* (Pluto Press, 1993) 68
12. Drucker, 62
13. Drucker, 68
14. Eriksen, *Ethnicity and Nationalism,* 8
15. Eric Schlosser, "The Prison-Industrial Complex," *The Atlantic Monthly,* December 1998
16. Natasha Lennard, "America's incarceration rates are highest in the world," *Salon.com*, October 15, 2012 http://www.salon.com
17. Hugh Thomas, *World History,* 462

5   Agents of Historical Change

1. Georg Wilhelm Friedrich Hegel, *The Philosophy of History* (Dover, 1936) 19

6   Theories of World History

1. See Francis Fukuyama, *The End of History* (The Free Press, 1992) 59–69
2. Georg Wilhelm Friedrich Hegel, *The Philosophy of History* (Dover Publications, 1936) 23
3. Hegel 19
4. Hegel 6
5. Hegel 36
6. Hegel 17
7. Hegel 19
8. Lewis S. Feuer, editor. *Marx and Engels: Basic Writings on Politics and Philosophy* (Anchor Books, 1959) 43
9. Feuer, 43
10. Feuer, 44
11. Feuer, 265
12. Fukuyama, *The End of History*, 64
13. Fukuyama, 62
14. Feuer, 262
15. Feuer, 263
16. William Dray, *Perspectives on History* (Routledge & Kegan Paul, 1980) 102
17. Dray, 102
18. Dray, 121

202 NOTES

19. Dray, 103
20. Jerome Blum, Rondo Cameron, and Thomas Barnes, *The European World* (Little Brown, 1966) 398.
21. John Patrick Diggens, *Max Weber, Politics, and the Spirit of Tragedy* (Basic Books, 1996) 21
22. Blum, 739
23. Walter Kaufman, editor. *Friedrich Nietzsche on the Genealogy of Morals* (Vintage Books, 1967) 320
24. Diggens, 125
25. Diggens, 73
26. Diggens, 73
27. Diggens, 280
28. M. Mitchell Waldrop, *Complexity: The Emerging Science at the Edge of Order and Chaos* (Simon & Schuster, 1992) 9–13
29. Mohamed Rabie, *Conflict Resolution and Ethnicity* (Praeger Publishers, 1994), 200
30. Diggens, 125
31. Diggens, 125

7 The Train of Time

1. Robert D. Kaplan, *An Empire Wilderness* (Random House, 1998) 4
2. Jack Weatherford, *Savages and Civilization* (Ballantine Books, 1994) 50
3. Weatherford, *Savages and Civilization*, 50
4. Fukuyama, *The End of History* (The Free Press, 1992) 39

8 Ideology and History

1. Mohamed Rabie, *Conflict Resolution and Ethnicity* (Praeger Publishers, 1994) 8–12
2. Robert D. Kaplan, "The Return of Ancient Times," *The Atlantic Monthly,* June 2000, 16
3. World in Brief, *The Washington Post*, September 4, 1999
4. Hugh Thomas, *World History,* Harper Collins, 1979, 29
5. Thomas, *World History*, 32
6. Alive and Well, A special Report, *The Economist*, July 28, 2010
7. Huston Smith, The *Religions of Man* (Harper and Row, 1972) 58
8. Karen Armstrong, *A History of God* (Ballantine Books, 1993) 27
9. John Patrick Diggens, *Max Weber: Politics and the Spirit of Tragedy* (Basic Books, 1996)106
10. Smith, *The Religions of Man*, 86
11. Thomas, *World History,* 151
12. John A. Garraty and Peter Gay, editors, *The Columbia History of the World* (Harper and Row, 1972) 69

13. Georg Wilhelm Friedrich Hegel, *The Philosophy of History* (Dover, 1936) 215
14. Garraty, *The Columbia History of the World*, 63
15. Garraty, *The Columbia History of the World,* 727
16. Diggens, *Max Weber: Politics and the Spirit of Tragedy,* 106–8
17. Herbert Heaton, *Economic History of Europe* (Harper and Row, 1958) 217
18. Garraty, *The Columbia History of the World*, 731
19. Garraty, *The Columbia History of the World,* 725
20. Garraty, *The Columbia History of the World,* 727
21. Garraty, *The Columbia History of the World,* 586
22. Lenichi Ohmae, *The End of the Nation State* (The Free Press, 1995) 16
23. See Francis Fukuyama, *The End of History* (The Free Press, 1992) 59–69
24. Sophie Bessis, From Social Exclusion to Social Cohesion: A Policy Agenda (UNESCO, 1995) 13
25. Harvey Cox, "The Market as God," *The Atlantic Monthly,* March 1999, 18
26. Quoted in Michael Nicholson, *Rationality and the Analysis of International Conflict* (Cambridge University Press, 1991) 10
27. Van Doren, *A History on Knowledge*, 242
28. Diggens, *Max Weber: Politics and the Spirit of Tragedy,* 106
29. Thomas, *World History*, 188
30. George F. Kennan, *Around the Gagged Hill* (W.W. Norton, 1993) 93

9   Cultural Determinism

1. Chester A. Crocker, "The Global Law and Order Deficit," *The Washington Post,* December 20, 1992, A21
2. Kenichi Ohmae, *The End of the Nation State* (The Free Press, 1995) 97
3. Crocker, "The Global Law and Order Deficit," *The Washington Post,* December 20, 1992, A21
4. Francis Fukuyama, *Trust: The Social Virtues & the Creation of Prosperity* (The Free Press, 1995) 12
5. Fukuyama, *Trust,* 84
6. Jim Hoagland, "All Globalization is Local," *The Washington Post,* August 28, 1997, A21
7. Lester Thurow, "Building Wealth," *The Atlantic Monthly,* June 1999, 63
8. Samuel P. Huntington, *The Clash of Civilizations* (Simon & Schuster, 1996) 125
9. Huntington, *The Clash of Civilizations,* 125
10. Fukuyama, *Trust,* 5–6
11. Thomas Sowell, *Race and Culture* (Basic Books, 1994) 231
12. Huntington, 28
13. Howard Bloom, *The Lucifer Principle* (The Atlantic Monthly Press, 1995) 223
14. Huntington, 217
15. Huntington, 183
16. Huntington, 206
17. Huntington, 304
18. Huntington, 232

204 NOTES

19. Bloom, 238
20. MinuteMenNews, "Intelligence Report Strips US of Sole Superpower Status," December 16, 2012, http://minutemennews.com/2012/12/intelligence-report-strips-us-of-sole-superpower-status/
21. Karen Armstrong, *Jerusalem* (Alfred A. Knopf, 1996) 228
22. Armstrong, *Jerusalem*, 229
23. Armstrong, *Jerusalem*, 239
24. Armstrong, *Jerusalem*, 274
25. David Gilmore, "The 1948 Exodus," *Middle East International*, November 1986, 16
26. Gilmore, "The 1948 Exodus," *Middle East International*, November 1986, 16
27. Bogdan Denitch, "Tragedy in Former Yugoslavia," *Dissent*, Winter 1993, 28
28. Denitch, "Tragedy in Former Yugoslavia," 31
29. Samuel Huntington, "*The Clash of Civilizations*," 20
30. Huntington, 130
31. Fukuyama, *Trust*, 26
32. Fukuyama, *Trust*, 33
33. David S. Landes, *The Wealth and Poverty of Nations* (W.W. Norton, 1999) 516
34. Thomas Sowell, *Race and Culture*, 10
35. Fukuyama, *Trust*, 84
36. Georg Wilhelm Friedrich Hegel, *The Philosophy of History* (Dover Publications, 1936) 131
37. Lester Thurow, "Building Wealth," 57

10 A World in Transition

1. Ismail Serageldin, "Science and Technology and the Arab World Today," *Al-Muntada*, June 2000, 14
2. William Raspberry, "Market Idolatry," *The Washington Post*, April 10, 1998, A23
3. Quoted by Raspberry, "Market Idolatry," A23
4. Roger I. Conner, "Total Equality Debate," *The New Republic*, August 23–30, 1993, 4
5. William Drozdiak and Steven Pearlstein, "Protesters Paralyze Prague," *The Washington Post*, September 27, 2000, A16
6. The Ugly Truth about Food Waste in America, the National Public Radio, September 24, 2012, 1 PM
7. Raspberry, "Market Idolatry"
8. John Kenneth Galbraith, *The Good Society* (Houghton Mifflin, 1996) 60
9. Joel Rogers and Ruy Teixeira, "America's Forgotten Majority," *The Atlantic Monthly*, June 2000, 69
10. Steven Weinberg, "Utopias," *The Atlantic Monthly*, June 2000, 109
11. Michel Foucault, *The Foucault Reader*, (Vintage Books, 2010) Paul Rabinow, editor, 67
12. An American Perspective—Corporate Compensation is an Ethical Issue, "Still Pay to be on Wall Street", *New York Times*, October 10, 2012

13. http://www.ethicsworld.org/corporategovernance/executivecompensation.php
14. Robert Samuelson, "The Next Evil Empire," *The Washington Post*, February 19, 1997, A23

Concluding Remarks

1. Chester A. Crocker, "The Global Law and Order Deficit," *The Washington Post*, December 20, 1992, A23
2. Paul Kennedy, *The Rise and Fall of the Great Powers* (Vintage Books, 1987) 439–40

Bibliography

Books

Adams, Robert, *Paths of Fire, An Anthropologist's Inquiry into Western Technology*, Princeton University Press, 1996

Adams, Michael, editor. *Islamic and European Expansion, The Forging of a Global Order*, Temple University for the American Historical Association, 1993

Alterman, Eric, *What Liberal Media?* Basic Books, 2003

Anderson, Benedict, *Imagined Communities*, Verso, 1991

Armstrong, Karen, *A History of God*, Ballantine Books, 1993

———, *Jerusalem: One City, Three Faiths*, Alfred A. Knopf, 1996

Balaam, David and Michael Veseth, *Introduction to International Political Economy*, Prentice Hall, 2001

Banerjee V. Abhijit and Esther Duflo. *Poor Economics: A Radical Rethinking of the Way to Fight Global Poverty*, Public Affairs, 2011

Bartlett, Robert, *The Making of Europe: Conquest, Colonialism and Cultural Change 950–1350*, Penguin, 1993

Bessis, Sophie, *From Social Exclusion to Social Cohesion: A Policy Agenda*, UNESCO, 1995

Bloom, Howard, *The Lucifer Principle*, The Atlantic Monthly Press, 1995

Blum, Jerome, Rondo Cameron and Thomas Barnes, *The European World*, Little Brown & Company, 1966

Brecher, Jeremy and Tim Costello, *Global Village or Global Pillage*, South End Press, 1994

Brockway, George P. *The End of Economic Man: Principles of any Future Economics*, W.W. Norton, 1995

Bushrui, Suheil, Iraj Ayman and Ervin Laszlo, editors, *Transition to Global Society*, Oneworld Publications, 1993

Carr, Edward Hallett, *What Is History*, Vintage Books, 1961

Chase, Stewart, *The Proper Study of Mankind*, Harper & Row, 1962

Cipolla, Carlo M. *Before the Industrial Revolution: European Society and Economy 1000–1700*, W.W. Norton, 1980

Clark, Gregory, *A Farewell to Alms, A Brief Economic History of the World*, Princeton University Press, 2007

Clinton, Bill, *Between Hope and History*, Times Books, 1996

Collier, Paul, *The Bottom Billion*, Oxford University Press, 2007

208 BIBLIOGRAPHY

Cook, Michael, *A Brief History of the Human Race,* W.W. Norton, 2003

Davidson, Basil, *The Black Man's Burden: Africa and the Curse of the Nation-State,* Random House, 1992

De Blij, Harm, *Why Geography Matters,* Oxford University Press, 2012

Diamond, Jared, *Guns, Germs and Steel: The Fate of Human Societies,* W.W. Norton, 1999

————, *Collapse: How Societies Choose to Fail or Succeed,* Viking, 2005

Diamond, Stanley, *In Search of the Primitive: A Critique of Civilization,* Transaction Books, 1974

Diggens, John Patrick, *Max Weber: Politics and the Spirit of Tragedy,* Basic Books, 1996

Dionne, J.R., *Why Americans Have Politics,* Touchstone, 1991

Dray, William, *Perspectives on History,* Routledge and Kegan Paul, 1980

Easterly, William, *The White Man's Burden,* Penguin Books, 2006

Eriksen, Thomas Hylland, *Ethnicity and Nationalism,* Pluto Press, 1993

Esposito, John L., *The Islamic Threat: Myth or Reality?* Oxford University Press, 1995

Feuer, Lewis S., editor, *Marx and Engels: Basic Writings on Politics and Philosophy,* Anchor Books, 1959

Frank, Andre Gunder, *Capitalism and Underdevelopment in Latin America,* Monthly Review Press, 1967

Freeland, Chrystia, *Plutocracy,* The Penguin Press, 2012

Fukuyama, Francis, *The End of History and the Last Man,* The Free Press, 1992

————, *Trust: The Social Virtues & the Creation of Prosperity,* The Free Press, 1995

Galbraith, John Kenneth, *The Affluent Society,* The New American Library, 1958

————, *Economic Perspective: A Critical History,* Houghton Mifflin, 1987

————, *The Culture of Contentment,* Houghton Mifflin, 1992

————, *The Good Society,* Houghton Mifflin, 1996

Garraty John A. and Peter Gay, editors, *The Columbia History of the World,* Harper & Row, 1972

Gatlung John, *The True World: A Transnational Perspective,* Free Press, 1980

Gellner, Ernest, *Plough, Sword and Book: The Structure of Human History,* Collins Harvill, 1988

Gilpin, Robert, *The Challenge of Global Capitalism,* Princeton University Press, 2000

Goldin, Ian and Kenneth Reinert, *Globalization for Development,* Palgrave, 2007

Gough, Leo, *Asia Meltdown: The End of the Miracle?* Capstone, 1998

Greenfeld, Liah, *Nationalism: Fire Roads to Modernity,* Harvard University Press, 1992

Halliday, Fred, *Islam and the Myth of Confrontation: Religion and Politics in the Middle East,* I. B. Tauris, 1996

Hardt, Michael and Antonio Negri, *Empire,* Harvard University Press, 2000

Harrison, Lawrence E. and Samuel Huntington, editors, *Culture Matters; How Values Shape Human Progress,* Basic Books, 2000

Hawking, Stephen W., *A Brief History of Time,* Bantam Books, 1988

Hawking, Stephen and Leonard Mlodinow, *The Grand Design,* Bantam Books, 2010

Hegel, Georg Wilhelm Friedrich, *The Philosophy of History,* Dover Publications, 1936

Heaton, Herbert, *Economic History of Europe,* Harper & Row, 1958

Heilbroner, Robert,*The Making of Economic Society*, Prentice-Hall, 1968

———, *Marxism, For and Against*, W. W. Norton, 1980

———, *The Nature and Logic of Capitalism*, W. W. Norton, 1985

———, *21st Century Capitalism*, W. W. Norton, 1994

Hill, McKay, *A History of the World Societies*, Houghton Mifflin, 2000

Himmelfarb, Gertrude, *On Looking into the Abyss,* Vintage Books, 1994

Hopkins, A. G., editor, *Globalization in World History*, W. W. Norton, 2002

Hugh, Thomas, *World History,* Harper Collins, 1996

Huntington, Samuel P., *The Clash of Civilizations and the Remaking of World History,* Simon & Schuster, 1996

Jacob, Margaret C., *Scientific Culture and the Making of the Industrial West,* Oxford University Press, 1997

Kaku, Machio, *Visions: How Science Will Revolutionize the 21st Century,* Anchor Books, 1997

Kaplan, Robert, *An Empire Wilderness,* Random House, 1998

Kaufman, Walter, editor, *Friedrich Nietzsche on the Genealogy of Morals*, Vintage Books, 1967

Kennan, George, *Around the Cragged Hill,* W.W. Norton, 1993

Kennedy, Paul, *The Rise and Fall of the Great Powers,* Vintage Books, 1987

———, *Preparing for the Twenty-First Century,* Random House, 1993

Kerr, Clark, and John T. Dunlop, *Industrialism and Industrial Man*, Oxford University Press, 1964

Kissinger, Henry, *Diplomacy,* Simon & Schuster, 1994

Kriesberg, Louis, *International Conflict Resolution,* Yale University Press, 1992

Kitschelt, Herbert, Peter Lange, Gray Marks, John D. Stephens, editors, *Continuity and Change in Contemporary Capitalism,* Cambridge University Press, 1999

Korten, David, *The Post Corporate World: Life After Capitalism*, Berrett-Koehler, 2000

———, *When Corporations Rule the World*, Berrett-Koehler, 2001

———, *The Great Turning: From Empire to Earth Community*, Berrett-Koehler, 2006

———, *Agenda for a New Economy: From Phantom Wealth to Real Wealth,* Berrett-Koehler, 2009

Landes, David S., *The Wealth and Poverty of Nations,* W.W. Norton, 1999

Lewis, Bernard, *The Muslim Discovery of Europe,* W.W. Norton, 1982

Marshall, Ray, and Marc Tucker, *Thinking for a Living: Education and the Wealth of Nations,* Basic Books, 1992

Marx, Karl and Friedrich Engels, *The Communist Manifesto,* Vanguard Publications

Mernissi, Fatima, *Islam and Democracy: Fear of Modern World,* Virago, 1993

210 BIBLIOGRAPHY

Mirsky, Yehuda and Matt Ahren, editors, *Democracy in the Middle East,* The Washington Institute for Near East Policy, 1993

Nicholson, Michael, *Rationality and the Analysis of International Conflict,* Cambridge University Press, 1991

O' Conner, Anthony M., *Poverty in Africa: A Geographical Approach,* Belhaven, 1991

Ohmae, Lenichi, *The End of the Nation State,* The Free Press, 1995

Pomeranz, Kenneth, *The Great Divergence: China, Europe, and the Making of the Modern World Economy,* Princeton University Press, 2000

Pounds, Norman, *An Economic History of Medieval Europe,* Longmans, 1974

Rabie, Mohamed,, *The New World Order,* Vantage Press, 1992

————, *Conflict Resolution and Ethnicity,* Praeger Publishers, 1994

————, *The US-PLO Dialogue,* University Press of Florida, 1995

————— Saving Capitalism and Democracy, Palgrave, 2013

Rabinow, Paul, editor, *The Foucault Reader,* Vintage Books, 2010

Rapoport, Anatol, *Peace: An Idea Whose Time Has Come,* University of Michigan Press, 1992

Reich, Robert B., *After-Shock,* Alfred A. Knopf, 2010

Rodrik, Dani, *The Globalization Paradox,* W. W. Norton, 2011

Rubenstein, Richard, "Unanticipated Conflict and the Crisis of Social Theory," in John Burton and Franks Dukes, editors, *Conflict: Readings in Conflict Management and Resolution.* St. Martin's Press, 1990

Schlesinger, Arthur, Jr., *The Coming of the New Deal,* Houghton Mifflin, 1958

————, The *Disuniting of America,* W.W. Norton, 1992

Schumpeter, Joseph A., *Capitalism, Socialism and Democracy,* Harper Brothers, 1950

Sen, Amartya, *Development as Freedom,* Anchor Books, 1999

Sharabi, Hisham, *Nationalism and Revolution in the Arab World,* Van Nostrand Company, 1966

Sorkin, Andrew Ross, *Too Big to Fail,* Viking, 2009

Smith, Huston, *The Religions of Man,* Harper & Row, 1972

Sowell, Thomas, *Race and Culture,* Basic Books, 1994

Spence, Michael, *The Next Convergence,* Picador, 2011

Stiglitz, Joseph, *Globalization and Its Discontents,* W. W. Norton, 2003

————, *Making Globalization Work,* W.W. Norton, 2006

————, *Freefall, America, Free Markets, and the Sinking of the World Economy,* W. W. Norton and Company, 2010

————, *The Price of Inequality,* W. W. Norton and Company, 2012

Thomas, Hugh, *World History,* Harper Collins, 1979

Thurow, Lester, *Fortune Favors the Bold,* HarperCollins Publishers, 2003

Thompson, W. Scott, Kenneth M. Jensen, Richard N. Smith, Kimber M. Schraub, editors, *Approaches to Peace,* United States Institute of Peace, 1992

Toffler, Alvin and Heidi, *Creating a New Civilization: The Politics of the Third Wave,* The Progress and Freedom Foundation, 1994

Trevor Roper, H. R. *Religion, the Reformation and Social Change,* Macmillan, 1967

Van Doren, Charles, *A History of Knowledge,* Ballantine Books, 1991

Waldrop, Mitchell M., *Complexity: The Emerging Science at the Edge of Order and Chaos,* Simon & Schuster, 1992

Wallerstein, Immanuel, *Geopolitics and Geoculture,* Cambridge University Press, 1991

Weatherford, Jack, *Savages and Civilization,* Ballantine Books, 1994

———, *Genghis Khan and the Making of the Modern World,* Three Rivers Press, 2004

Wei-Ming, Tu, editor, *Confucian Traditions in East Asian Modernity: Moral Education and Economic Culture in Japan and the Four Mini-Dragons,* Harvard University Press, 1996

Articles

"A Loss of Nerve in the News Business," *The Washington Post*, November 2, 1995

An American Perspective—Corporate Compensation is an Ethical Issue, http://www.ethicsworld.org/corporategovernance/executivecompensation.php

Chester A. Crocker, "The Global Law and Order Deficit," *The Washington Post,* December 20, 1992, A21

David Broder, "Frontline in Exaggeration," *The Washington Post,* January 13, 1996

Diana Johnstone, "After Socialism's Debacle," *World Policy Journal,* Summer, 1991, 523

Edwin M. Joder, Jr. "Tele-Tunnel-Vision," *The Washington Post,* February 14, 1993

Eric Schlosser, "The Prison-Industrial Complex," *The Atlantic Monthly,* December 1998

George Soros, "Toward a Global Open Society," *The Atlantic Monthly*, January 1998

Ismail Serageldin, "Science and Technology and the Arab World Today," *Al-Muntada*, June 2000, 14

Jim Hoagland, "All Globalization is Local," *The Washington Post,* August 28, 1997

Joel Rogers and Ruy Teixeira, "America's Forgotten Majority," *The Atlantic Monthly,* June 2000

Lester Thurow, "Building Wealth," *The Atlantic Monthly,* June 1999

Michael Naumann, "A Dialogue of Culture," *Deutschland,* June/July 2000

MinuteMenNews, "Intelligence Report Strips US of Sole Superpower Status," December 16, 2012, http://minutemennews.com/2012/12/intelligence-report-strips-us-of-sole-superpower-status/

Natasha Lennard, "America's Incarceration Rates are Highest in the World," *Salon.com*, October 15, 2012, http://www.salon.com

Peter F. Drucker, "The Age of Social Transformation," *The Atlantic Monthly*, November 1998

Richard Harwood: "Thinking Small," *The Washington Post*, March 25, 1994

Robert Reich, *The Washington Post*, April 5, 2000

Robert Samuelson, "The Next Evil Empire," *The Washington Post,* February 19, 1997

Roger I. Conner, "Total Equality Debate," *The New Republic*, August 23–30, 1993, 4

Ariel Rosenblum, "Digital Knowledge," *Civilization,* April/May 2000

Steven Weinberg, "Utopias," *The Atlantic Monthly,* June 2000

" Still Pay to be on Wall Street", *New York Times*, October 10, 2012

212 BIBLIOGRAPHY

The Ugly Truth about Food Waste in America, the National Public Radio, September 24, 2012, 1 PM

William Raspberry, "Market Idolatry," *The Washington Post*, April 10, 1998, A23

William Drozdiak and Steven Pearlstein, "Protesters Paralyze Prague," *The Washington Post*, September 27, 2000

Index

Al Akhawayn University, 8
Albanians, 163
Africa, 6, 16, 141, 142, 148, 208, 210
African, 10, 24, 25, 116, 148, 159, 160, 174, 188
Algeria, 174, 188
Alon, Yigal, 163
America, 16, 31, 37, 49, 50, 52, 57, 64, 66, 71, 116, 157, 160, 161, 168, 172, 192, 200, 201, 204, 208, 210, 211
American, 7, 8, 16, 17, 23, 30, 31, 36, 38, 52, 64, 66, 67, 70, 71, 102, 103, 116, 147, 148, 155, 156, 159, 161, 163, 164, 165, 169, 170, 171, 174, 179, 181, 182, 187, 189, 190, 191, 192, 208, 211, 212
Amsterdam, 116
Apple, 188
Aqsa, 162
Arab, 3, 37, 101, 119, 128, 139, 148, 157, 158, 159, 160, 162, 163, 164, 174, 188, 195, 199, 204, 210, 211
Arabic, 88, 132
Arabic-Islamic, 162
Arnold, Matthew, 41
Artigiani, Robert, 11
Armstrong, Karen, 133, 162, 202, 204, 207
Asia, 8, 38, 116, 141, 142, 157, 172, 208
Asian, 10, 24, 25, 30, 133, 134, 148, 156, 157, 159, 160, 172, 181, 189, 211
Australian, 24
Aztec, 28
Aztecs, 135

Babylonians, 134
Bangkok, 17
Barbarians, 119, 160, 160
Beirut, 7
Belgium, 16
Berlin Wall, 159
Bin Al-Khattab, Umar, 162
Bloom, Howard, 160, 161, 199, 203, 204, 206
Bloomberg News, 74
Bolivia, 16, 171
Book of the Dead, 134
Bosnia, 163
Bosnians, 163
Brazil, 188
British, 5, 17, 159
Burundi, 24
Byzantine, 163

Cairo, 7, 17, 172
Calcutta, 17
California, 74
Caliph, 162
Cardo Maximums, 162
Catholic Church, 63, 87, 102, 136, 139
Catholicism, 139, 162, 171
Charisma, 77
Charismatic, 77, 135
China, 5, 16, 25, 37, 38, 49, 67, 116, 129, 133, 148, 156, 157, 159, 160, 166, 171, 172, 188, 193, 194, 210
Christian, 37, 102, 133, 157, 160, 161, 163, 162, 164, 165, 166, 170, 179
Christian Crusaders, 162

214 INDEX

Christianity, 86, 98, 102, 103, 127, 133, 134, 146, 149, 160, 163
Christmas, 164
Clinton, Bill, 8, 76, 207
Cold War, 60, 146, 154, 155, 165, 193, 194
Collingwood, R.G., 5
Columbia, 18
communism, 54, 60, 89, 127, 128, 141, 146, 147, 149, 150, 152, 155, 159, 193
Confucian, 156, 157, 171
Confucianism, 133, 171
Conner, Roger, 179, 204, 211
Constantine's Martyrium, 162
Croatia, 177
Croatian, 163
Croats, 163
Cox, Harvey, 147, 203
Crocker, Chester A., 155, 196, 203, 205, 211
Crusaders, 162

Day of Judgment, 134
Denitch, Bogdan, 163, 204
Diamond, Jared, 24, 80, 91, 199, 200, 208
Drucker, Peter, 69, 201, 211

East, 17, 95, 161, 166, 175, 188, 198
Eastern Europe, 51, 156, 164
East Germany, 159
East-West, 165
Easterly, Williams, 208
Egypt, 2, 16, 25, 116, 133, 164, 171, 172
Egyptian civilization, 16, 28
Egyptian, 3, 16, 37, 53, 116, 134, 172
England, 22, 31, 37, 116, 123
Enlightenment, 18, 136
Erfurt University, 8
Eurasia, 25
Europe, 6, 8, 17, 30, 31, 35, 51, 63, 64, 83, 87, 95, 116, 117, 191, 135, 136, 139, 140, 148, 156, 165, 175, 183
European, 24, 25, 30, 31, 45, 62, 114, 116, 117, 119, 135, 137, 139, 140, 141, 142, 148, 156, 157, 157, 159, 160, 163, 169, 181, 190, 191
European Union, 158, 188

Fascism, 141
Federal Reserve, 156
Foucault, Michel, 9, 10, 109, 185, 199
France, 5, 16, 49, 74, 140, 159
Fregoso, Ottaviano, 77
French revolution, 64, 140
Freud, Sigmund, 148
Fukuyama, Francis, 9, 153, 156, 158, 167, 171, 172, 173, 200, 201, 202, 203, 204

Galbraith, John Kenneth, 59, 182, 200, 204, 208
Galilee, 163
Germanic, 92, 95
Germany, 5, 7, 8, 49, 74, 95, 116, 120, 128, 150, 163, 172
Georgetown University, 8
Ghofshi, Nathan, 162
Gibbon, Edward, 13
Glazer, Nathan, 70
Great Britain, 74
Great Recession, 69, 147, 166, 170
Greece, 95, 196
Greek, 16, 17, 92, 95, 196
Greenspan, Alan, 156
Gypsies, 142

Harwood, Richard, 52, 200, 211
Hegel, Georg, 79, 92, 94, 95, 96, 98, 99, 104, 109, 112, 116, 134, 143, 145, 172, 200
Hegelian, 94, 97, 112, 143
Herodotus, 134
Himmelfarb, Gertrude, 5, 199, 209
Hindu, 160, 170
Hinduism, 133, 134
Historical discontinuity, 9, 10, 11
Hobbes, Thomas, 140
Holland, 16
Holy City, 162
Hong Kong, 159

INDEX **215**

Hugh, Thomas, 51, 63, 199, 209
Huntington, Samuel, 153, 157, 158, 159, 160, 161, 163, 166, 200, 209

Inca, 135
India, 16, 28, 37, 38, 116, 133, 148, 183, 188
Indian, 16, 37, 157, 172
Industrial Revolution, 17, 21, 22, 23, 31, 32, 33, 35, 36, 37, 39, 49, 54, 64, 67, 87, 108, 119, 135, 156, 157, 174, 176, 207
International Monetary Fund (IMF), 165, 182, 188, 196
Iraq, 25, 159, 161, 192
Iran, 76, 116, 130, 171
Ireland, 164, 171
Islam, 86, 98, 103, 119, 127, 133, 134, 139, 146, 149, 159, 160, 162, 171, 179
Islamic civilization, 16
Islamic fundamentalism, 163
Israel, 3, 130, 159, 162, 163
Israelis, 5, 133
Italy, 62

Japan, 57, 67, 74, 171, 188
Japanese, 16, 17, 141, 158
Jena, 95
Jericho, 7
Jerusalem, 7, 162
Jews, 37, 133, 134, 139, 142, 161, 162
Jordan, 8
Judaism, 86, 98, 133, 134, 139

Kennan, George F., 152, 209
Kennedy, Paul, 31, 80, 196, 209
King, Martin Luther, 189
Kissinger, Henry, 165, 209
Kuwait, 7
Kuwait University, 7

Lagos, 17
Landes, David, 37, 167, 209
Latin American, 30, 36, 37, 58, 148, 159, 171, 174, 189

Latin language, 139
Lebanon, 174
Lenin, Vladimir, 146
Lewis, Charles, 50
Liberia, 159
Libya, 53, 188
London, 172
Luther, Martin, 102, 137

Madrid Peace Conference, 3
Malaysia, 37, 157
Manila, 17
Mao Tzu Tong, 146
Mauritania, 188
Meritocracy, 183
Martyrium, 162
Marx, Karl, 33, 36, 65, 79, 92, 94, 96, 97, 98, 99, 104, 109, 112, 140, 143, 144, 146, 167, 168, 173
Marxism, 67, 83, 96, 97, 98, 131, 143, 144, 145, 146, 189
Marxist, 83, 94, 96, 97, 102, 112, 143, 146, 159
Mayan, 135
Mexican, 16, 24
Mexico, 16, 17, 159, 171, 172
Mexico City, 17
Middle Ages, 31, 156
Middle East, 3, 8, 24, 142, 148
Morocco, 8, 16, 188
Moynihan, Daniel A., 70
Muslim, 104, 133, 139, 157, 160, 161, 162, 164, 166, 170
Mutuality of enmity, 166

Napoleonic, 196
National Intelligence Council, 161
Nationalism, 7, 37, 40, 46, 54, 67, 68, 89, 127, 128, 129, 130, 131, 136, 138, 150, 151, 152, 163, 164, 176, 187, 189
NATO, 188
Naumann, Michael, 15, 211
Nazism, 128, 141
Netherland, 74
New Guinea, 25

216 INDEX

new world, 31, 45, 137, 175, 187, 195
new world order, 188, 189, 196
New York, 172, 187
Nigeria, 164, 172
North America, 17, 30, 31, 64
North Korea, 76, 156

Obama, Barack, 161
Ohmae, Kenichi, 54, 210
Orthodox Christians, 163
Ottoman Turks, 163

Pacoma, 16
Pakistan, 159
Palestine, 25, 133, 162
Palestinians, 3
Persian, 16, 37, 88, 101, 119
petroleum society, 8
Pharoanic, 16, 134
Protestant Reformation, 35

Ramadan, 164
Reagan, Ronald, 8
Reformation, 35, 63, 101, 137, 139
Renaissance, 18, 87, 114, 136
Roman, 16, 92, 95, 119
Roman empire, 133, 158
Rome, 95, 172
Rubenstein, Richard, 11, 210
Russia, 74, 188, 189
Rwanda, 24, 159

Sadat, Anwar, 3
Saudi Arabia, 52, 76, 133, 159, 164, 171
Schlosser, Eric, 74, 211
Serbia, 128, 164
Serbian, 173
Serbs, 163
Singapore, 37, 74
Sinic, 166
social capital, 69, 167
social trust, 74, 156, 167, 169, 170, 171, 172, 174
Somalia, 24, 159, 174
Sophronius, 162
South America, 8, 16, 116

South Korea, 159, 193
Southeast Asia, 172
Southern European, 62
Soviet Union, 67, 128, 141, 146, 165
Sowell, Thomas, 158, 210
Spaniards, 139, 174
Spanish, 17, 138
Sub-Saharan Africa, 16
Sudan, 76, 174
Sweden, 163
Syria, 25, 53
synagogues, 162

Ten Commandments, 134
The Clash of Civilizations, 166, 209
Theobald, Robert, 177
Third World, 7, 17, 18, 30, 36, 37, 46, 51, 52, 53, 67, 68, 150, 165, 169, 172, 191, 194
Thurow, Lester, 57, 157, 210, 211
Tokyo, 17
Toynbee, Arnold, 100, 101, 104
traditional trust, 169, 170, 171, 172, 173, 174
transitional period, 6, 7, 8, 12, 19, 36, 40, 41, 44, 45, 51, 57, 63, 67, 68, 71, 87, 105, 116, 117, 118, 119, 124, 135, 136, 152, 155, 169, 175, 176
Tunisia, 53, 188
Turkey, 7, 157, 159
Turkish, 159, 163

United Nations, 7, 17, 141, 188, 192
United States, 3, 7, 8, 17, 23, 38, 49, 50, 65, 70, 71, 74, 75, 104, 123, 133, 142, 148, 155, 159, 160, 161, 163, 165, 171, 172, 174, 179, 182, 186, 188, 192, 194
Van Doren, Charles, 23, 149, 210
Van Gogh Museum, 16
Vatican, 163

Washington DC, 8
Wall Street, 187
Weatherford, Jack, 16, 31, 211

INDEX **217**

Weber, Max, 26, 79, 80, 101, 102, 103, 140, 167, 168, 173
West, 175, 188, 189
Western Europe, 17, 159
Western civilization, 17, 35, 101, 163
Westphalia Treaty, 137, 139, 196
Wilson, Woodrow, 141
World Bank, 179, 188
World order, 155, 156, 188, 189, 194
Wolfensohn, James D., 179

World Trade Organization, 188
World War II, 141, 157, 158

Yemen, 37, 53
Young, Michael, 183
Yugoslavia, 163
Zimbabwe, 76

Zionism, 162
Zionists, 162
Zurayk, Constantine, 15, 199

Printed and bound by CPI Group (UK) Ltd, Croydon, CR0 4YY